LEYTON ORIENT
The Road to Wembley (1967-1999)

LEYTON ORIENT
The Road to Wembley (1967-1999)

A journeyman supporter's tale

MARTIN STRONG

First published 2016 by DB Publishing, an imprint of JMD Media Ltd, Nottingham, United Kingdom.

ISBN 978-1-78091-538-8

Printed and bound in the UK by Copytech (UK) Ltd Peterborough

Every year come Cup Final day, the two teams who get to Wembley are highlighted on whichever channel happens to have the rights to cover the big event in the afternoon/early evening. It's a journey that for them started in January and has concluded some four months later. My Oriental road to Wembley took a little longer, however. It all began at Brisbane Road in April 1967 with Stanley Baker, and finished at the end of May 1999 with Matty Lockwood. This is the story of what happened in between.

Acknowledgements

Thanks a million to my non-Orient family, despite the fact that none of the following ever go to Brisbane Road these days: My lovely wife of thirty years, Sonia, our two wonderful daughters Barbara and Becky, my magnificent mum and dad and my three sisters, Carol, Susan and Elaine, not forgetting mum-in-law Baka, and sis-in-law Atzi round the corner.

Thanks a million to my Orient family for helping to give me so much pleasure over the years at our beloved little east end club: Dave, Brenda and Suzanne Randlesome, Lotte Gatward, John and Elle Hurlock, Peter Collins, Bob Seaman, Glenn Strongitharm, Dave Staplehurst, Jay Gilbert, Gary McCullum, Paul and Matt Hiscock, Dick Richards, Dave Groves, Keith Davies, Keith Saville (1,000 not out), Paul Burrell, Rachel and Kevin Ellen, Paul Morant, John Parke, Alan Harvey, Ken Mortimer, Tony MacDonald, Alan Chandler, Arthur Godfrey, Paul Roberts, Ron Lambert, Charlie Hasler, Dave Chapman, Joe Durston, Mike Gold, Terry and Val Gregory, Christine, Caroline Doig, Val and Ian Jacobs, Jim Boyce, Glenn Ford, Chris Smith, Martin Smith, Peter and Geoff Eveling, Bruce Rixen, Ian Bermange, Martin Dixey and the other Tom Davies.

To Dave Dodd, Simon Fellman, Keren Harrison (super SLO), Rhiannon and Nathan, Linda Broughton (despite all the losing raffle tickets), Rose Hambleton, Tim Hayden, Martyn Rolfe, Steve Jenkins and all the other heroes at the Supporter's Club. To Caroline – 'today is an O's day' – Burkinshaw, Julian and Jay Lillington, Bill Linnell, David Boon, Mat Roper, James Masters, Matt Simpson, Neil Irvine, Brian Long, Barri Twinn, Elliot Byrne, Louise and Riley Teenans, the lads at the Orient Outlook Podcast, and other social media 'friends' and 'followers'. To fellow Orient supporters up the road, Andy, Sharon, Daniel and George, Bob around the corner and Dennis Dawkins. To nephew Robert, thanks for all the progs and Graham, and to Mike, Tinks, Kevin, Paul, Malcolm and Sonia, plus Herb of course.

To the great guys at *The Orientear*, thanks for all the sterling work with the comic over the past thirty years: Dave Knight, Tom Davies, Steve Harris, Jamie Stripe, Matt Arnot, Rory McQueen, Sean McNeill, Jim Nichols, Dave Winter and to anyone that's ever bothered to read any of the 'Martin Strong Diaries' in that time.

To celebrity fans Bob Mills and Julian Lloyd-Webber, and celebrity non-fans Sir Roy Strong and Sir Rod Stewart.

Legendary fans, Suzanne Randlesome over 1,000 consecutive games and the late George Gatward supporter for 72 years.

Thanks to the lot I sit with, high in the West Stand, every other Saturday: Terry, Steve, John, Al, Andy and Layers, along with the rowdy lot in front of me, Ted, Jim and the rest of 'em.

To honorary O's fans, Malcolm Cook, Cliff Wakenshaw (COYI) and Derek Baker (COYS), and all sadly departed supporters, notably George Gatward, and the Clapton Orient players that gave their lives for our country in the First World War. Plus any other fans that I know but have forgotten. And last but not least, of course, to all of the players I've seen proudly wearing the famous Leyton Orient shirt over the past fifty years. You may not have been world-beaters (Jamie Snowcroft excepted) but I'm sure you've all given your everything for our wonderful club and left me with so many happy memories in that time.

Here's to the next, God knows how many years, of watching Leyton Orient. We may not be best in the world on the pitch, but off it we're unbeatable.

Up the O's.

Contents

CHAPTER 1

1966 – SETTING THE SEEDS

It all began with the 1966 World Cup. My Dad had no real interest in the great game, but the tournament was being played in our country, so everybody was watching, and the Strong's were no exception.

We saw England's first game against Uruguay, played at Wembley, on our tiny black and white Pye television, but along with the rest of the nation had been disappointed with the result. After the goalless draw however, I had been cheered up by Alf's promise after the game that we would still win the competition.

Then came the second match. To begin with it had started in much the same way as the first, with no goals and not a lot of action. Indeed I may have begun to get distracted but then a wonderful thing happened. I can still picture it now some fifty years later – Bobby Charlton entered the Mexico half and let fly from thirty yards. The ball flew past the 'keeper and into the net. Bobby's jump for joy, his puff of the cheeks. My life had begun. I had my first hero. No not actually Sir Bob, but Kenneth Wolstenholme. He had predicted as Charlton had received the ball and advanced that he might try one from a distance and he had been spot on. The man was a genius. How on earth did he know that I thought to myself?

It could be said that from that moment my life started. Fifty years of watching twenty-two men chase after a small white (or yellow, or pink in the FA Cup) thing trying to put it between a couple of round posts (or square in the early days if you were in Scotland).

I can remember every England game in that World Cup as if it were yesterday. That quarter-final against those 'animals', as Sir Alf called them, from Argentina with Hurst rising Colin West like to head home the winner. There was Bobby's double in the semi and of course the Final.

Watching on that July afternoon back in 66, I remember how West Germany took the lead yet I recall Kenneth saying at the time that the team who scored first in World Cup Finals never usually ended up winning, and as he was the man who knew everything we were surely on our way to becoming World Champions. 0–1 became 2–1, but then came the killer blow. Only minutes remaining and a free-kick to the Germans. Given the same scenario now, having watched the O's for some fifty years I would have expected an equalizer, but in 66 a young seven-year-old just did not believe it could happen.

Yet a German shot, a lucky ricochet, the ball breaks to Weber and the ball ends up in the back of the net. At the time I was devastated. Indeed my devastation then was almost, but not quite of course, on a par with my devastation felt after the 2014 Play-off Final. If I shut my eyes now I can still see Sir Alf geeing up the players on the sacred Wembley turf as they prepared for extra-time, telling them that they had won the trophy once and that they had to go out and win it again. And win it again they did.

Eleven heroes we had that day, indeed twelve including Wolstenholme who, as if it wasn't enough to tell the nation that Geoff Hurst was steaming forward ready to hit the fourth, had even noticed that certain spectators had encroached onto the turf in the belief that the game had already finished. It had seconds later.

The whole afternoon is still as clear as anything. Mooro climbing those steps to collect that twelve-inch pot of gold. Nobby's dance for joy around the pitch and the tears of Sir Bobby Charlton. Indeed the whole tournament I remember as if it all happened only last week.

All these matches I had watched at this magical venue called 'Wembley'. I had fallen in love with the place already. England played all of their matches there, but games too were played there I understood, by club sides from our country. The team that I was to follow in our domestic game had yet to be decided, but I already knew that whichever one I picked I would look forward to seeing them grace the turf of this bit of heaven, some fifteen miles north-west of where I lived in Chingford.

It really did look such an awesome place. I knew at the time, England were unbeatable there and I was sure that which ever team I chose to follow in the coming years, they too would be unbeatable there.*

It's a tiny bit sad I know, but I can still picture pretty much everything from that tournament even now, some fifty years on. My memory generally is awful. Ask me what I had for dinner last night, what I did last Sunday or what the weather was like yesterday and I could not tell you. Yet anything connected to the great game and my memory, and indeed especially when it comes to matters concerning Leyton Orient suddenly seems to come good.

One listen to the classifieds at 5.00pm on a Saturday afternoon and the results are all up there glued to the brain. They only seem to fade away a week or so later, except of course the Orient ones, which for some reason (despite repeated attempts at forgetting so many of them) seem to get implanted up there for ever and ever.

When folk around me have found out about this ability I have with footballing and O's facts it has been suggested that I should maybe enter Mastermind. Many a time I have been told that I would have been in with a shout of bringing home that little glass bowl that the winner gets. Actually my entry could have been interesting. After my specialist round, chosen subject 'the Goals of Peter Kitchen (1977–84)', I would have fancied myself to have had a good lead going into the second half of the show.

When it came to the general knowledge section however, it would have been an entirely different ball game. As I can only ever remember getting one question correct from the second half of the programme in all the years that it's been going, I believe I may have struggled somewhat.

I can actually remember the question I rightly answered quite vividly. It was, 'who is the current Director of the Victoria and Albert Museum?' The fact that the answer at the time was Sir Roy Strong, and he happens to be my uncle may have aided me somewhat, but I can still remember doing some wild celebrations at the time.

No, an appearance by me on the programme would have been the ultimate 'game of two halves.' My collapse on the show would have been almost as dramatic as Orient versus Hull City in 1984, when we led 4–1 with twenty minutes to go, only to lose the game 5–4.

* *England lost 3–2 to Scotland there ten months later, and after fifty years I'm still waiting to see an Orient victory at Wembley Stadium.*

CHAPTER 2

1966-67 – THE BEST SIXPENCE MY DAD EVER SPENT

By the end of the 66 World Cup I had broken up from school, with the final whistle having been blown on Larkswood Infants in Chingford for me, as I was to move up to the Junior school. The real significance of this was that in the new playground us youngsters were allowed to play ball games in the dinner hour and at play times too, unlike in the old one. This basically meant an hour and a half of football for most boys from Monday to Friday.

It always amuses me, even today, when I read about areas like Merseyside and Tyneside and what great footballing hotbeds these places have always been. How the boys in these areas grew up only wanting to kick a ball, and how they only lived for football. No disrespect to these areas, I'm sure the youngsters there did love the great game and played at every opportunity, but it was the same, certainly in the late sixties after our World Cup win, throughout the country and Chingford was certainly no exception. The bell would go for playtime, that third of a pint of free milk, which we all got in those days would be downed in an instant and it would be out onto that tarmac to play make believe Bobby Charlton, Geoff Hurst or Rodger Hunt. We were all the same.

The week would build up to a climax on Saturday. We had all been hooked by the events in England during the summer of 66. The lucky lads at school with claret and blue dads were taken to see the three World Cup heroes at Upton Park. Others may have been led to White Hart Lane to see Greavesy sticking them in. A few went to Arsenal or Chelsea. Basically it all depended on your father. They were the days of discipline. If your old man supported a team and he took you to see them, then you jolly well followed them too or else.

How different it all was then to what it is like these days. I now work at WH Smith and nothing depresses me more than when the kids come into the shop decked in Man Utd, Liverpool and Barcelona shirts. Regrettably the footy on the box these days, where you can watch all the top teams live on your sofa, seems to have put to an end the 'support your local team' culture

Fifty years ago I had something of a problem however concerning my dad. My father I consider to be a great man. As a person I have only ever found two traits to his character. One was his dislike of Esso petrol, which came to a head in 1970 (*see* chapter five) and the second was that he had no interest at all in football.

On 30 July 1966 the whole nation was glued to the television or at the very least the wireless, to follow England's World Cup winning achievement. Apart that is from my dad. He was in the garden doing some weeding. A feat made all the more remarkable by the fact that the afternoon saw a fairly heavy shower and my dad got drenched.

I must admit just why my father never took to the great game remains – like the fact that Karren Brady has anything to do with running a football club – one of life's great mysteries. Being one of three boys he did not have to encounter the kind of problems I had to face, with myself having three sisters and no brothers. Unlike me he at least had two others he could kick a ball around with (in those days it was extremely rare for girls to kick footballs around). Although I remember my grandad was keener on fishing, I recall he did have some interest in football. Yet of his sons my father had no time for the game. While of my dad's two brothers one liked only cricket and the other, Sir Roy was to turn into the Lionel Messi of the arts world.

There was absolutely no danger of me taking a lead from any of them however and from the start of the 1966–67 season my poor father was constantly pestered into taking me to see a game. He was given eight months of grief before – and some might argue the date was significant – he succumbed to the pressure on 1 April 1967.

I don't think he wanted to take me to a match, but I fancy he realized that I was not going to give up the harassment so he took me to see Leyton Orient versus Swindon Town. This I feel he saw as some kind of compromise. Leyton Orient versus Swindon Town in the Third Division was a football match as such, but unlike other venues in the area where games were being staged he would not have to encounter a big crowd at Brisbane Road. This meant that it was easier for parking so that he would not have to leave so early to get to the match. He could therefore still get in a good mornings gardening. It was also cheaper for him taking me to see the O's rather than one of the 'big boys' in the area. Sure it's one of the oldest 'funnies' around – my dad didn't like football so he took me to see Leyton Orient – but in my case its 100% true.

I can still picture him now as we sat in the north wing of the main East Stand that afternoon, sitting next to me doing the *Telegraph* crossword while I sat riveted to a 0–0 draw. I loved it. From that day on Leyton Orient were to be my club. This was the team that I was going to watch regularly playing at Wembley. A fifty-year-old marriage was born that's still going strong today. Despite the fact that there were no goals it was lovely just being there. After watching all those games on our black and white television the best part about the afternoon was seeing the colours of the players' shirts. The Leyton Orient team donned blue tops for the afternoon, while the Swindon side wore red. I told my Dad that the Swindon players were wearing the same colours as England had done on the afternoon that they had won the World Cup, but that I would still be supporting Leyton Orient that afternoon. My Dad laughed, though deep down I'm sure he was more concerned at the time with getting six across correct.

Another interesting take on that afternoon was the presence of cameras around the ground. They were there to film for the Stanley Baker film *Robbery,* a fact which one of my daughters found out about some thirty years later and which led her to buy the DVD of the film for me at Christmas. I had hoped to spot myself in the crowd but alas it was not to be. My fifteen minutes of fame through supporting my club would have to wait until sometime after 1967, but come it eventually did some years later. (*see* chapter 20)

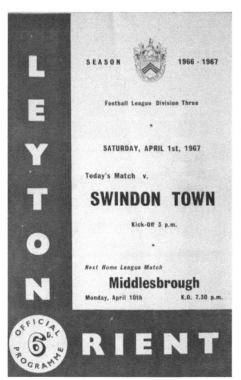

One monumental event did come out of the afternoon, occurring some ten minutes before the kick-off just as we were entering the ground. My father uttered five immortal words to me that were to have a vast significance on the rest of my life: 'Do you want a programme?' At the end of the day my Leyton Orient programme collection numbered one. When Sonia these days opens our bedroom wardrobe, or looks in our spare bedroom and sees 3,000 of the little buggers, I fancy that if she had one wish in life it would be to turn the clock back to 1967. She would wish that she would then be able to hide that sixpence that my dad gave to the man selling programmes that afternoon.

The season ended with the O's in fourteenth place in Division Three. Of the hundreds of games I've seen our boys involved in at Brisbane Road, the Swindon encounter remains the only one I've ever seen them play there wearing blue tops. In the close season the club colour was changed back to red, which it has been ever since. I suspected at the time, that some clever person at the club had spotted that England had defeated West Germany wearing red a year earlier and that a change of colour would bring about a change of fortune for Leyton Orient. Fifty seasons later and I'm still waiting for that change of fortune for the O's to come.

CHAPTER 3

1967-68 – AN EARLY DISLIKE OF NEWPORT COUNTY

My mother I consider to be a great lady. Having known her for over fifty years I can honestly say that I've only ever known her to have one fault, when I was at school in the early days she made me go home for dinner at lunchtime. Whilst my classmates were becoming useful footballers between 12.30 and 1.30pm I was busy travelling to and from school to have my lunch. I'm not saying that if I'd have stayed and had school dinners and afterwards played the game in the playground that I would have developed into a Wayne Rooney or a Dean Cox, but it may have given me at least some kind of footballing ability.

Sure there was the fifteen minutes playtime in the morning and afternoon, but by the time the free bottle of milk had been downed and the teams had been picked any serious chance to improve ones skills were gone.

And then there was Jeffrey Perkins. He was the leader of our class, a John Terry type figure. It was he who decided around December 67 that there was not enough time for a proper game of football during playtimes. Perkins changed the rules so that the teams that were picked after the morning bottle of milk would remain the same at lunchtime and for the afternoon session. Alas as I was not around during the main period of play I was not even considered for selection at all. As far as I was concerned it was a stupid rule change (Perkins I think must have gone on to work for the FA or maybe even FIFA in his later years), which meant that I was to get no football to play at all during the day.

The fact that my footballing prowess began to fall behind that of my mates was not helped by the fact that I was blessed with my three sisters. In those days there was as much chance of seeing a female kicking a ball as there was of spotting a Barcelona shirt in WH Smith.

Consequently when I got home at night and had no one to play with I turned instead to reading about the game. Hence the seeds of me becoming somewhat of a footballing 'anorak' began to be sown. I got stuck into the *News of the World Football Annual*, as well as reading *Shoot* and *Goal* magazines. Indeed by the turn of the decade, although I was only eleven, I already knew every FA Cup winner since 1872 and every English and Scottish league champion in the twentieth century (though I soon found out that learning the Scottish champions was easy, as it only ever appeared to be one of two teams, for some reason). I knew the nicknames and grounds of every League and Scottish League club, though I must confess I always had a weakness when it came to ground capacities and record attendances.

Returning back to my footballing skills, by the time of the first trials for the school team early in 1968, I had been relegated to 'last pick'. This really was the supreme humiliation for any youngster in those days. The boys that were picked just before me I remember, generally started to lose interest in the great game and looked around for other interests. I suppose if I'd been a normal sort of chap I'd have done the same thing, yet it seemed that the worse I became at playing the great game, the more enthusiastic I became in finding out about it and watching it.

Needless to say as soon as the season had started my poor dad was constantly harassed into taking me into seeing another game. He actually succumbed to the pressure early on in 67–68 and I saw my first match that year on 14 October against Southport. It turned out to be a good day for everyone. We were treated to my first Orient win 3–0, and the crowd was only three and a half thousand, half of what it had been for the Swindon game, which pleased my father greatly.

Our boys were now playing in all red and they had dropped the 'Leyton' from their name so that I was now simply watching 'Orient'. There was also one more highly significant change from that first game against Swindon. The shape of the programme had changed from eight and a half by five and a half inches to a new smaller five and a half by four inch format, which had a plain white cover. With the size of my collection doubling that afternoon to two, I made the momentous decision that from then on I was going to collect them as a record of every Orient game I had been to.

My dad took me to four more home games that season. I did not see us lose although generally it was another wrenched campaign for the O's as they finished nineteenth just avoiding relegation. I always insisted on my father getting to the game in plenty of time so that I could note the team changes in the programme. One of my favourite parts of the little white magazine however, was the page for half-time scores. About five minutes after the second half had started a man in a white coat would leave the player's tunnel and go to the corner of the ground where the half-time scoreboard was situated. He would have a box of numbers, which he would put up against the corresponding letters in the programme, so that we would know what was happening in games up and down the country. The numbers would correspond of course to the number of goals that the teams had scored in the first half. For about ten minutes, while careful not to miss any of the action on the pitch, I would meticulously fill in the scores onto my programme so that it was complete.

At the time, it was a vital part of the match-day experience for me. From my wonderful seat high up in the West Stand at Brisbane Road these days, I see countless folk, old and young fiddling around on their mobile phones below me, looking up scores and relaying them to those around them, while the game is going on. It really has become so easy these days to keep abreast of events up and down the country. Yet I have to say that I feel somewhat sorry for the youngsters when I see them doing this now. Little do they know the fun some of us had in the sixties and seventies given to us by the man in the white coat. They really do not know how they have missed out being born some thirty years too late. I really am so thankful I was born in the fifties and was not deprived of my half-time scoreboard fun.

It was as a result of this ritual that an early hatred of Newport County was born. Team rivalries as we all know are part and parcel of the British game. Spurs and Arsenal, Liverpool and Everton, Celtic and Rangers the list goes on and on. Healthy banter takes place between rival supporters up and down the country in schools, offices, factories, pubs and clubs, as it has done since the start of time.

Supporters love to have a club that they can despise and fans that they can wind up when a match against their team goes in their favour. Alas at the Orient in the late sixties I had no one at school that followed anyone who we ever played. West Ham, Tottenham, Chelsea and Arsenal were all in a different division to us, so that I must admit here was one part of being a footy fan where I was missing out. The team that I got to know and dislike in those days however came to be Newport County.

The bastards always kicked off their home games at 3.15. As a result when it came to filling in the half-time scores in the programme if County were at home there was always a blank. My hero in the white coat who would do such a sterling job keeping us abreast of events in the rest of the leagues could not tell us what was happening at Somerton Park because they were always late kicking off. Just why Newport started their matches after everyone else was, and indeed still is one of life's great mysteries. As life's great mysteries go this has to be on the same scale as to why John Jackson never won an England cap in the seventies,

Newport home ticket – note the kick-off time.

or why Dean Cox has never played at a higher level than League One in present times.

In those days of course I could have filled County's half-time score quite easily the next day from the *Sunday Mirror* which we always got, but somehow I felt it would not have been quite right, not having done it 'live' at the time, so I just left a gap.

Even now when I delve into my programme collection in my wardrobe at home and come across those old relics from the late sixties I see the blank spaces and it makes my blood boil. Certain other things have happened in the years since, (*see* chapters 18 and 23), so that nearly five decades later I still hate Newport County.

CHAPTER 4

1968–69 – THE FIRST LITERARY WORK OF ART FROM A STRONG

An indication of just how my enthusiasm for football had grown in only a year was the fact that I had started to harangue my dad about going to see the O's during the close season in 1968. A year earlier the pestering had not begun until the new season was underway. Indeed my intimidation had about the same degree of success as Alex Ferguson had on match officials in the nineties, in that my dad relented and agreed to take me to the first home match of the new season.

The Rotherham game on 10 August was for sure a cracker. I had been building up to it for weeks and was not disappointed in the resulting 3–3 draw. All I had to make do with during the summer months were a few black and white highlights from the European Championships on the television. Now however we were back in the real world. Red shirts and green grass, the half-time scoreboard and the 'official' programme. I could never understand why they always insisted on calling it the 'official programme', as I never found anyone selling 'the unofficial programme', although I'm sure that if they did I'd have started collecting them.

Memorable as the game that afternoon was however, the Rotherham match will forever be remembered by me for events before the contest started. At around ten to three the man on the public address, Keith Simpson – he did the job for well over twenty years – made an announcement. He said that from then on the O's would be led onto the field of play at home games to the accompaniment of *Tijuana Taxi*. As the team made their way onto the pitch that afternoon, courtesy of Herb Alpert, my dad burst into laughter. I must admit that even I found it highly amusing at the time that such a non-footballing tune with no connection at all to the Orient, would be leading our boys into battle every other Saturday.

Many a supporter will be able to reminisce about memorable days they have spent with their fathers at football watching their team play Cup Finals and the like. I have to report however, that the happiest I ever saw my dad at a game was as our team ran onto the pitch before that regulation Third Division fixture, laughing at a tune being played on a record by a brass band.

It all seemed a bit bizarre at the time, yet the most remarkable thing about it all is that nearly fifty years on our boys still take to the field to the same tune. *'Taxi'* has become part of Brisbane Road folklore. When I eventually emulate my uncle Sir Roy and appear on Desert Island Discs on the radio, *Tijuana Taxi* will for sure be there as one of the eight records selected to accompany me on my journey to the island.

If that was a high point for my dad that year watching the O's, there was a definite low later in the season before the home match that we went to against Reading. Another part of the match-day routine for us in the late sixties came before matches, just after we had bought the programme. We always bought a 'Goalden Goal' ticket for a shilling, which you would open up and there would be a time printed on it, which you hoped would be the time of the first goal that afternoon. If you were successful you would win a cash prize. Although we had never won, it was all part of the match-day experience for me, adding even more to the excitement of an afternoon at the football.

The tickets were sold by the 'Goalden Girls' around the ground who were young female O's fans. Orient were doing their part at the time to promote the 'swinging sixties' with the nicely dressed ladies. There were a fair few of them and I got to like them almost as much as I liked the man in the white coat who went round the ground with the half-time scores. Indeed a couple of them still

Goalden girls 68. Rose and Brenda top row, far right.

venture to Brisbane Road some fifty years on – Brenda Gregory, who is now Brenda Randlesome, and Rose Larratt, now Rose Hambleton can still be spotted in the Supporter's Club at every home game on a match day.

There was however mass controversy over the tickets at the match we went to in January. As per usual we had bought our 'Goalden Goal' ticket before we had taken our seat, but upon opening it, it showed a time of 00.04. In other words we wanted the first goal to be scored after four seconds. My dad went berserk. 'What the hell is all that about?' I remember him saying. 'How in their right mind can the club print a ticket with that time on?' I tried to argue that the record fastest goal was actually scored in four seconds by Jim Fryatt for Bradford Park Avenue against Tranmere Rovers in 1964 and that we were still in with a shout of winning the money, but my dad was having none of it. 'That's the last time we are ever buying a 'Goalden Goal' ticket,' he said. We did not win the money that afternoon and sure enough he was true to his word and we never again parted with a shilling before the game to participate in the contest.

Back at school my soccer skills were showing little sign of improvement. As I entered the third year of the juniors a career for me as a professional footballer was beginning to look a little unlikely. As far as I know no scout had ever come to watch me play during PE lessons, and I don't think any of them had ever approached my dad to discuss my football skills. Larkswood Junior School had always enjoyed a very good reputation when it came to all sports, especially the great game, but it soon became clear that I was going to do little to enhance that reputation.

I remember being particularly thrilled one Friday when headmaster Mr Harries announced at morning assembly that not one but two ex-pupils of the school were going to play in a Wembley Cup Final the next day. The match in question was the League Cup Final and the two boys were twins, Roger and Ian Morgan playing for Third Division Queen's Park Rangers against West Bromwich Albion. I felt a really proud eight-year-old when I heard the news. Boys from all over the country I felt would have given their right arm to swap places with me and go to a school where ex-pupils appeared in Wembley Cup Finals.

Yet as if all this had not been enough, after the weekend Mr Harries told us all at assembly on the following Monday that one of the boys, Roger had scored the first goal for Rangers and that they had gone on to win the game

3–2, after being 2–0 down. Upon hearing this of course I thought it was truly wonderful. It really was up there at the time, along with the day that England won the World Cup in 1966, as one of the proudest days in my life. I was indeed a lucky boy to be a pupil at Larkswood Junior School in Chingford.

It also made me realize that although I supported a Third Division team in Orient, it would still be possible for me to see them play and win at the magical place that was Wembley, as Third Division QPR had done. Surely it was only a matter of time before I would be watching the Orient play and win there.

Although I was about as near to making the school football team as Leyton Orient have ever been to producing an England centre-forward (although if Gianvito Plasmati had been born in this country I'm sure Roy Hodgson would have taken a look at him in 2014), I still followed our school football teams results at the time, with great interest.

Every Monday morning Harries would read out the school side's scores from the Saturday, which I would meticulously write down in a notebook. The side that Larkswood was putting out at the time was actually much better than any other in the area. The scores always heralded news of a win for our school, ranging from anything between 6–0 and 18–0. At the end of the 1968–69 season the team had a 100% record. Having written down every result, I decided to write my first book entitled *The Great Larkswood Football Team*. With Perkin's ban on me playing still in force it gave me something to do at playtime, so that by the end of May my first literary work was complete.

Looking back now, it may have assisted my writing if I had actually watched a few of the games. It may also have helped if I had known the names of at least a few of the boys who had turned out to play for the school. I was in the third year at the time and the side was made up exclusively with boys from the year above us, who I did not know.

Despite the fact that I only had the results of matches involving Larkswood, remarkably I still managed to produce a final league table involving all ten schools. With our boys playing eighteen and winning eighteen I thought it fairly likely that we would have won the league and so placed us top. As we defeated Selwyn 15–0 and 18–0 I decided to put them in last position, thinking that it was a fair bet that they had finished bottom.

After working on the project for about a month I presented the finished article to games teacher and school football supremo, Mr Shepherd. If I say so myself it must have been brilliantly written because upon reading it he never questioned me as to whether I'd actually seen any of the games. He didn't even seem to notice that none of the player's names were ever mentioned. He was so impressed that he presented it to Mr Harries and he too must have found it a sixties version of *Fever Pitch*, so much so that I was called up before the entire school one day at morning assembly and given a round of applause. For any pupil of Larkswood Junior School at the time this was the supreme accolade. Being called up by the Head and climbing onto the stage was the equivalent of mounting those thirty odd steps at Wembley to collect a trophy. I can even remember wiping my sweaty palm on my short trousers before the handshake, in much the same way as Bobby Moore had done before shaking the hand of the Queen in 66.

Thanks to my uncle, who has written many a book, the Strong family is able to boost many a much-acclaimed piece of literature over the past forty years. Even Sir Roy though would have been hard pressed to have produced a classic in the mould of *The Great Larkswood Football Team*, which I wrote back in 1969.

Football in those days was my one and only hobby. Whilst nowadays of course if you've got the money to have pay-per-view television you can watch a live game virtually every day of the year if you so desire, in the late sixties of course, that was far from the case. There really was no live football on the television save for the Cup Final and a few really big matches. Indeed there were not even any highlights on the box before 10 o'clock during the week. I was thrilled however in May 1968 when I was able to watch Manchester United win the European Cup by defeating Benfica at Wembley, with the match shown live on the television. I recall there was much debate between my mum and dad after ninety minutes with the score at 1–1 as to whether I should be allowed to stay up past my bedtime and watch extra-time. It was thankfully agreed that I could, as a one off, though I remember having seen United's three goals in the added thirty minutes I was sent straight upstairs at the final whistle, unable to view the presentation of the trophy. I went to bed that night once again in awe at that wonderful place called Wembley, dreaming that one day the O's would lift the European Cup there, and I would be present to witness it.

Although there was no live football that I could see on the small screen in those days, there was usually live football on the radio every Wednesday evening, if there was an important match on. Even then though, they were only allowed to broadcast the second half of the game for fear that, bizarrely, relaying the whole ninety minutes would encourage people to stay away and listen to the game on the radio instead of actually going to the match.

I used to really look forward to Wednesday evenings, if I knew there would be live footy that I could listen to on my little pocket transistor radio in my bedroom from 8.30pm onwards. (I was never allowed to stay up if there were any late night highlights on the television) It meant that I could at least get some kind of 'football fix' in the middle of the week. Many an evening in the late sixties and early seventies was spent straining to hear the poor reception on my not-very-good tranny. The reception at the European away matches was the worst. I can remember finally giving up half way through the second half of Newcastle United's tie in Ujpest Dozsa for the second leg of the Inter-City Fairs Cup Final in 1969. I went to sleep that night feeling dreadful that an English team had played the final of a major European competition and I did not even know the result.

Nearly fifty years on I have to say that I'm still a big fan of listening to football on the radio. I'm quite happy to retire up to my bedroom and listen to a match on the radio even if it's on the television. The commentaries I find are generally better – if the games is rubbish they actually tell you the game is not the best, unlike on the television. My pocket tranny has now of course been replaced by a digital model, so that there's no problem with the sound quality anymore. (I don't think, mind, I'll have the dilemma of worrying about the reception of any second half of a European final involving Newcastle these days.)

My dad took me to see six home games during the season. 1968–69 was (just for a change) not a good one for the O's. Of the six matches I saw five were draws. In March, manager Dick Graham resigned to make way for a player-manager, Jimmy Bloomfield. Only by winning our last two games, away at Bournemouth and at home to Shrewsbury did we avoid ending up in the Fourth Division. *The Great Orient Football Team* was never a book that was going to be written by me that season.

Many boys in my position supporting such a crap side may have started to get disillusioned with the O's I guess and start to look beyond Brisbane Road for their footballing thrills. My mates had mostly seen their sides appear in at least one Wembley final. Spurs and Chelsea in 1967 and Arsenal in 68 and 69.

The West Ham lot may not have done so, but they could still boost the three heroes from the 66 World Cup side. Yet here I was with my club having ended the campaign in nineteenth position in the Third Division. The roots of a hard life as an Orient fan were there for all to see in the late sixties.

Another event occurred during the year that made me further realise that the next forty odd years as an O's supporter were not going to be easy. Once again the controversy centred around the programme. Orient had introduced a policy whereby the price of the little white magazine was included in the cost of admission, so that everyone who went to the match got a programme. This did not please my father, however. He resented the fact that he had to pay for one of the things for himself when he took me, when he had about as much interest in reading it as he had in reading my mum's *Woman's Own*, or my *Goal* magazine.

It was a policy that I had no reason to dislike at all, however. Not content with making my poor dad arrive early so that I had plenty of time to list the team changes, I now made him stay behind when the game had finished. This was so that I could collect any programmes that supporters had decided that they did not want and left them on their seats. I thought at the time that there must be something wrong with these people that had gone to the game yet did not want to keep a record of it in the form of the programme – how could anyone in their right mind not want to keep and collect the things? There were, indeed some strange folk around, I thought at the time.

However I thought that it was great that I could collect up to fifteen of them that were seemingly unwanted, and then take them into school the following Monday to swap them. It was on the Monday morning that the aggravation would start however. I tried to exchange my Orient ones I had for those that the Spurs, West Ham and Arsenal boys had from their teams, to boost my general collection. They though would always argue that one of their First Division programmes was worth four or five of mine from Brisbane Road. That was always their deal and I had to take it or leave it.

At the time I remember that this really bugged me. I found it a hard theory to grasp. A Tottenham programme was sixpence, the same price as one bought from Leyton Stadium. True the White Hart Lane version was slightly bigger and had a few more photos, but no way was it five times better than ours. So why was the swap deal so bad for me? In fact it took me eight years before the conundrum was solved and I found the solution, when I was studying at school for my economics 'O level'. It was then that I found out about 'supply and demand' – as Tottenham were a more popular team, (God knows why, but they were) there was a greater demand for the item from our north London friends than there was of one from the Orient, and so it could attract a better price. I knew nothing of this back in the late sixties, however. All I knew at the time was that I used to go to school with fifteen programmes on a Monday morning, and come home with just three or four. Yes by now of course it was really starting to hit home that being an Orient supporter was not going to give me an easy existence.

CHAPTER 5

1969–70 – A PROMOTION SEASON – THE FIRST OF MANY?

Despite all the setbacks that I'd had in the few years I'd been an Orient fan, it never once occurred to me to change my allegiance and start following a decent team. I knew from an early age that anyone with any feeling for the game only ever supported one club. (Unless of course your name was David Cameron, in which case you could claim you were both an Aston Villa and West Ham fan.)

I always felt towards the end of the sixties, that my loyalty would eventually be rewarded with a successful team. And as it was I did not have to wait long at all, because in 1969–70 we were unbelievably Third Division Champions and were promoted to the second tier. Having finished the previous season avoiding relegation by just one place, our final league position in 69–70 was to put it mildly, something of a surprise.

Looking back now, some forty-six years later, it remains one of my great Oriental regrets that I never really made the most of our fabulous 1969–70 season. My thinking at the time was along the lines that being a football supporter of any team, including the O's, would mean seeing a successful season at least once every few years. In those days I'd already seen enough *News of the World Football Annuals* to know that teams such as Orient drifted between divisions. We might have got ourselves relegated but we would be able to recover within a few campaigns, which would mean seeing a winning team again. Little did I know the truth at the time, however, that over the next forty-five seasons I would only have two more promotions to celebrate at Brisbane Road. Looking back now I wonder how my football watching career, indeed my life as a whole might have developed if I had known that fact at the time.

As it was, the pestering of my father began around mid-July so that once again my dad was given little option but to take me to the first home game of the season. I had already been delighted that we had won our first game 3–0 away at Rochdale and was even more ecstatic after witnessing myself a 1–0 home victory over Halifax in mid-August. After an excellent start to the season however, crowds started to rise, which meant that my dad was less keen to take me. As regulars to Brisbane Road will know parking has always been a major problem at our ground, it being in the middle of a highly residential area. When there's a big crowd, for one to get parked anywhere remotely near to the ground has always meant arriving well before kick-off time. Much as I badly wanted to see our boys, I did not want my dad to suffer too much on a Saturday, so I cooled down on the harassment for the rest of the season.

Saying that though, I still saw a couple of fine games in our wonderful campaign of 1969–70. There was a fine 4–2 victory over Barnsley in February and I also saw the penultimate match of the season, when we defeated Shrewsbury 1–0 to clinch the Third Division Championship. It remains something of a regret though, that I did not see more of one of our better seasons and indeed may have pestered my poor father a little more if I'd have known then that I'd have to wait another thirty-six more campaigns before we once more achieved an automatic promotion.

The way that results went in 1969–70 it appeared that the board at the Orient had been really shrewd in appointing Jimmy Bloomfield as player/manager back in March 1969. The truth was in fact, that it was a move made mostly with the clubs finances in mind. By upgrading Bloomfield we carried on getting the services of the former Arsenal inside-forward as a player, and did not have to pay for a new manager recruited from outside.

Indeed the team that Bloomfield had assembled in the triumphant season was actually very good indeed. Goddard was reliable in goal. Denis Rofe was a brilliant full-back, eventually sold to Leicester City for £110,000. Tommy Taylor and Terry Mancini were like rocks as central defenders. Peter Allen and Barry Dyson both played every game and were wonderful in midfield. We had Mark Lazarus and Peter Brabrook as wide men, both highly experienced, and to score the goals in the middle were Mickey Bullock and Barrie Fairbrother. Between them the pair scored thirty-two times, a most un-Orient like tally for a pair of strikers. Even though I only saw half a dozen games in all, I saw more than enough to know that they were a fine side.

The club continued to produce the little white programme and by the end of the season my collection had grown to about thirty. I had a few more from other London clubs, which I had swapped at school, and they all sat nicely stacked at the bottom of my wardrobe in my bedroom. Of greater prominence in the same place at the time however, was my compete set of *Scorcher* comics, which I had been getting and collecting every week, much to the annoyance of my mother. For the first yet not the last time in my life there started to be the makings of a conflict between myself and a female regarding wardrobe space and football related stuff.

Champions ! The first of many!

Women seem to have developed this rather strange idea that wardrobes were invented to hold clothes. It's a fact of life that the person who thought up the things wanted them to be used to hold football related items. Let's be honest you don't spend hours looking at a pair of trousers that's hanging there reminiscing about the old times when you have worn them. Yet you can pick out that 1977–78 Orient versus Sheffield United programme that's there on the shelf and remember that Peter Kitchen hat-trick on the day that helped us towards Second Division safety that day. You see the Leyton Orient versus Notts County matchday magazine from 2015–16 and you straight away think of

Sammy Moore's 35 yarder that screamed past the County custodian into the top corner that afternoon. The housing of such articles is surely the true purpose of wardrobes, not clothes.

I can never remember having any kind of argument at all with my mother, although with my football comic collection rising steadily in 1970 we were getting close to it, because of my refusal to let any of the football magazines get the red card to the dustbin. Our close relationship was possibly saved however, by an incident involving the comic at the end of our promotion campaign, which made me dump the entire *Scorcher* collection.

As well as the football stories which made up most of the magazine – Lags Eleven and Billy's Boots were my favourites – there was also factual stuff, which filled a few pages every week. At the end of each season there would be a double page spread paying tribute in turn to all the champion teams throughout the English and Scottish divisions. There would be drawings of key players and key goals throughout the campaign. One of the major rewards for Orient's magnificent season would be that two page spread in the comic, highlighting our wonderful achievement that year. I can still remember now being unable to sleep properly the day before the comic was due out in anticipation of the momentous event.

When I saw the magazine the next day however there was a major, major disappointment. The double pager had started off brilliantly. Fine drawings of Bullock, Allen and Fairbrother (they had even got his beard right) and nice sketches of key moments throughout the nine months. Then I saw it. They had a drawing of Mark Lazarus scoring the goal against Shrewsbury that had won us the title. It was shown in the comic as a right foot shot. Now there was the rub. The whole world knew that the goal that our winger had scored that afternoon was in fact a header. I knew because I was there. I remembered it well.

I was devastated. As devastation went this was on the same scale as that suffered after our relegation under Liverani, at the end of the 2014–15 season. How could the comic blatantly lie? How could they unashamedly make something up? My parents had always told me that lying was one of the worst things possible, yet this comic, which I had religiously been buying and believing for the past three years had done just that. And they had done it to my club too.

I had been so looking forward to cutting the pages out and sticking them on my bedroom wall next to my Orient rosette, but that was now obviously out of the question. Most children around my age at the time would have got their ultimate sense of devastation by finding out the truth about Father Christmas. For me though it came when finding out that you could not always believe everything that you read in football comics. The impact it had on me at the time was so great that I immediately stopped spending my shilling a week pocket money on the thing and consigned my entire Scorcher collection to the dustbin. I just thought it was so wrong what they had done and I never bought *Scorcher* again.

Whilst saying good riddance to one part of my football collection, one thing I was never going to say goodbye to was my *Soccer Stars in Action Picture Stamp Album*. Back at school as far as I was concerned playtimes, thanks to Perkins, remained football free, at least so far as playing the game went. I had discovered a much more rewarding way of passing the fifteen minutes in the morning and afternoon however: swapping the doubles that I had collected in my *Soccer Stars in Action* collection. The stickers were collected at the time by practically all boys to put in their albums. You bought them in packets of six at the corner newsagent. Everyone would get lots of doubles. As a result many

an hour was spent showing the other boys your duplicates, hoping they would have ones you did not have. 'Gottit, gottit, gottit, gotitt, no ain't got that one' became standard playground terminology. Football, as we all know has changed so much in the past forty years or so, sadly a lot of the changes have been for the worse, yet the sticker swapping ritual I know is one that still goes on today. At WH Smith I sell many a packet of Panini stickers every week. Many of these I'm sure will end up being exchanged in the playground. When I sell the packets at work, it is indeed the kind of thing that restores ones faith in the great game today.

It became standard practice in my youth that when you had completed your album you took it into school and proudly showed it off. I guess most of the lads who had assembled their complete sets kept them for a few years before becoming teenagers, finding more mature interests and so ditched their collections. I'm a little bit embarrassed to have to say that a few of us never grew up and I still have my album today.

Looking back at my collector's book now, the stickers of the players were to say the least, interesting. The soccer stars were often superimposed onto photos of other games. Thus Stoke's Tony Allen for instance could be seen wearing blue shorts and socks in front of a Stoke teammate who was attired in white shorts and socks. Liverpool's Alec Lindsay can be seen on a mazy dribble being chased by someone all in yellow, who in turn was being tracked by someone in white. Lindsey of course was attired in Liverpool red, so that there were three different kits being worn on the pitch. They would not get away with it these days, the stickers now are a lot more professional, I'm sure, but in the sixties and early seventies the discrepancies didn't seem to bother anyone.

Then there were the biographies of the players. They were quite magnificent. In the album midfield men did not exist. Instead they were 'schemers'. Players who were essentially markers were in fact 'shadowers'. Tall centre-forwards were

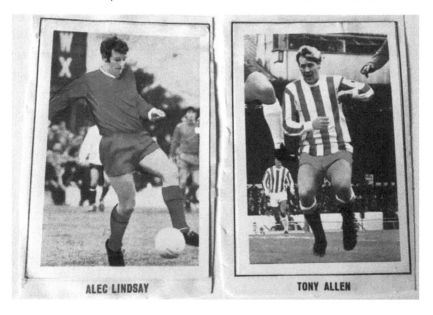

ALEC LINDSAY   TONY ALLEN

'spearheads'. Bobby Gould was thus described as a 'bulky, bustling spearhead who kept defences on their toes'. Eddie Gray, we learnt was, 'a Scot who had grown in stature and ability and was essentially a clever and adept schemer'.

I can remember feeling a lot of envy at the time that the other boys at school could collect the heroes from their teams, Arsenal, Spurs and West Ham, and put them in their books. Alas though, there was no page for the Orient. I had to be content with a few mentions of the O's, in certain players' pen pictures, such as David Webb, who once played for us. The joys of being a ten-year-old Orient supporter continued.

Another happening occurred at the end of the season, which was to make me question once more whether being an O's fan was giving me a deprived childhood. Events centred on my eleventh birthday party. Other lads at the time would have football parties on their days of celebration. Essentially that meant jellies and ice cream followed by a birthday cake and then a kick about over the park. On my big day however I did not want to be humiliated by being 'last pick' in a match so that my mates were asked to come round to my house for a Subbuteo party instead. Subbuteo was a football game with small figures which in those days was to youngsters what the 'FIFA' play station game is today. There were little miniature footballers you used to 'flick to kick'. Every boy at the time had a Subbuteo set.

I woke up on the Saturday morning of my party in June with great anticipation. As anticipation went this was on a par with that experienced before any of the last three Leyton Orient Play-off Finals. You could buy miniature Subbuteo teams of clubs and countries and I had requested two as birthday presents from a couple of the lads that were coming for the entertainment at my Chingford abode. Norman Blight had promised me the England team, while Michael Attwood was to bring me the all-red Orient side in miniature. Sure there would be somewhat of a colour clash between the red shirt/white short team that I already owned – this was the one that had come with the standard Subbuteo set – but from then on with the proper Orient team in my possession I would truly be able to play with my heroes. The little one-inch figures could be Allen, Bullock or Dyson.

What a let down however, the day turned out to be. As let downs go this was on a par with the feeling after any of the last three Play-off Finals. I can still remember now my supreme disappointment as I opened Blight's gift. Sure it was a Subbuteo team. Sure all the players had mostly white shirts. But England? No it

Not England and Orient footballers.

was Peru. He had got me bloody Peru. Now I'm no racist now and I wasn't then, but these were pre Laurie Cunningham and John Barnes days. An England team then with eleven black players was about as believable at the time as the thought then would have been of the O's ever being owned by an Italian. And then there was that red sash across the Perivian shirts. Of all the games I'd watched England play on the television and all the pictures I'd seen of them in books they'd always had plain white shirts. Not once had they had a red diagonal stripe across their fronts like the Peruvians. I was gutted. Blight explained it by saying that with the high demand caused by the 1970 World Cup, which was going on at the time, the miniature England team had sold out everywhere. The nearest he said he could get me to England was Peru. Bloody Peru.

My party had just begun but it had already got off to a poor start. Worse though was to follow. Attwood arrived. I could see by the shape of his present that I'd got another Subbuteo team. Things were looking up – or were they? Upon undoing the wrapping paper I saw on the side of the box the word 'Liverpool'. I opened the box. The players were attired in mostly red but crucially they had white collar and cuffs. I was of course once more gutted. The whole world knew at the time that Orient – unlike Liverpool – played in all red including collar and cuffs. Attwood could see how my face had dropped. 'I asked for Orient but they said they did not have your team,' he said. 'Liverpool with their white collars and cuffs was the closest they had.'

With this double whammy my party had been well and truly ruined before a single Subbuteo player had been flicked that afternoon. I tried to make the most of the rest of the day but as you can imagine it was hard. Indeed for a brief period afterwards I recall I even started to question whether I could support a football team that they could not even produce a proper miniature Subbuteo set for.

It was around this time that my father's other character fault came to light. The first, as already mentioned was his dislike of football. The other was his dislike of Esso petrol. All the other boys at school were lucky. Their dads all used Esso. The significance of this was that around May 1970, with every four gallons of petrol bought from an Esso garage you got a free World Cup coin – a member of the England squad to put on the blue collectors board. You never knew if you were going to get Brian Labone or maybe Geoff Astle before you opened it, so that swapping once again came into play, a la stickers in the playground. All the boys at Larkswood collected them. My dad however did not go to Esso for his petrol but instead went to BP. At the time they had a rival promotion with the promise of winning money. This was done by matching up halves of specimens of paper notes ranging from ten shillings to fifty pounds. These too were given away free with four gallons of petrol from BP garages everywhere. My dad argued that our Morris Oxford ran better on BP petrol than it did on Esso fuel, but to be honest I'm sure he was just lured into their garages because of the prospect of winning some cash.

The sad consequence of this was that by the end of May I was the only one at school without a growing World Cup coin collection and it was hurting. My poor dad was being harassed constantly at the time into changing his fuel. Eventually it all got too much for him and he succumbed to pressure and abandoned BP for Esso around mid-June. (In hindsight I think it had much to do with the fact that after a month he had still not won anything from the matching notes at BP.)

By the time I started collecting however some of the other boys were already starting to take their completed boards into Larkswood to show them off. My dad was harangued into doing as much driving as possible, but alas as the World Cup drew to a climax and the Esso promotion ended I was still five coins short. Whilst any normal person would have kept their collection for a few years then thrown it away having grown up, I have to report that I've still got mine at home. And to this very day it still bugs me somewhat that Alan Mullery, Martin Peters, Peter Thomson, Brian Labone and Peter Bonetti are missing. (Though if

Alas, 5 coins still missing.

I remember correctly Bonetti's absence didn't bother me too much some forty-five years ago after his quarter-final display against the Germans.)

Loathe as I am to ever criticize my father, what I found really annoying about the whole sorry affair was that there did not appear to be any difference in the performance of our car after the change from BP to Esso. In fact it took about a year for my dad to fully redeem himself in my eyes. Cleveland petrol stations then started to give away little plastic busts of the heads of British players, again given away free with every purchase of four gallons at their garages. My dad happened to be a Cleveland fan, so much so that my collection was the first at school to be completed. The busts themselves were in fact absolutely dreadful looking nothing like the players they were supposed to be, yet it was still a proud day for me when I carried my completed collectors case into school one Monday.

The summer of 1970 then was truly a summer of setbacks. The one concerning the World Cup coin collection, the *Scorcher* 'comic of deceit' scandal and the Peruvian/Liverpool Subbuteo team shocker. Despite all of these setbacks however the biggest blow for me was seeing England get knocked out of the World Cup in Mexico. After 66, I had only ever known World Cup success for our country. The nation had gone football mad in 1970 despite the fact that kick-off times from across the Atlantic were often in the middle of the night. Everyone was stunned when West Germany had overcome a two-goal deficit to defeat us 3–2 in the quarter-finals. Indeed the only consolation for me at the time was that Brazil had defeated those horrible Peruvians at the same stage of the competition. It still could not hide the fact though that after the ecstasy of Orient winning promotion, the following few months had been for various reasons, real relegation material for me.

CHAPTER 6

1970–71 – GRAFFITTI PROBLEMS

The summer of 1970 was to be sure a 'summer of two halves.' The first forty-five minutes – June and July – had seen many a trauma, but it's fair to say that things picked up considerably after that. There were three massive alterations to my life during August and September. A change of school, a change of division for the O's and last but not least a change to the size of the match-day programme at Brisbane Road.

I had left Larkswood in the summer moving along with the rest of the fourth year to Chingford Junior High School for eleven to fourteen-year-olds. The new school was a lot nearer to our house, so that if I had wished I could have gone home for lunch, then nipped back for the lunchtime game of football. Perkins was still the boy in charge but I never asked him for my place back in the 'football squad'. I had taken the momentous decision at the age of eleven that I was going to retire from the playing side of the game. To be honest it was not a tough decision. I was just no good at football. Looking back now maybe if I'd have known then about some of the non-footballers I was to see wearing an Orient shirt over the next forty odd years, I may have been tempted to carry on and could have ended up playing for the O's, but at the time giving up the game seemed the right thing for me to do.

It would have been nice to have become a professional footballer and have written a book now about a life winning one hundred England caps, scoring a hat-trick in a Wembley cup final, becoming England manager and obtaining a knighthood, awarded for services to the game, but unfortunately it was never meant to be. Instead I'm left writing a book about my lots of years following a not-very-good football team from east London.

I liked the new school though many of the boys were upset that the official sport played there was not football, but some other strange game where it appeared the ball had gone out of shape. With my anorak on, I knew of course that the ball had burst during the 1946 FA Cup Final between Derby and Charlton, but I had never heard of any game being played with the ball not being round. Also in this new game there appeared to be fifteen players per side on the pitch at any given time, which seemed bizarre. Goal nets (which I knew of course had been invented by a certain Mr Brodie in 1890) were not allowed and somebody had forgot to cut the posts off connecting them to the crossbar, so that they rose about one hundred feet in the air. Somethings never changed however, and with this new game I was still hopeless and was last pick every PE lesson.

More tribulations of being an Orient supporter surfaced again at the new place of education. This time the traumas concerned graffiti. From my earliest days at Chingford Junior High School I could see that writing stuff on classroom desks was an integral part of a boy's day there. Everybody did it during boring (ie all) lessons. The secret was to do it when the teacher was not looking. Getting caught would always mean getting a detention where you had to clean all the desktops. I did my share of scribbling, though was always careful not to be seen. The problem arose however with the kind of prose that was being written. There was plenty of stuff regarding Tottenham, Arsenal and West Ham on all of the desks.

Because of the quantities of lads supporting these teams it was impossible for the teachers to work out just who had written 'Ralph Coates is magic', 'Radford is better than Osgood', or 'I love Geoff Hurst'. Some of the cleverer members of staff however had fathomed out that there was only one Orient supporter in the year. As a result the author of 'Mickey Bullock for England', 'Fairbrother is God', and 'there's only one Barry Dyson', was not overly difficult to work out. I may actually have got away with my misdemeanours but for the fact that I was one of only three or four of us in our class who were left handed. Whilst most of the writings were all on the right side of the desk, mine were on the left and therefore always stood out.

It was at the beginning of an English lesson one afternoon that our teacher Mr Clegg pulled me out to the front of the class. He was a northerner, who reminded me a little at the time of Nobby Stiles, though he did have teeth. He told the whole of the class that he knew who the culprit was who had plastered all the desks with Orient graffiti because there was only one person in the class stupid enough to support such a hopeless team. The whole class laughed and I must admit that having become somewhat immune to all the Orient related stick I'd received over the years, even I managed to raise a smile. Mr Clegg had not finished his speech, however. He carried on by saying that he was going to make an example of me and that I would have to stay behind every day after school for a full two weeks to scrub all the desks clean. At once the laughter stopped as he read out my sentence. Two weeks detention as a punishment everyone agreed was extremely harsh for the crime committed. Past offenders had only ever been given at most two or three days desk cleaning, yet I'd been handed a massive ten.

It was while staying behind on one of my detention days however, that I got to find out the real reason for the severity of my penalty. I happened to notice on Clegg's desk a Doncaster Rovers versus Barnsley programme. He told me that he was from Yorkshire and that he was a staunch supporter of the Rovers. Everything suddenly fell into place. We had done the double over them the previous season (2–0 at home – Mancini and Bullock, 1–0 away – Robertson own goal) and I decided that he saw my punishment as a way of inflicting some kind of revenge for our two victories. He probably felt a lot of jealousy in that whilst his boys had finished the season in eleventh place we had won the league. It has to be said that following the graffiti incident for a few years after I hated Doncaster Rovers, although they more than redeemed themselves a few years later of course by giving us Peter Kitchen. Yes, it's fair to say though, that at the time the troubles of being a (left-handed) Orient supporter were continuing.

My new school was greeted with a new division for my team, but my dad was not a great lover of Division Two. I'm sure he longed for the days of 1967–68 and 68–69 with crowds of three and four thousand. We went seven times in 1970–71 and eight and nine thousand regularly visited Brisbane Road. Tommy Taylor was sold to West Ham, but basically it was still the promotion winning side from the year before. The team struggled somewhat however only scoring twenty-nine times in the league and finished seventeenth.

The good news for me however, was that the programme was now bigger and better. The old four by five and a half inch with the same plain white cover for every match had been replaced by a new five and a half by seven and a half inch version and it even had a photo on the front page. As it was now Second Division fare as opposed to Third, I was able to negotiate a better rate on my swap deals at school. We were now talking of just three Orient programmes in exchange for one from White Hart Lane, Highbury or Stamford Bridge. The ritual of staying behind after the final whistle to collect left overs remained a successful policy, even if it did mean sacrificing watching the start of Dr Who on a Saturday evening for me and my dad.

The late summer of 1970 saw another momentous event in the history of mankind. As momentous events in the history of mankind goes this was on a par with Barry Hearn taking over Leyton Orient in 1995. In September 1970 the first *Rothmans Football Yearbook* was published. Ask any football anorak in the seventies, eighties or nineties who their best friend was and their answer would be either their football programme collection or their bible of the great game, 'the Rothmans'. Sure we had the News of the World and other similar annuals to entertain us in the sixties, but now we had the much bigger, definitive article, loaded with many more facts. At last for the first time we could instantly find out that Torquay beat Aldershot 6–1 in Division Three (South) during the 1951–52 season. That East Fife's record attendance was the 21,515 that packed Bayview Park to witness the Fifers entertain Raith Rovers in 1950. That H.H. Barnett won his only England cap against Ireland in 1882 (he was playing for Royal Engineers at the time.)

When my dad bought that first one for me some forty-seven years ago, I could barely believe what I saw. It gave me a feeling at the time comparable to that of seeing my two daughters for the first time when they were born in 1987 and 1991. Flicking through it initially, I just did not know where to start looking at it. In the months that followed I spent hour upon hour reading it. It's fair to say that I could sadly find something to interest me on every one of the nine hundred and ninety-two pages.

The complete collection.

It may have been the winners of the John White Footwear Crowd Behaviour Award in 1969–70 (Cardiff City) or the victors of the Arthur Dunn Cup (Old Reptonians) but at the time every page held some fascination for an eleven-year-old Statto. The big blue magic book is still going today, though it's now called the *Sky Football Annual*, and I've just bought the forty-seventh edition. Sadly I can still find something to interest to me on every page of the damn thing.

Looking back to those days, I can remember at the time my mum telling me that I was foolish to want to buy the second edition a year later. Her argument was that as many of the statistics were repeated in the book from the previous year, it was a waste of money to buy it again. I suppose she had a bit of a point, but I countered at the time that I was going to get it every season and that in years to come the complete set of Rothmans books would form a valuable collection. I'm sure my mother thought that a few old football books would never be worth much, yet I could now probably get around five or six hundred pounds for the lot of them that grace my bedroom. There's about as much chance of me not buying an edition now as there was in 1970 of me joining the Doncaster Rovers Supporter's Club.

CHAPTER 7

1971–72. – PLANET EARTH'S GREATEST DAY?

By simply surveying the league table for the season and looking at the results for the year, 1971–72 appears on the surface to have been a pretty mundane campaign for the O's. However a final position of seventeenth for the second time running does not tell the true story of a memorable season.

Being the lone O's fan in my year I had always struggled to hold my own with the Spurs, Hammers and Arsenal boys. Their teams included players who played for England and they were all even able to own proper Subbuteo teams of their clubs. I was old enough by now however, to realize that there was one particular area of our game in which my mates could not get excited about. It was an area of the game though, in which the Orient were able to participate in. It is the phenomenon that was known then, and indeed is still known today as 'giant-killing.' Every year certain teams from the First Division would be defeated by those from lower division teams in the FA and League Cups. Thus – although no one would actually lose their life – a giant would be 'killed', metaphorically speaking. To be a proper giant-killer the victors would have to be in the Third or Fourth Division or, in extreme cases not even be in the league at all. However I had decided at the time, that as we were in the lower half of the Second Division any win over a top club could in our case still be considered an act of 'giant-killing.'

In 1972 we entered the FA Cup in January in the Third Round, and were drawn at home to Wrexham. We were victorious in that match and were given an away tie in the next round at First Division Leicester City. The game I remember was given added spice by the fact that Leicester's manager at the time was Jimmy Bloomfield, the man who had guided us to the surprise promotion a couple of seasons earlier. In June 1971 he had been 'poached' from the O's by the Midlands club. George Petchey had been brought to the Orient as his replacement, having previously been Youth Team Manager at Crystal Palace.

Since I had started to follow the Orient we had had no success in the FA Cup at all. I had yet to go to Wembley to see them play in the Final. The Fourth Round tie at Filbert Street was a few years before I started to follow the team away from Brisbane Road, so that the afternoon saw me completely devoid of any developments at the game.

The first time I knew about what had gone on was at 4.45pm courtesy of the legendary *Grandstand* teleprinter on the Beeb. There it was in all its glory: 'Leicester City 0 – Orient 2'. Needless to say I was elated. It was for sure a great result. We were 'giant-killers' and would surely have our match plastered all over the back of the Sunday papers for a change. Just for once our boys would take prominence over the Tottenhams, Arsenals and West Hams of the world. Was I looking forward to seeing the newspapers the next morning.

That Sunday some forty-seven years ago there was great anticipation as I intercepted the paper boy around eight o'clock in the morning. I grabbed the *Sunday Mirror* from him and turned to the back pages expecting to see a wonderful write up about our boys, with even a few pictures of our lads thrown in for good measure.

There was however, one small problem that I had overlooked. One of the other results that Saturday. Hereford United 2 – Newcastle United 1. Now although I must admit to being a little biased towards the O's, even I would have to reluctantly concede that being non-leaguers at the time, Hereford probably deserved the adulation and publicity that day more than we did for their victory over a First Division side, but why the hell did they have to pick that day of all days to have their moment of glory? Our win was quite simply the finest individual result for our club since I had started supporting them, yet it had been relegated in the papers to the 'other matches' section. I was gutted.

Although at the time I was understandably more than a little upset, I looked upon it as being akin to the 1966 World Cup Final at the end of ninety minutes. After the Germans had snatched that last minute equalizer, Alf went round to all of the players before extra-time started. He told them they had won the thing once and now they would have to win it again in the extra thirty minutes. And win it of course they did.

I envisaged George Petchey going into training on Monday morning and seeing the glum looks on the player's faces. I fancied that they would have all been devastated by the fact that they had hardly got any praise for defeating a top flight club two days before. I pictured him going round telling them they had been 'giant killers' once, and that now they would have to go out and do it again in the next round. And indeed go out and do it again in the next round they jolly well did.

Twelve-thirty lunchtime, the Monday after any Saturday of the FA Cup (bar the first round and the semi-finals), the *Jimmy Young Show* on Radio Two. Bryan

Butler was always there in those days at the Headquarters of the FA at Lancaster Gate for the draw for the next round. There was always mega anticipation all over the country as to whom you would get next if your team was still in the competition. School at this time was always out for me at twelve-twenty as the lunch break started, and I would be home just in time for the first ball to be drawn out of the bag. Needless to say the Monday after the Leicester game saw me rush home with extra relish. It was the Fifth Round draw and Orient's ball was unbelievably still in the hat. It was something that I had never known to have happened before, since I had been following them.

The old boys who pulled the things out of the bag at the FA, always sounded on the radio as if they were about a hundred and five years old. They were people such as the heads of the FA County Associations in Suffolk and Cornwall, top dignitaries within the Football Association who I'm sure went around everywhere wearing smart suits. One of the old codgers picked out the home team, then the other the away side. They were not household names. It always seemed to me that they sounded as if they might drop dead at any point, or at least drop the bag with the balls in it. Yet remarkably drop the bag they never did. In fact cock it all up they never did. The bag was always shaken in front of the mike before each ball was picked out, as if to reassure those listening at home that there was no cheating taking place. When you did not hear the rustle any more, you knew that there was just one team in the bag left to pull out. The fact that the wonderful event was never televised added to the mystic of the whole glorious affair. You just had to shut your eyes and imagine what was going on at Lancaster Gate.

Nowadays alas, the wonder of the FA Cup draw has for me all gone. It is now celebrities on the television on a Monday night, an occasion that can happen anywhere around the country with hundreds of idiot fans in the background all hoping for their twenty seconds of fame, their ugly mugs live on the BBC. It's all a bit like watching an evening in a bingo hall. It's a great shame that those glory days of the FA Cup draws at 12.30pm on Monday lunchtime have well and truly gone for good, but I suppose that's football in the twenty-first century.

Back in 72 the air was punched in triumph on the February lunchtime after the Fifth Round draw as the old codgers contrived to give us Chelsea at home. We had been heroes once that year by beating Leicester, but thanks to Hereford it had not really counted. Now though we had the chance to do it all again against a big team, Chelsea, who were the holders of the European Cup Winners Cup at the time, the League Cup finalists and a team in the top six of the First Division.

So 26 February 1972 saw what many still consider to this very day to be the greatest ninety minutes in the history of the world. It still remains (despite the Oxford game in 2006, and Arsenal at home in 2011) the best day of my Orient supporting career to date. Yet though he would never admit it, I'm sure my dad hated every minute of it. In fact looking back now, he deserves a medal for simply taking me in the first place on that historic afternoon. He was unable to get a ticket for us in the north wing of the Main Stand, where we always used to sit. In those days of course there were seats only in the East Stand at Brisbane Road and nowhere else in the ground. The rest of Leyton Stadium was for standing, which my father did not like doing, especially when it was packed, which it certainly would be for the Chelsea game. He knew just how much it meant to me to be there that day however, so he managed to acquire two standing tickets for the South Enclosure at the ground, just in front of the seated area in the East Stand.

We had to leave on the day of the game at a ridiculous time, just as *Grandstand* was starting, yet we still had to park what seemed like fifty miles away. The worst part about it for him though, was the fact that he was unable to do the *Telegraph* crossword because of the amount of people there. The South Enclosure was new territory for me and it was packed. The chances of cramming thirty thousand into Brisbane Road these days are about as remote as the thought of watching us play Premier League football there now, yet back in 1972 the club somehow managed to cram all the punters in. From where I was, being a not particularly tall twelve-year-old I could barely see anything at the far, north end of the ground. The half-time scoreboard was out of eyeshot, so that I would have to go home with my programme incomplete, yet for that one glorious afternoon it did not matter.

The Chelsea side in those days was good. Arrogant, but good. Household names like Hudson, Hollins, Cooke, Bonetti and Osgood rolled off the tongue. Our pitch on the day, as was so often the case in the early seventies was awful, but as the game started, the visitors passed it around well and deservedly went 1–0 up through a David Webb header after twenty-seven minutes. It came as no great surprise when Osgood doubled their lead some eight minutes later. Both goals had come at our end just in front of us so that I had a near perfect view of them. I could also see the Chelsea hordes crammed in at the Coronation Gardens end behind the goal going ecstatic.

At the time the only team I had ever seen come back from being two goals down to win 3–2 was West Germany against England in the 1970 World Cup.

In true anorak style at the time, I remember turning to my dad and relaying to him this wonderful fact, adding that Peter Bonetti was the England goalkeeper for the losing side that day back in 1970, and that he was in goal for Chelsea that afternoon. My father did not appear too interested in my observations however, he was more concerned with trying to avoid getting crushed. The chances of history repeating itself and Bonetti conceding three again, this time at Brisbane Road, certainly seemed very remote as half-time approached, but I for one had not given up hope and amazingly in the next hour my optimism was unbelievably rewarded.

With around forty-five minutes gone the ball disappeared down the other end. I strained my neck but could see nothing. Then there was an almighty roar. I knew instantly that Orient had scored. I had not seen the goal, but remember jumping up and down wildly for the first time that day. It has become a well-known fact of football that the best time to score a goal is just before half-time and if anybody needs proof of it they should just take a look at that Orient versus Chelsea game from 1972. Phil Hoadley's goal for us that day transformed a game that we were at one point losing badly, to one where victory was grasped in the closing moments. Though 2–1 down at the break, was I keyed up big time for the second half when the interval was taking place. Not least of all because Orient were kicking towards our end and I would at last be able to see all of our attacks. I was convinced that we would equalize at some point in the second half, yet even I at the time didn't think it would take barely a minute to do so, after the restart.

Right in front of me there was a dreadful mix up between Bonetti and Webb with forty-six minutes gone, which left Mickey Bullock looking at an empty net with the ball at his feet. Mickey Bullock was what you might call a typical Orient centre-forward. One of a series that was to include such legends of the game as Moores, Marks, Cooper, West and more recently Plasmatti and Palmer. Basically this meant, and indeed still means today, that given the ball at their feet with an empty net in front of them, a goal is far from guaranteed. On this occasion however, our man Bullock seemed to forget that he had an Orient shirt on and hit the back of the onion bag. I went delirious. The O's had equalized and under our noses at that. Unbelievably it was 2–2. Could we pull off the greatest result in the history of football by going on to win the game?

The rest of the second half saw many a chance for both sides but as the game approached ninety minutes a replay looked the likely outcome. By this time I had given up straining my neck in the hope of seeing any of the action at the north end of the ground. Instead I contented myself with eyeing up the reaction of the Chelsea fans behind the south end goal whenever the blues attacked. I had not seen them celebrate ecstatically, so I knew that we were still ok. Then with just minutes of the ninety remaining a long Tom Walley through ball for the O's, once more saw mass confusion in the Chelsea defence. Our forward Ian Bowyer lunged at the ball, Bonetti fumbled and the ball broke to Barrie 'the beard' Fairbrother, who side footed it gracefully into the middle of the empty net. Incredible. I went balmy. My celebrations were wild, jumping up and down. Even my dad, if I remember rightly, was seen to look happy, though his smile that day was not on the same level as when they had played *Tijuana Taxi* for the first time at the ground, some three years earlier.

Mass confusion reigned at Brisbane Road for a few minutes as the Chelsea mob tried to invade the pitch to force an abandonment and when order was finally restored four minutes, which seemed like four hours injury time was added, all of it understandably played at the other end. A huge scream went up from the away supporters behind the Coronation Gardens end. I knew that something dramatic had happened, but by their reaction I knew that thankfully that it had not resulted in a goal. Moments later to my great relief, I saw Barrie Fairbrother catch the ball centre field and run triumphantly down the tunnel, as the referee blew for full-time.

We had done it. It was simply wonderful. With due respect to the 1966 World Cup Final, that afternoon saw the greatest game of football ever played. Once again we were 'giant killers', yet this time the glory was all ours. As we fought

THE GOALS

THAT SUNK

CHELSEA

These are the goals that rocked the football world. The goals that sunk Chelsea here at Brisbane Road in the fifth round of the F.A. Cup.

(1) Above, goalkeeper Peter Bonetti dives in an unsuccessful attempt to stop Phil Hoadley's 30-yard drive to cut Orient's arrears after going 2-0 down.

(2) Top right opposite, Bonetti and David Webb caught in a moment of confusion which allows Mickey Bullock (right) to go through and hit Orient's equaliser.

(3) Bottom right opposite, Barrie Fairbrother about to crack home the winner in the dying minutes of the match watched by a grounded Ian Bowyer.

our way out of the ground, along with the other thirty thousand, my dad hated it. The car was miles away, the traffic back to Chingford was terrible so that we arrived home just as Dixon of Dock Green was starting. For the first time ever after coming home from a game at Brisbane Road we had missed the whole of *Dr Who* that evening. But who cared.

It was for sure a glorious day. I was on cloud nine that evening. It was truly a day of firsts. The first time I had been there to see us beat a First Division club. The first time I had seen them win after being two goals down. The first time my dad had arrived home without having done the *Telegraph* crossword. Yet there was still one more first to come that super day. I had never been allowed to watch *Match of the Day* on the television on a Saturday night. The programme was never allowed to start before 10 o'clock and that was always considered too late for me to stay up and watch it at my tender age. Someone at the FA had decided upon this silly rule – probably the same person who decreed that Newport County's home games should all kick-off at 3.15. On that February day back in 1972 I had seen the BBC cameras at the ground and had watched at around 2.30pm as Barry Davies had climbed the ladder in the west stand onto the television gantry. I hoped in the evening, that I would be allowed to stay up and watch my heroes that night, especially after the result at Brisbane Road that afternoon.

As per normal however, I was given the red card and sent to bed at 9.30pm. This time though, I was given the proviso that if the Orient versus Chelsea game was the first match they showed on *MOTD*, then I would be allowed back downstairs to watch all of the action again. Sure enough to round off a memorable day, our match was indeed the initial game on, and I was therefore able to relive the afternoon all over again. And while it was on my dad was finally able to do the *Telegraph* crossword.

And then there was the commentary. One wonders if Barry Davies knew then that when he climbed those steps onto the west-side gantry that afternoon that he was about to give the greatest verbal display in the history of televised football. His summing up of the historic day epitomized the kind of form he was on: 'A tie that started as a purely London affair now belongs to the whole nation.' Magic stuff. With this one match Davies instantly replaced Wolstenholme as my commentating hero, an accolade that he still holds today. There used to be a big debate, especially in the nineties, pre-satellite television days, as to who was the BBC's number one commentator, John Motson or Barry Davies. Never any contest in my eyes after 26 February 1972. Anyone with any doubt only had to delve into the Beeb's archives and play again their coverage of Orient versus Chelsea. Presumably that was what someone did in 1994 when they awarded the World Cup Final that year to Davies, but no one can have done it four years later when the big match was inexplicably this time given to Motty. In the years that followed, they gave our Barry all sorts of sporting topics to cover at the BBC as well as the football. I'm sure though that when he was sitting there commentating on the two-man bob-sleigh in the winter Olympics, I bet he was sitting there wishing he could turn the clock back to that famous afternoon and be back there at Brisbane Road watching the best game of football ever played.

I remember going into school two days after the wonderful event and being treated by everyone as a hero. There were only a few Chelsea boys in our year. Most of the other lads hated them as they had won a few things in recent years, and they were generally thought of at the time as being somewhat arrogant. They could even boost a top ten hit with *Blue is the Colour*, a feat that even Spurs could not match in those pre Chas and Dave days. For a short time anyway it was a real pleasure being an Orient supporter and I revelled in it.

As a mark of respect to that remarkable day, and being the sad bloke that I was turning into then (and still am today) I took the decision never again to stand in the South Enclosure at Brisbane Road to watch another Orient game. That terrace, I decided must always be linked to the Chelsea match and nothing else. Any sane, normal person would have looked upon the place where we stood as a lucky omen and raced back there for the next home game, but I was rapidly turning into a bit of a footballing saddo in the seventies and normality is not a word always associated with such beings.

Nowadays that part of the ground is still there, but it is all seated. It is currently where away fans are located when there are a lot of them. From my wonderful seat high up in the West Stand during boring passages of play now (which is actually quite frequent with the O's these days) I look down at that terrace and still reminisce about that incredible afternoon. My plan is that on the nearest home game to 26 February 2022 I shall go and sit there to mark the 50th anniversary of planet earth's greatest day. Hopefully, too I'll be able to take my dad with the knowledge that being all seated he'll be able to do the *Telegraph* crossword this time round.

Whilst the Chelsea day remains one of the great days in the history of Leyton Orient Football Club, it must also be remembered that the afternoon had drastic repercussions for our opponents. The following week Chelsea were due to play Stoke City in the Final of the League Cup at Wembley. It was a match that they were expected to win easily against an ageing Potteries side. Yet after the result at Brisbane Road, the blues were clearly deflated and lost the game 2–1 with thirty-eight-year-old George Eastham scoring the winner.

I watched the final on *The Big Match* the day after it was played and I must confess to feeling very proud when I heard forty thousand Stoke supporters chanting 'Orient' before the game. The Chelsea slump after their defeat to us did not stop there. Indeed the club had problems aplenty for the rest of the decade after we beat them in 1972. A new East Stand was built at Stamford Bridge, the cost of which almost caused the club to go bankrupt. There was continual trouble with hooliganism amongst their fans and relegation to the Second Division followed. Even today veteran Chelsea followers say that the problems of the seventies all started for the Blues on that fateful day for them at Brisbane Road.

Given where the two clubs are these days it seems remarkable now to look back and remember that there was actually quite a rivalry between Orient and Chelsea in the seventies, and indeed the early eighties. We had some good wins against them in the league in this period – 3–1 at home on Boxing Day in 75, with Laurie Cunningham scoring a cracker sticks in the mind – and of course there was another famous cup win for us in 78.

The nearest we have come recently to even playing them was when the winners of our Cup replay against Scunthorpe were given Chelsea away in the FA Cup third round draw during the 2015–16 campaign. In true Orient style, of course we alas lost the replay 3–0, thus scuppering any thoughts we might have had of a 72 or 78 repeat.

There is indeed one more chapter to write about Orient verses Chelsea in 1972. For this we have to turn the clock forward some twenty-two years from the famous day. Season 1994–95 was even by Orient's standards a really poor one. We were rapidly sinking into the bottom division and on the brink of going bust. It was one continuous nightmare at the time. Making my way to the ground in October 1994 with the prospect of enduring another home defeat, this time against Plymouth, I saw a wonderful sight, however. A man selling videos of that Chelsea game some two decades earlier. I was stunned. Was I dreaming? Was this for real? It was pre YouTube of course and I had not seen the classic game again since the day of the match. No I was not dreaming. It certainly was for real. The man assured me that the video contained the full BBC match coverage of the game that afternoon back in 72, together with the legendary Davies commentary. Needless to say a copy was bought there and then. Indeed it was so tempting at the time to turn around and head straight back to the tube station, go back home to Loughton and watch my new purchase immediately. I resisted the temptation however deciding that I would wait until the evening to give it its first viewing. After witnessing the inevitable 2–0 defeat to the west country club that afternoon in 94, I went home and watched my new video some four times that night. It may only have been black and white, but it was still magnificent. Memories came flooding back of that super day, some twenty-two years earlier.

The quarter-final back in 72 saw us paired at home to Arsenal. My father and I did not go. He told me he tried but was unable to get a ticket. In fact I did not mind too much at the time. I knew just how much my dad had suffered in the previous round, and I did not expect us to beat Arsenal anyway. We ended up losing the match 1–0, albeit somewhat unluckily by all accounts. Actually I can remember quite enjoying the afternoon of the game. On the television on a Saturday afternoon *Grandstand* on the BBC and *World of Sport* on ITV had started flashing up the updated scores of the day's top encounters from time to time on their respective programmes. We may have lost against Arsenal that afternoon, but for me it was quite nice at the time to see our name actually appear on screen some six or seven times between three o'clock and four forty on the day. It never usually happened on a Saturday. As a follower of a small club, these were the things at the time that you had to make the most of when they occurred.

The rest of the season petered out somewhat disappointedly for the Orient in the league. My dad and I saw six or seven games, but they inevitably paled into insignificance when compared to the Fifth Round cup thriller. Although only twelve I remember even at the time thinking that if I carried on watching the O's for another fifty years I'd be hard pressed ever again to see a game as memorable as the Chelsea one. Well we are indeed approaching that fifty years and it has to be said that to this day the 3–2 thriller remains for me the all-time number one Orient/Leyton Orient match I've ever seen. As mentioned, Oxford in 2006, and the first Arsenal cup game in 2011 pushed it very hard, but just not quite hard enough to overtake it as my favourite ever game.

I was now closing in on becoming a teenager and I was basically becoming a football fanatic. It was of course a lot more difficult for those addicted to the great game in those days than it is today, of course. These were pre video and satellite times so that the only football I was able to watch all week was *The Big Match* on ITV on a Sunday afternoon and the preview programmes on Saturday lunchtimes. (After the Chelsea game for the time being *Match of the Day* on a Saturday night was still considered as being on too late for me to stay up, and had therefore gone back to being out of bounds for me.)

Around this time I can remember being thrilled at receiving free 'flick books' that were being given away with the *Daily Mirror*. These were six books that you could flick through from start to finish showing twelve goals (six on one side of the book, six on the other) from the past few years' football. Starved of any regular footy to watch I played them over and over again. Amongst others they had Best's goal against Benfica in the European Cup Final, and Clarke's winner against Arsenal in the 1972 Cup Final. It was not as good as watching any football on the television, of course but it was, I decided at the time a pretty good substitute for a soccer-starved youngster.

I was also ecstatic at the time to get a collection of 3-D footballers that were being given away at the time in *The Sun*. The rivalry between the two newspapers was intense at the time, indeed it remarkably still is today, of course. It was on the same scale as Celtic and Rangers, Spurs and Arsenal or even Orient and Newport County, so that when *The Mirror* brought out their football flick-book promotion, *The Sun* felt obliged to do something similar to rival it. They came up with cards of footballers in 3-D. We did not actually get *The Sun* in our household, but not for the first time my parents were harassed intensely, so that for three weeks my dad brought it home from work every day. I thought that the cards they gave away were great. It was more stuff to put in my wardrobe, so that even without the ditched *Scorcher* comics, with my programme collection ever increasing, my wardrobe was rapidly becoming a utopia of football related material.

CHAPTER 8

1972–73–A GUINEA PIG NAMED BOWYER

After all the dramas of the previous year, 1972–73 was a quiet season for the Orient. The O's ended up finishing fifteenth in the league, but alas we were knocked out of the cup in the Third Round, at home to First Division Coventry City. After the thrills of the previous campaign, *Match of the Day* cameras were once more sent to Brisbane Road for the game in the obvious hope of seeing another upset. To the great disappointment of myself and the rest of the nation, the Chelsea experience was not repeated however and we were well beaten 4–1. We did not go to the game, but at least it had been decided at the start of the season that I was old enough to be allowed to stay up on a Saturday evening and watch *MOTD*, so I witnessed the loss from the comfort of my home at 10 o'clock that night.

My father actually took me to a fair few games during the season. He knew that the time was rapidly approaching when I would be old enough to go to all of the games by myself, and he would be free to tend to the garden every Saturday afternoon.

The big news to break during the season was a change of name for my guinea pig at home. For a couple of seasons Ian Bowyer had been my favourite Orient player. This had stemmed from a home match in 1971 when he had scored a hat-trick against Cardiff City. I was not present at the game, but as it was the first time I had ever known any O's player to score three in one afternoon, he instantly became a hero of mine. My guinea pig, which we kept in the garage became 'Bowyer' overnight, named after Ian. (Not the sausages, which were big at the time.)

Indeed if I could have changed just one little detail about that near perfect day, 26 February 1972, it would have been that the ball could have broken to Bowyer and not Barrie Fairbrother in the 89th minute so that he could have stroked home the winner that afternoon.

However in 1973 Ian Bowyer was transferred to Manchester City. There were strong rumours of a training ground fight at the Orient following a reported fall out between manager George Petchey and Bowyer. No guinea pig of mine was going to be named after a Brisbane Road troublemaker, so I decided to change his name to Fairbrother.

CHAPTER 9

1973-74 – PROMOTION NEAR MISS AND A LONG WALK HOME

Having finished at Chingford Junior High School in July 1973 I moved up to Chingford Senior High School at the end of the summer. The even bigger news during the close season was that it was agreed, after a few family conferences that I was finally old enough to venture to the games at Brisbane Road alone, without the need for my father to accompany me. This obviously suited my dad, and it was of no great discomfort to me going to the games using public transport. The 69 bus went from outside our house through South Chingford, Walthamstow and Leyton before arriving at the High Road in E10, just a minutes' walk from the heaven that was Leyton Stadium.

I could now go to every home game that I wanted to go to, which basically meant every home game. This would have other knock-on effects, of course. I was now able to acquire more programmes to boost my collection. I could also now stand at matches, something that all the other lads at school were doing but something which I had never done, with the exception of the Chelsea cup game.

It was great watching the boys on a regular basis, but there was an even bigger bonus for me that season. Quite unbelievably, after three seasons of mediocrity in the league, Orient actually started to win a few matches. The story was that Malcolm Allison had had a massive clear-out at Crystal Palace during the summer. Our manager George Petchey knew their players from the time he had spent as a coach at Selhurst Park, and snapped up six of the better ones, notably John Jackson, Gerry Queen and David Payne. This proved to be a very smart move.

From October through to the beginning of December we played eight games, winning six and drawing two of them to leave us in second position behind Middlesbrough. We lost the first home game 1-0 against Bristol City, but after that I saw some cracking games. We beat Nottingham Forest 2-1, Bolton 3-0 and Luton, who at the time were in second place, 2-0. I liked to feel that the team knew that for the first time I was attending games regularly at Brizzy Road and were so turning it on just for me. I was for sure in a dream world just before Christmas. The Chelsea game was ninety minutes of happiness but this was now a continuous bliss. At the time (and I hope this doesn't sound too rude) I only lived to stand at the bus stop every two weeks and wait for my '69'.

On Boxing Day Crystal Palace, who were near the foot of the table were defeated 3–0 at Leyton Stadium. Our team that day included four of the players who Allison had kicked out. It was however the one home game that I missed, as Christmas in our family was always seen as a time for family visiting. I remember I did have the small consolation that Yuletide of receiving an Orient silk scarf as a present from my grandma. Silk scarves in the early seventies were **the** football fashion item. I have to say that it always brings a smile to my face these days when people complain about supporters being ripped off by the price of replica shirts, as if being ripped off is a new phenomenon. It's fair to say that football fans have been taken for a ride for decades. Silk scarves some forty odd years ago were the ultimate rip-off. They were useless in the cold weather because they gave no warmth at all around the neck, so that everyone wore them around the wrist. After normally one wash half the letters came off, so that by mid-January 1974 I found myself supporting 'Or e t F '. By this time I had also lost around 60% of the club dragons that had initially graced the other side. What's more at a pound a time they were flipping expensive too.

Another example of exploitation in those days were 'sock-tags', as popularized at the time by the hated Leeds United. These were funny little things that were supposed to hold your socks up with the player's number on them. A lot of the players wore them, yet if you were more than two rows up in the stand they were totally useless because you were too far away to identify the numerals. Like the scarves however everybody bought them. Although I still had the odd kick about over the park, my early retirement from the playing side of the great game was still pretty much in force, yet even I bought a pair of these utterly worthless, yet again very expensive football accessories, out of the Christmas money I got that year.

I went on to eventually work in a Bank for thirty-one years and as such I like to think that handling financial affairs is one of my stronger points, yet looking back now I cringe at some of the pounds that I have thrown away in the Orient club shop over the years. As spending cock-ups go some of my transactions over the years have been on a par with Leyton Orient paying Darius Henderson's wages for a whole year during the 2014–15 season.

The Orient team even made a dreadful record in 1973, which I bought, of course, quite imaginatively titled *Football, Football*. Bad as it was, it was still played relentlessly at the time on our mono Decca record player at home and it included such classic lines as 'football, football is the game we play, every

Saturday come and join us.' The likes of Cassidy, David Essex and the Sweet were never seriously challenged in the charts at the time. Thankfully it never replaced Herb in leading the team out every other Saturday.

The 1973–74 season peaked in the middle of January when we defeated Sunderland at home to stay second in the table behind Middlesbrough. As any O's veteran will tell you now, the rest of the season alas, was one largely of despair. Over the years the post-Christmas collapse has become something of a tradition at Brisbane Road. There were plenty in the nineties – indeed in 1997–98 we even fielded illegible players, which gave us a three-point deduction, thus giving us a helping hand to go down the league. More recently there was the 2013–14 season under Russell Slade in League One where we won our first eight and spent the first five months of the season never out of the top two, but still ended up not going up. And of course having won our first five league games in 2015–16 under Ian Hendon, we decided to start the downturn early in that most recent of seasons, winning only four out of the next 25 to finish eighth and outside of the play-off places. Looking back now though, it's fair to say that back in 1974 most of us had not seen any kind of dramatic collapse happen before at our club, so that we were totally unprepared for it at the time.

Before Christmas we had, as the expression goes, been 'scoring goals for fun'. Our three strikers Mickey Bullock, Gerry Queen and Barrie Fairbrother had all been hitting the back of the onion bag regularly. To have a forward line that could all score was then (and of course still is) almost unheard of at the Orient. Every thirty years or so, a miracle has happened and we've found ourselves with a proper goalscorer – a Peter Kitchen or a Jay Simpson – but to have more than one scoring at the same time for our club, has been virtually unheard of at our theatre of flats over the years. After being spoilt before Christmas back in 74 however, from February onwards the goals just dried up. Only eleven were scored in the last fifteen matches and as a result, we were to win only two of them.

Yet the football league in their wisdom had brought in 'three-up, three-down' for the first time in 1973–74, so that with the other sides in the promotion race also faltering, by the time of the last game of the season remarkably we still had a chance of going up. Play-offs of course had yet to be invented so that it was Carlisle or ourselves for that final third promotion place. The Cumbrians had finished their programme, so that we all knew that all we had to do was to defeat Aston Villa at home in a rearranged game, the Friday night before the Cup Final, to join the elite in the First Division.

Nowadays with the Orient, I inevitably expect things to go wrong, but back then like most O's supporters I entered the evening with supreme confidence. I was convinced that we were going up. Villa were mid-table and had nothing to play for. We would have the backing of a massive crowd with everybody rooting for us. What could possibly go wrong? I still felt that I had possibly not made the most of our previous promotion back in 1970 when I was only ten, so that this time I wanted to make the most of what I thought was going to be a great night.

Arriving home from school at four o'clock, I was outside waiting for the 69 bus at four-fifteen. First in the queue at Leyton Stadium at around a quarter to five, I had arrived at the ground well before any of the Orient players had, and I guess just as the Villa coach was leaving Birmingham. I was the first one to enter the ground when the turnstiles opened, and so was just about ok to secure my normal position just to the left of the goal, at the front of the North Terrace.

By kick-off time 29,766 were packed into our ground. Over the years we've had some great atmospheres in E10. We have had the two Play-off semi-final victories against Hull in 2001 and Peterborough in 2014, the Play-off Final win against Wrexham in 89 and the Arsenal game in 2011. Yet even to this day for me nothing has ever topped the atmosphere at Brisbane Road before that Villa game back in 74. The game was not all-ticket, three sides of the ground were standing so that everyone turned up early to try to get a decent place to watch what was going to be a bit of Orient history being made. By 6.15, seventy-five minutes before kick-off, you couldn't move on the north and south terraces or in the west-side. The singing was constant from all sides of the ground and there was not an away supporter in sight. It was glorious. This was going to be the night of nights, nothing could surely go wrong. But of course we are Leyton Orient so it therefore goes without saying that events – more often than not on the big occasion – very often do tend to go horribly wrong. Wembley in 1999, The Millennium in 2001, Wembley again in 2014, Swindon away last game of the season, 2015 – need I go on?

As the game started back in 1974, we were all over the Midlanders, but just could not score, a phenomenon we've witnessed countless times over the years watching the O's. Then the almost inevitable happened at the start of the second half. There was a Villa breakaway, an Orient player fouled inside our own area and from the resulting penalty the team with nothing to play for went 1–0 up. There was a stunned silence inside the stadium. We still had time though to put things right. Finally one of the countless Orient attacks resulted in a Mickey

Villa Pen.

Bullock equalizer right under our noses on the north terrace. Just one more needed. With the lads kicking towards us we were all trying to suck the ball into the net. The game went into injury time, we had a great chance for the winner but Villa custodian Jimmy Cumbes pulled off a wonderful save. The ref blew for time. Failure. We had blown it, big time. A massive cloud of disappointment descended over Brisbane Road.

I really did feel at the time that it was the end of the world. When we all signed that contract to become Leyton Orient supporters – in my case after the Stanley Baker game on 1 April 1967 – we were basically resigning ourselves to a lifetime of heartache and misery, broken only by the odd flash of glory usually every dozen years or so. There have indeed been many huge disappointments for me in the past fifty years, yet for me the one felt after the Villa game back in 1974 remains up there as the worst disappointment of the lot. I think that deep down at the time, I knew that we had blown the best chance that we would ever have of seeing our team play in the top division. I knew at the time that it had been a bit of a freak season for us to be up there at the top of the second tier. I knew that the chances of it repeating itself the next season, or indeed any season afterwards, were to say the least, slim. And so indeed that has proved to be the case. In the forty odd years since that Villa game, we have never again got remotely close to being in the First Division or, as I believe it is called today 'the Premier League'.

At the end of that infamous game I was truly gutted. My normal routine after the game in those days was not to stand at the bus stop outside the ground. I normally walked up to the previous one so that I could board an empty 69, thus avoiding the queues. The night of the Villa game though was different. I was devastated and just wanted to be left alone. I thus walked all the way home from Leyton through Walthamstow and back to Chingford. I arrived home at 125 Old Church Road at around eleven o' clock, some six and three quarter hours after I had left for the game. The Villa team were probably already back in Birmingham. Upon seeing my mum and telling her the result I recall her saying at the time, 'oh well, at least they didn't lose.' It was actually exactly the same thing that she had said some eight months earlier after England had drawn 1–1 with Poland which meant that they did not go to the World Cup Finals in 1974. Great person as my mum is, her football knowledge, it has to be said, is about on a par with that of Robbie Savage or Karren Brady.

The truth was that back in 1973–74 the Second Division was very ordinary. Middlesbrough won the title by fifteen points which, bearing in mind it was only two points for a win in those days, was a massive margin over the other sides. They were clearly a class above anyone else. Luton and Carlisle who went up with them not surprisingly both came straight back down the following season. The O's doubtless would have done the same thing, but nevertheless it would have just been nice to have seen them rub shoulders with the games best, if only for one season.

Looking back now some four decades on, despite the disappointment felt at the time, it had still been a remarkable year for the O's. When I first found out that the rules were being changed to three up/three down in our division, like most Orient fans I feared that it would be bad news for our team. With another side going down it would surely make it more difficult for us to preserve our status in the second tier. I don't think anyone actually considered that we would in fact be challenging at the top all season. The prospect of a year spent watching my team in the Second Division promotion pack at the time would have been about as believable then as the thought that one day Leyton Orient would be the subject of a reality TV show in Albania.

Our side that year, though we ultimately missed out, was actually very good. Ray Goddard and John Jackson shared the goalkeeping duties, and both were very competent. David Payne and Bill Roffey, the two full-backs, were dependable – I remember Roffey scoring an absolute screamer at home to Fulham in December. In midfield Peter Allen, Ricky Heppolette and Terry Brisley held things together, whilst our forward line had scored thirty-three between them by Christmas – to say the least a very un-Orient like total. Manager George Petchey had certainly done a fine job on limited resources, which of course was always the case at Brisbane Road.

The day after the infamous Villa night was the day of the FA Cup Final, yet I had no enthusiasm at all for Liverpool versus Newcastle that day. That fact alone shows just how much the events of the previous night had taken out of me, because normally Cup Final day was one of the highlights of my year, as indeed it's fair to say it was then for almost everybody with any interest in the great game. It's hard to believe now but looking back, the whole country came to a halt in the seventies on Cup Final afternoon. Come three o'clock on the big day the roads and shops were empty as everyone watched the big match on the television. Unlike now of course, it was virtually the only time of the year when you could watch a live game on the box, and folk made the most of it.

And the football would not just be on the television for the duration of the match with the Beeb and ITV starting their build up well before kick-off. *Cup Final Grandstand* and *Cup Final World of Sport* would both start well before mid-day. As opposed to the half hour football preview programmes you normally got on a Saturday for this one day there was a whole utopia of football related rubbish for obsessives like myself to get excited about.

To begin with both channels would have cameras inside the two team's hotels. We could gauge the mood of the players on the morning of the match and try to tell who was 'up for it' for the big day. Then the real fun would start in the battle for supremacy between the two channels. It would be *It's a Cup Final Knockout* and *Cup Final Mastermind* on the Beeb, against *Cup Final Wrestling* and Dickie Davies with *Meet the Cup Final Celebrities* on the commercial side. The latter would be live from the VIP lounge at Wembley. Davies would introduce the nation to personalities such as Susan George who, with large brandy in hand, would tell us all how she wasn't really interested in football, but liked seeing all of the players legs (ho! ho!) and was a big fan of Georgie Best.

The real curiosity for me however, was *Cup Final Wrestling*. Apart from the fact that Kent Walton who presented it, was moved three hours earlier than normal to accommodate the big game, I could never quite work out what the difference was between *Cup Final Wrestling* and *Wrestling*, which was on every other Saturday in the year. Still at least it meant that they ditched the *ITV Seven*, in other words the horse racing, which I hated, to make way for more football related material.

Any sane person subjected to either side from the start would have been totally sick of football by the time *Abide With Me* was sung at around at a quarter to three. I of course loved it all, though. 1973 had seen a classic Cup Final day, culminating in what remains my all-time favourite final as the mighty Leeds were humbled by second division Sunderland. The whole country had wanted the Rokerites to win as they were the massive underdogs, and also because the world at the time hated Leeds. And the whole country knew, of course that Sunderland included in their side an ex-O in Vic Halom, which obviously increased the north-easterners popularity everywhere. Just for one year however Cup Final day was different in 1974. I was in mourning. I just about mustered up enough enthusiasm to watch the game, but it was a poor one with Liverpool winning easily 3–0. Maybe if I'd have known at the time that the Newcastle side included a certain Frank Clark who was to become something of an Orient legend in later years, I may have paid a bit more attention to the match that afternoon.

So 1973–74, without the need for my dad to take me, had seen me for the first time go to virtually every home game at the Orient. By May our garden looked a lovely picture. Around Christmas I saw Sir Stanley Rous on a programme on the television. Rous was the world's football supreme in those days, a seventies version of Sepp Blatter without the alleged corruption. On the programme it was evident that like me the man was footy mad. He said that he had meticulously kept a record in a book of every football match he had ever been to over the years. I decided at the time that if it was good enough for Rous to do, then it was good enough for me. I therefore started to do the same thing, writing down every game I went to in a little black book. It probably goes without saying of course, that forty-two years on that little black book is alive and well. It is indeed still listing all the matches I go to along with all of the games results. I haven't bothered to write further details of the matches, as I figured from the start that I would have these details in copies of the *Rothmans Yearbooks* that I had. One thing that I have done however, is make a note of the end at which all the goals have been scored over the years in matches played at Brisbane Road. Also which way the O's have kicked towards in each half of the games, and at which end all of the penalties have been scored or missed. What use has this been to me over the past forty years? None whatsoever. So why have I done it? I haven't got a bloody clue.

CHAPTER 10

1974–75 – A DISLIKE OF MANCHESTER UNITED

It's laughable now but in the mid-seventies, a lot of people said that the introduction of three-up and three-down between the top two divisions in English football would be a disaster for the game in this country. Many said that the new innovation would never last. At the end of its first season in 1973–74, little old Carlisle (much to the sadness of Orient supporters, of course) were promoted to the First Division for the first time in their history, while the mighty Manchester United ended up getting relegated to join us, for one season in Division Two.

When the new seasons fixtures came out for 1974–75, our first game paired us at home to the Red Devils. In those dark days of football hooliganism, it was part of football tradition that Manchester United supporters would riot at every away game. Whilst most of the clubs in the top league had done their best to control it to a large degree, when they went down to the Second Division the majority of clubs there were totally unprepared for it and simply could not cope.

Leyton was completely invaded by the Mancunian hooligans on 17 August 1974. By about mid-morning they were apparently running riot all over E10, smashing shop windows and causing general mayhem in the area. In those days Brian Moore would introduce ITV's Saturday football preview programme, *On The Ball* live from the ground where he would be commentating from for the game on *The Big Match* the next day. As our game against United had been chosen as that Sunday's match, Moore previewed the day's action live from the television gantry in the west-side at Brisbane Road.

Needless to say in those days, when there was very little footy on the box I loved the two football preview programmes on the BBC and ITV on Saturday lunchtime. The little football tasters had started in the late sixties with Sam Leitch's slot on the Beeb, which always kicked off *Grandstand*, after David Coleman had done the programme's necessary introductions. The beauty of it for me in those days was that for the first time I was able to see all the goals from the previous weeks *Match of the Day*, which I had not been allowed to stay up and watch. It was indeed the first football a soccer-starved youngster had seen since the previous Sundays *Big Match*. Eventually ITV followed suit with a lunchtime programme *On The Ball*, as part of *World of Sport*. It usually followed straight on from the Beeb's offering, so that there was normally about fifty minutes of continuous football coverage on a Saturday lunchtime. It would get you in the mood for the great game, especially if you were going to a match that afternoon.

On the Saturday of the Man U. game however, you could see behind Moore that all hell was going off at Brisbane Road. In those days ITV were never allowed to officially say where they were doing the preview show from, as it would give away which game was going to be on *The Big Match* the next day. It seems incredible looking back now, with all the live footy we have these days, but it was thought that if folk knew that the match was going to be on the box the following day they would not bother attending the game. With all the turmoil in Leyton during the morning, the decision had been made to let all the United fans into our ground early as it was thought that the idiots would be easier to control if they were inside Leyton Stadium, rather than on the streets of east London. You did not need to be a football genius to recognize that the cameras were at the Orient that afternoon and that the Manchester following were going berserk inside Brisbane Road. Brian Moore looked petrified. Witnessing all the chaos I made the decision to give the game a miss for my own safety. Even though United won the game 2–0 the trouble continued throughout the game and afterwards in London. The next week ITV took he decision to transfer *On The Ball* to the safety of the studio and as far as I remember it was never transmitted live from a ground again after that Brisbane Road experience.

Brisbane Road 17 August 1974. I missed this.

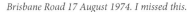

To this day it still bugs me greatly that I missed that Orient versus Manchester United fixture, on 17 August 1974. One of my (sad) ambitions following the O's over the past six decades has always been to be able to eventually say that I've seen them play at least once against every one of the other ninety-one clubs in the football league. Presently, I've currently seen them encounter eighty-seven of the other teams at least once. The only ones I've not seen them play against are Liverpool, Manchester City, Burton Albion and Manchester United. We've never played Burton, and Liverpool and Manchester City we haven't encountered since the sixties, but Man U. was the one of those four that I could and should have been at when we faced them. But I wasn't all thanks to the United yobbos.

Nowadays many people hate Manchester United. For many it's a question of the arrogance of their supporters, with their cockney and west-country accents. The fact that they think it's their right to win trophies year after year and that if they go eighteen months without silverware then they are all living deprived lives. They think they support the biggest club in the world, despite the fact that they are often not even the top team in their own city. Many dislike them remembering that for so long they were led by a man called Sir Alex, reason enough to forever hold a grudge against them. For me however the animosity felt is all a matter of what happened on 17 August 1974 when they tried to wreck my club and indeed Leyton, and made me miss a game at Brisbane Road when I should have been there.

After the first home match debacle I attended most of the home games during the 1974–75 season. We ended up finishing twelfth. The writing was always on the wall that it was going to be a bit of an anti-climax after the previous campaign. The undoubted highlight of the season was a Third Round FA Cup tie at home to Derby County. Derby were an exceptional side that year, and actually went on to become League Champions at the end of it. An excellent crowd packed Brisbane Road in January to watch the match, and after just twenty minutes we were incredibly 2–0 up thanks to goals from Derek Posse and Gerry Queen. There were rightly thoughts of another famous afternoon along the lines of the Chelsea one some three years earlier. Derby defender Colin Todd ruined the script however, scoring twice to peg us back to 2–2 and condemn us to a replay. Both the goals were deflected, and indeed they ended up being the only goals he got all season. For years to come I hated Colin Todd. Somewhere in his career I'm sure he must have played for Newport County or Peru.

The BBC covered the Derby match, it was the main action that night on *Match of the Day*. The Beeb made the massive mistake that day however of sending John Motson to commentate on the game. If the job had been given to Barry Davies I felt at the time, we'd surely have won.

The replay was the following Wednesday. I knew that the game would be shown on ITV's football show late that evening, *Midweek Sport's Special,* which was aired straight after the *News at Ten* on the commercial channel. It was before I was allowed to venture to away games, but I blanked myself out from listening to the results on the radio that evening, so that I could watch the later highlights show without knowing the result. The O's gave another sterling performance. With just a few minutes of the programme remaining the score was 1–1. You knew watching though, that someone had to get a winner before the ninety minutes were up because there was no time left for them to show any extra-time.

Orient had brought on a young substitute, a winger called Laurie Cunningham in the second half. With the end of the game approaching, he broke away from Colin Todd and the rest of the Derby defence, and found himself one on one against the County 'keeper. This surely had to be it, more giant killing for the O's and our passage through to the next round. Alas no, like all good Orient forwards the youngster missed, shooting wide of the custodian but also wide of the post.

Needless to say Derby went up the other end almost directly from this and scored, so that we ended up losing 2–1 despite another more than admirable performance. At least the two games against the eventual league champions gave us something to remember the season by. The league by contrast gave us very little. Our forward line, which had stopped scoring the season before around February, this time round decided to shut up shop around September. We ended up scoring just twenty-eight times in forty-two matches. Derek Possee ended up top scorer with a massive seven. Twelve games ended up 0–0 and twenty-two of the forty-six competitive matches played were draws. Most exciting team in the football league we definitely were not in 1974–75.

Quite remarkably though we managed to obtain a 0–0 draw at Old Trafford in the return fixture against the Red Devils in March. Over 41,000 saw a game, which by all reports we could easily have won. Tom Wally 'scored' what many considered a perfectly good goal, but it was ruled offside. Some things in life simply have not changed over the past forty odd years, and one is the fact that you never get any decisions as an away team at Old Trafford. Still along with

Bristol City we were the only team to keep a clean sheet there all season. I never read reports of any trouble at the game, so I presume that the Orient fans that travelled up to the match that day resisted the temptation to smash up Manchester as an act of revenge for what had happened in Leyton, back in August.

Home life for me continued to go well, it was a big year for me at school, but a successful one as I finished it by passing nine 'O' levels. Yes, 'O' levels. What a wonderful name for an exam. Not only were my club the only one in the Football League ever to have a Christmas carol written in their honour, but they were also the only one to have a national exam named after them.

CHAPTER 11

1975–76 – SAINS-BURIED ON A SATURDAY AFTERNOON

I made two major decisions during the close season. The first was that I was going to stay on at Chingford Senior High School to study Mathematics, Economics and History 'A' levels in the sixth form. Chingford Senior High School, or Chingford Foundation School as it is called these days has built up a reputation for producing footballers over the years. On display within it now I believe, are a signed shirt donated by David Beckham, who was once a pupil, and a pair of boots again signed by another ex-pupil, Harry Kane. Regrettably nothing of mine is hung anywhere in the building as far as I know, though they may have framed an old O's programme somewhere, in recognition of my wonderful collection of 3,000 of the things.

The second decision, and it seems somewhat incomprehensible these days, was that I decided to get a part-time job at Sainsbury's supermarket on a Saturday. Since the sixties I have been a football nut. Saturday afternoon when the season is on has always meant just one thing and one thing only, and that's footy. Even if I am not at an O's game I will follow their score and if they are not playing I will follow the other scores. The world always stops for the great game at three o'clock on the first day of the weekend.

As a Christmas present the wife got me a ticket to see Jersey Boys last December on a Saturday afternoon – the O's were playing at Mansfield that day. The matinee performance started at 3.00pm. Around ten to three I took my seat and expected to hear *Tijuana Taxi* sounding from the speakers at any minute. It never came. The interval arrived just before four o clock. I went to the loo and was amazed to find myself looking at so many happy faces. Usually when I go to relieve myself at that time on a Saturday afternoon, it's at Brisbane Road, and more often than not I am surrounded by doom and gloom and unhappiness. It all seemed a bit weird at the time. I enjoyed the show though I would have enjoyed it more had we got more than a 1–1 draw at Field Mill that day.

The thought of me missing Saturday afternoon matches at Leyton Stadium these days is about as believable now as the thought in the seventies would have been of any Orient owner being wanted for extradition by the Albanian authorities. Yet I spent two seasons – 1975–76 and 1976–77 stocking shelves in a supermarket rather than being at our little piece of heaven in east London. Naturally I feel a little ashamed of myself these days looking back, but at the time I was busy studying and needed the money for things like real ale and clothes so I virtually stopped going to football for a couple of years.

That's not to say, however that I lost interest in the O's or indeed football during my sabbatical. Finishing work around six I would stroll home and wait outside the newsagents for the classified results edition of the *Evening Standard* to be delivered there at around 6.40pm. In those pre-mobile and Internet days the *Evening Standard* classified results edition on a Saturday evening was a really popular newspaper. There would be a queue of people outside the newsagents early evening waiting for the van to arrive with the football results edition. For many of us it was the first time we had had news of the afternoon's goings on up and down the country. It was a real rush job for the printers, I remember thinking at the time that they must have been miracle workers to get all of the results to us within an hour of the matches finishing. The match reports would be roughly ninety per cent about the first halves of the games, and then there would be a couple of lines stating the scorers in the second periods. It could make for hilarious reading if a team made a dramatic late comeback.

I remember one Saturday Chelsea playing Bolton Wanderers and going 3–0 down by half-time. They proceeded to make a dramatic recovery however and actually won the game 4–3. The headline in the *Standard* that evening read, 'Chelsea hammered by the Wanderers.'

For Orient, 1975–76 was another unremarkable campaign. We finished thirteenth in the league, were knocked out of both the League and FA Cups at the first attempt and could still not average a goal a game. The only bright spot was the form of Laurie Cunningham who was clearly going to be a star of the future. I did not really miss much however, by only going to Brizzy Road a few times that season. A sign of how I'd just temporarily lost a bit of interest at the time can be gauged by the fact that Barrie Fairbrother had been transferred to Millwall, yet I hadn't even bothered to change the name of our guinea pig.

CHAPTER 12

1976–77 – THE ANGLO SCOTTISH SKELETON IN MY CLOSET

One of the big regrets I've got in my life as an O's fan is that I never made the most of the Anglo-Scottish Cup run in 1976–77. It still hurts now that Orient made it to a Cup Final and I was not there to see it. Ok so it was only a relatively minor tournament, we lost 5–1 on aggregate to Nottingham Forest and the Final was not played at Wembley, but it was a final nevertheless and I was not present home or away. It also bugs me that I missed out on seeing our lads play at Aberdeen and Patrick Thistle in Scotland, as part of our run in the competition. How good would that be to have on your Orient CV that you saw them play at two venues north of the boarder? I'm currently up to 146 when it comes to the number of grounds I've witnessed the O's play competitive matches on, but it could easily have been 148 had I started following them away a year or so earlier than I did, which would have enabled me to have included Aberdeen and Patrick on my list.

The truth at the time however was that I really was up to my eyes in it studying for my 'A' levels and unbelievably as it seems now, pretty much nothing else, not even my beloved O's, mattered at the time. The Brisbane Road team that I was not watching were really struggling in the league, especially (just for a change) when it came to sticking the ball in the back of the net. We managed a massive thirty-six goals in the forty-two league games in 76–77. Not surprisingly Laurie Cunningham was transferred for £100,000 to West Bromwich Albion in March having played the first twenty-four games. At the end of the season however, he was still the top goal scorer with just half a dozen. There were big problems with the pitch at Brisbane Road, so that with postponements galore we ended up playing what seemed like half the season's home games in April and May.

With the season drawing to a close, for the first time in a few years, despite the fact that we had for some time had games in hand over the other strugglers, relegation looked a distinct possibility. In the end it all came down to the final match of the season, at home to Hull City on 17 May. We needed a draw to stay up. It was a Tuesday night and my exams were only a month away, yet I knew I just had to be at Brisbane Road that night. In hindsight it turned out to be one of the most important evenings in my fifty years of supporting east London's finest.

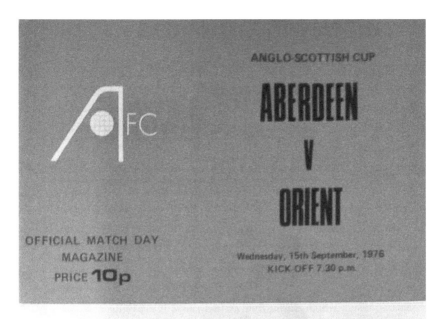

Alas, I missed this one.

As you can imagine the game itself was very tense. We took the lead through Allan Glover, who had come to the club along with big Joe Mayo, as part of the deal that had taken Cunningham to West Brom. A very rare mistake by 'keeper John Jackson however, enabled Hull to equalize and ensure a desperate nail-biting finish for the eight and a half thousand present. By all accounts Jackson had been brilliant all season and if it had not been for him our passport to the Third Division would have been booked long before the last game. Despite his aberration though, we held on for a 1–1 draw and Second Division football was thankfully assured for at least another season.

At the end of the match there were huge celebrations at the ground. The evening highlighted just what a strange phenomenon it can be at times being a football supporter. Just three years previously, we had again seen our team draw 1–1 at home in the last game of the season against Aston Villa, and we had all gone home as if it was the end of the universe. Now here we all were witnessing the same result, which meant that we had thus finished fifteen places lower in the league than we had done on the previous occasion. Yet the way we were all acting on the terraces, this time it was as if we had just won the European Cup. Bizarre.

One of the things you soon realize about supporting a crap team like the O's over the years is that you really do have to make the most of any kind of success, or actually anything remotely resembling any faint kind of triumph, when it does eventually come along. This was one such occasion, and we all wanted to make the most of it. We were also presented with a novel way of celebrating that night against Hull. It had been decided that because of the poor state of our pitch, it was all to be dug up and re-laid during the close season. Supporters were invited onto the playing area after the match to take home any turf they so desired. Having spent years of being told at Leyton Stadium to stay off the pitch at all times, this in itself was a real novelty that evening.

I managed to acquire some grass just to the right of the penalty spot at the Coronation Gardens end of the ground, which accompanied me home on the 69 bus that night. I liked to think of it as being from the actual spot where Barrie Fairbrother had slide home the winner against Chelsea some five years earlier. Upon arriving home that night my mum did not seem too keen on having my sacred piece of turf inside the house, so I therefore took it to the garage. I placed it next to Fairbrother's cage and sat looking at it. A sudden feeling of guilt came over me. I started to feel rather ashamed that I had virtually abandoned the

Orient, my first love, for the past couple of seasons. I decided there and then that in 1977–78 it was all going to be so different and that I was going to be a born-again dedicated supporter of the club. Whenever even now, however I meet up with O's veterans, I still pray they do not bring up seasons 75–76 and 76–77. For two years I was hardly there at Brisbane Road, and to this day it still hurts to own up to that sorry truth.

CHAPTER 13

1977–78 – CUP N' KITCH GLORY

I celebrated my eighteenth birthday in June 1977 and two months later had more cause to be over the David Mooney as news came through that I had passed all three 'A' levels. I decided that I would take a year off from studying before going to university to do a four-year business management degree starting in September 1978. I booked myself in for a course at Aston University in Birmingham some twelve months later. I got myself a job as a pension's clerk with Spillers who made Homepride flower as well as dog food, so that I could save some money for the time that I was going to have studying up in Birmingham.

Having had my appetite well and truly whetted by the Hull game, I was eagerly awaiting the start of the new season. Little did I know it then but 1977–78 was going to shape the rest of my life.

With no Saturday job for me anymore, I was now free to go to east London's piece of heaven for all the home games. It all started for me on 3 September with the season's first Saturday Brisbane Road encounter against Oldham Athletic. Standing at the bus stop outside my house waiting for that '69' I realized just how much I had missed not going to football the previous two years. I decided there and then that I was going to go to all the home matches that I could that year. Indeed over the next eighteen months I was to develop into a real Orient addict, so that it would eventually get to the stage where, for a period, I would go to every game home or away, no matter what.

Arriving at the ground and looking at the programme that day, I felt really ashamed that I knew very little about the Orient team. Names like Mayo and Chiedozie meant nothing to me. And then there was the number ten. A fairly short, little bit tubby bloke, who was evidently a new signing bought from Doncaster Rovers. A chap named Peter Kitchen. This guy, by all accounts had been scoring goals aplenty for the Yorkshire club who were two divisions below us.

But we all knew that he would not do the same at the Orient, of course. We never had anyone who knew where the back of the net was. It was a well-known fact that our top scorer never made it into double figures. Since I'd been watching them Orient shirts seven to eleven seemed to have generally been filled with some of the great non-marksmen of the era. The seventies for sure had been dreadful as far as goal scoring was concerned. To get the ball rolling we had hit the target all of twenty-nine times in 70–71, top scorer being Mark Lazarus with six (he could have had eight but had Jewish holidays off) It was for sure a malaise that continued throughout the decade. The O's were barely averaging a goal a game since their promotion in 1970.

On the afternoon of the Oldham match it took me all of ninety seconds to decide that I liked Peter Kitchen. By then he had already scored. Orient strikers just did not score a mere ninety seconds after the kick-off. By the end of the afternoon he had scored again and I liked him even more. Unbelievably we ended up winning the match 5–3. Games at Brisbane Road just did not end up 5–3. Kitch looked a little overweight, a touch lazy and he seemed to have a problem when it came to defending. He also sported a rather silly Mexican bandit like moustache. Yet it was clear that he knew where the goal was. Ok so there was the small matter of my team reaching the semi-final of the FA Cup in 1978, but of just as much significance for me that year was the fact that we had at long last found a goal-scoring hero.

The O's though, despite Kitchen, really struggled results wise for the first three months of the season. I was finding Spillers really boring, yet I always had the consolation at the time of Kitchen. I waited for the '69' at two o'clock every other Saturday afternoon in high anticipation of seeing that Peter Kitchen goal, and I was rarely disappointed. 3 December 1977 was a particularly big day. None of those present at Brisbane Road that day will ever forget the first hat-trick scored by an Orient player for over six years. Arguably more memorable than any of his goals that day against Mansfield was his attempt at a somersault after the third. After nearly breaking his back in the process Kitch never again attempted the feat. O how I loved the man

By the turn of the year he had notched up fourteen of the twenty-two we had managed in the league. I can remember at the time, sitting and staring for ages at the 'leading scorers' listings in the Sunday papers. It just seemed incomprehensible that an Orient player could be up there with the Latchfords and Dalglishs of the world. Looking back I'm glad now I did all of the staring at the time because it was to be another thirty-eight years before I was able to do similar with an 'O' once more top of the goalscoring pile, this time through Jay Simpson in 2016.

After my two year sabbatical from the game despite the indifferent results, by Christmas I was well and truly back in the Orient groove. I was there at every home game and I was even keeping my eyes open for those Newport results in the division below us. It was as if I had never been away. I was going to the games on my own, but that did not bother me at all.

I still had a special passion for the FA Cup after the events of February 72 and hoped that in my comeback season the lads would give me a nice little run in the competition as a welcome back. What transpired in 1978 however, was something beyond my wildest dreams. The Third Round draw gave us First Division Norwich City at home. It signalled the start of the most remarkable run by any team in the entire history of the FA Cup.

The FA allowed the O's to stage the match against the Canaries on the Friday night, the day before all the other ties were to be played. To anyone under thirty reading this it may seem hard to believe now, but the date of the game was not changed to suit the television companies. It was the Orient who requested the change so that we could attract a bigger crowd with both West Ham and Tottenham having home ties on the Saturday. In fact the decision was fully justified as fourteen and a half thousand were lured to Brisbane Road that night to watch the mighty O's. From my normal position on the north terrace, which I had reclaimed after my two-year absence, I went bananas as Kitch (who else) gave us a first half lead. We were going to be 'giant-killers' all over again and with no other games being played on the night we were guaranteed to have all the glory in the morning newspapers. Alas it was not to be however, as Norwich equalized in the last minutes through Roger Gibbins. Although whilst not quite on the same level as the Villa game some three and a half years earlier I still felt gutted at the end of the evening. We had been so close to a memorable win but in the end we had to settle for a draw and a replay at Carrow Road.

I felt even more sick at lunchtime the next day. City manager John Bond had seen his team luckily sneak into the Fourth Round draw and he had been invited on to the BBC's *Football Focus* programme that lunchtime as a studio guest. He sat there throughout the interview looking ever so smug with a silly grin on his face. After hearing him answer questions about the previous night's game in the nauseating west-country accent he possessed, he joined Colin Todd as one of my footballing cult hate figures, a seventies managerial version of Steve Evans.

It was generally accepted that by failing to win at Leyton Stadium we had blown our best chance of progressing into the Fourth Round. Amazingly though we won the replay 1–0. It was the only game of the wonderful cup campaign that I missed that season, though as you can imagine I was just a bit pleased when

I found out the result. Needless to say Kitchen got the night's only goal, but by all accounts our real hero that night was keeper John Jackson. If Kitch was to become my all-time Orient hero, then Jacko to this day, runs him a close second.

I could always relate to goalkeepers. Partly because in those days I always stood behind the goal at matches I went to, and partly because on the few occasions when I did happen to play the game myself, I always stood between the sticks. Though officially retired from playing, if I did venture over the park with a few mates I normally ended up as the goalkeeper. Basically this was because I was a little on the tubby side and I did not like running, having all the speed of a seventies Jamie Snowcroft. I therefore developed a soft spot for goalkeepers, and in my opinion John Jackson is the best I have seen play for the O's.

My development as somewhat of a footballing anorak had been somewhat knocked back at the time by my two years in the wilderness during the 75–76 and 76–77 seasons. By early 78 however I was back on track to becoming a 100% footy saddo. For a start my Orient programme collection was really beginning to take off again. I started to try to fill the gaps in my portfolio. I would turn up to Brisbane Road early to delve through the old ones in the programme shop. I started to write to dealers for certain ones that I was missing.

Season 1977–78 to this day remains my all-time favourite season at the Orient. There is though just one dark spot about that memorable campaign. The ridiculous size of the programme. For some inexplicable reason the Orient home match-day magazine for the season was a quite ridiculous oblong shape. By making the things a daft eight inches by six inches they were near impossible to keep in good condition during the match. I tried various tactics like putting the buggers in an envelope and a Tesco carrier bag, but this was abandoned in October when the bag got badly trodden on after celebration of a Peter Kitchen goal against Cardiff.

There was the option of having them posted to me, but programmes really do have to be read on the day of the game and I also reckoned that you could always rely on the Post Office to lose at least one a season, so this idea was given the red card. How I longed at the time for a return to the late sixties and the little plain white cover jobs when they fitted nicely into a side pocket and always arrived home in pristine condition.

Some thirty-seven years on and I look back now at my Orient homes of the 77–78 – and indeed the 78--79 ones when the shape did not change – and I have to report that it marks a low point in my Orient programme collecting career. Alas some of them are in a bit of a sorry and creased state. It's all very sad. Indeed things did not get any lower than for the visit of Charlton Athletic on 4 February. Having just acquired the magazine it started to pour with rain. I thus had a predicament. Did I fold the article and put it in my pocket, thus getting it creased but keeping it dry, or did I hold it meaning it would be uncreased but open to the elements? I chose the latter option. However it did not stop raining all afternoon from two o'clock onwards. Luckily, however the referee could see my predicament from the middle of the pitch and to save my programme from further punishment took the decision to abandoned the match at half-time. Looking at the programme now it really suffered getting wet that afternoon and is to this day in a sorry state, but as the game was not finished it begs the question is it a proper match-day mag anyway?

The Fourth Round draw gave us Blackburn Rovers at home. Though in the same division as the O's, they were well above us in the league and in the game at Brizzy looking much the better team for the first hour. They took the lead, but Jacko was having another blinder to keep the score down to 1–0. Then in a totally unexpected turnaround Kitch got two and big Joe Mayo another to send us into the Fifth Round. On the way to the semi-final in 78 we defeated three First Division sides, yet in my opinion the best team we encountered before we played Arsenal was that Blackburn side. They really should have beaten us that afternoon.

As the cup run was gaining momentum, we continued to struggle in the league. Though I did not think that we were playing that badly, results were just not going our way. After a poor start to the season George Petchey had been replaced by a returning Jimmy Bloomfield. This was a popular choice as Bloomfield had done so well in his first stint as manager. Despite the magnificent Kitch, scoring goals remained a problem for the rest of the team, though with Jacko around there was always a fair chance of keeping a clean sheet. We had a settled team as well, with five of the better players being ever presents that season. For some reason though it was really difficult for us to get points on the board in the league.

When the O's were drawn at home to Chelsea in the FA Cup Fifth Round, a flood of memories were brought back. This time I went to the match alone, my dad staying at home, and I stood on the north terrace. The Orient side this time around was totally different to that which played some six years before, only Peter Allen remained at the club from the time of the previous match. Some things were never going to change unfortunately, and the Chelsea following were as naughty as ever, breaking down the wall at the front of the Coronation Gardens end two minutes into the match. They had managed to injure a few of their own supporters with their surge forward and consequently the rest of the match fell a bit flat, ending goalless. Kitch had a goal disallowed when he was about three miles offside and Jacko pulled off one fine save, but it was a generally disappointing afternoon. As with the Norwich tie, it appeared that we had blown our best chance of progressing, by failing to win the tie at Brisbane Road.

Twenty-fifth February – two days before the Chelsea replay – will go down in as a big day in my O's supporting career. It was to herald my debut as an Orient away fan, with the O's playing at White Hart Lane. It was to be the first of hundreds for me as a visiting supporter, yet it cannot be said that it was a true reflection of what was to be the norm in the years to come, in so much as we did not lose on our travels that day, drawing 1–1.

I had been to many games at 'the Lane' over the years and had always stood on what was called, 'the Shelf', there. This was a wonderful place to watch football. The stand was high up above the half-way line and from it, you would get a great view of the whole pitch. There was rarely any trouble, as all the yobbos would stand behind the goal in the Park Lane Stand terrace to taunt the away supporters, who were housed in the adjacent section. Many folk in those days, used to arrive at grounds at least an hour before kick-off to secure their normal spot on the terraces. Up and down the country it was the same at all of the bigger clubs. As a result an excellent pre-match atmosphere had always been created by kick-off time. That's all so unlike today alas, where people have their designated seats and simply don't have to get to games early. The terracing back in those days, always created a much better atmosphere, and of course, the games in those days were affordable for the majority of people.

Hillsborough in 1989 was a shocking experience, of course, and standing at matches had to be made safer, that goes without saying. However, the demise of such wonderful terraces such as the Shelf, the North Bank at Arsenal and the Shed at Chelsea was in so many ways, still sad. At the end of the day there was also an easy excuse for the administrators to raise prices by making stadia all seater, which was exactly what they did.

Back in 78 for my initial Orient away game, I stood on the Shelf and mingled with the Spurs contingent rather than stand with my fellow O's behind the goal on the away terrace. As a result I was to experience a sensation at my first away match that I was to encounter many a time on my early away travels; that of going absolutely mad inside celebrating an Orient goal, while outwardly remaining as calm as anything. Many a time in the seventies and eighties, I blended in with the home fans rather than stand in the away end with fellow O's. Though it's thankfully a thing of the past now, at one time away fans were often charged more in their section than the home fans paid in theirs. You would get a view much worse as a visitor than the home lot would get and facilities were generally not as good for those who had travelled to follow their team. I often therefore went in the home end and learned quickly how not to go balmy when Orient hit the back of the onion bag. The Tottenham game ended 1–1, which was a fine result for us, against a team who were heading straight back to Division One, the Spurs having been relegated the year before.

Two days later saw the Chelsea replay. Although, in my opinion, it was not quite on the same level as the cup game with them some six years before, the 78 Chelsea cup experience is still certainly well up there in my list of all-time top Orient matches.

Since my dad had stopped taking me I'd always gone to watch matches alone. As has been previously stated all my school chums had been Spurs, Arsenal or Hammers fans, though going to Brisbane Road by myself had never bothered me at all. With the O's into the last sixteen of the cup this season however, a few of my mates had amazingly started to take an interest in the team from E10. I travelled across London that night with Mike, Tinks, Malcolm and Kevin, four friends from way back. Indeed, Mike was the same Mike Attwood of Liverpool Subbuteo team notoriety back in 1970, though some eight years later I'd just about brought myself to forgive him for not being able to get me the proper miniature Orient team on my eleventh birthday.

Along with a small group of Orient supporters we all stood in the away end that night for one of those truly wonderful football evenings. Although I knew that I could keep my mouth shut, I knew that no way would the other four be able to if our boys scored, so that standing with the Chelsea lads in the Shed was not an option. At half-time however the prospect of cheering an O's goal seemed highly remote. We were one down, our full-back Bill Roffey having wonderfully lobbed Jacko from twenty-five yards to give Chelsea the lead though an own goal.

But then came Kitch. Things had gone a little un-Orient like at Tottenham a couple of days earlier in that Joe Mayo had scored our goal rather than Kitch. Normal service was resumed that Monday, however. After forty-nine minutes the great man beat six Chelsea defenders – including Micky Droy three times – to score an absolute classic. Then twenty-four minutes later a long through ball saw our magnificent saviour slide the ball past Peter Bonetti to make it 2–1. Unbelievable. The goals were up the other end to where we were standing on the North Bank, but needless to say the small pocket of O's fans gathered there went absolutely balmy.

Being the Orient we all expected an equalizer to come any time before the final whistle, but miraculously we held on for a famous 2–1 victory and a quarter-final place for just the fourth time in our history. I escorted my four mates out of the ground, making sure that we all looked glum and kept quiet while walking back to the tube station. When we reached what we considered the safety zone of Stratford on the Central Line all hell broke out however. We all let out all of that pent up joy that had been bottled up inside us all since we had left the ground. It was for sure a glory, glory night and the elation continued the next day, with the game making all the headlines in the papers. I had known since the second minute of the Oldham game at the start of the season that Peter Kitchen was the greatest striker the world had seen since Pele, but now it seemed that the world was starting to recognize it too. In getting to the quarter-finals of the FA Cup we had scored seven times and the mustachioed messiah had scored six of them. He was already fast becoming an O's legend.

As well as a time of great excitement for the Orient, it was also a time of big change in my personal life. Being a pension's clerk at Spillers was about as interesting then as listening to a Roy Hodgson press conference is these days. I decided to call it a day there and go and work elsewhere. On 20 March I was to start work at the Australia and New Zealand Bank in the City of London – generally known as 'the ANZ'. The plan was that I was to stay there just six months to save some money, before university started in September. Although I was not intending to stay at my new place of employment for any great length of time, my salary rose from £2,400 at the dog food company to £3,000 a year at the bank. That was a lot of money in those days for a youngster and it was for sure a good transfer for me.

I left Spillers on Friday 10 March, and took a week off before I started work at my new employers. The eleventh saw the FA Cup quarter-final at Middlesbrough. It was to become a day that has gone down in Orient folklore. When veteran O's fans meet up even today, there's always a story or two about our legendary trip to Ayresome Park back in 1978. Two football specials left from Stratford station along with many a coach from Brisbane Road that day to see our big game. This level of support was unheard of for an Orient away game in those days, with everyone keen to see whether our boys could make it through to their first ever FA Cup semi-final. I was aboard one of the trains. Upon our arrival in the North East we were afforded a wonderful police escort to the ground. Two train loads sung cockney songs through the streets of Middlesbrough as we were determined to make the most of one of the great days in the club's history. The locals hated us, but we had the old bill there escorting us, so we knew we were perfectly safe.

It was when we arrived at the ground however, that things started to go downhill. Apparently Orient, despite the massive support, had not sold their full quota of standing tickets, so that consequently we were moved from the away terrace where we had been originally located, to the junior standing area which was high up in one corner of the ground. As a result a small three-foot wall separated us from the Boro faithful who were there in their numbers just below us. As well as it being a big day for our club, it was also a massive one for the home team as they too were looking to reach the semis for the first time in their history. Consequently the crowd of 36,000 was a record gate for them and they packed the fans in everywhere. It was apparent from the start to most of the eastenders present that there could be a few problems for us if the game was not going the way of the home team. After the wonderful actions of the police in getting us safely to the ground however, we did not think we would encounter too many major worries. The boys in blue would look after us, wouldn't they?

The game itself was a total backs to the wall job for our lads, as the northerners pounded our goal with attack after attack. Jacko was being his normal, wonderful, stonewall self though, so that with ten minutes remaining the score remained 0–0. It was at this time that there was an amazing act performed by the Tyneside police who had been standing with us for the duration of the game. They just totally disappeared. One of them passed me as he made his way to the exit. I stopped him and asked him where he was going. He told me he was leaving to direct the traffic. I told him that I could see major problems for us trying to get back to the station without an escort, to which he replied, 'that your fault for being bloody southerners.' Over the next five minutes or so our 'away' terrace suddenly became very crowded. There were lots of new folk around me whom I did not recognize as being Orient supporters. More were climbing over the three-foot wall in front of us from the home section to join us and they did not look very happy.

The game ended, we had got a draw but we all had more important things to worry about at the time, like making it back to the station alive. The next half an hour I have to say was one of the worst thirty minutes that I've ever had. How I ever made it back to our train in one piece remains one of life's great mysteries. Boro boys were everywhere in the streets looking for cockneys. At one point I found myself alone, confronted in a side street by three of them. I sacrificed my red and white scarf, throwing it at them and just running to nowhere in particular. Eventually I got back to the station well shook up by my first major encounter with football hooliganism, but thankful that at least that I was not in Middlesbrough hospital, where I might easily have ended up that night.

We had secured a wonderful result, yet all the talk on the way home was not of the match but of the nightmare trip to get back to the station for everybody. A few of our boys showed off bad cuts and bruises, so I had to be thankful that it was no worse for me. My scarf was now the proud possession of a Middlesbrough fan, though I had at least managed to cling on to my programme, of course. I might not have survived the day, but if I was going to die then it went without saying that I would go down clutching my match-day magazine. This was an FA Cup quarter-final programme after all, and it was not even a silly shape unlike the one I was going to get for the replay.

I got home around half past ten that night. It had certainly been some day. The Tyneside police had instantly joined Colin Todd, John Bond the Peruvian football team and anyone connected with Newport County onto the Martin Strong hate list. Over the fifty years I've been watching the game, the Middlesbrough experience of 1978 remains the worst instance of football hooliganism I've ever had to encounter. Making my way back to the station that day was a nightmare I would not even wish on Steve Evans or Karren Brady.

I was actually so devastated by events that I can even remember thinking at the time, did I really want to carry on going to watch football and should I go to the replay? I did a lot of thinking on the Sunday and Monday – it was my week off work before I started my new job at the bank. By Monday evening my attitude had mellowed a little and I decided that I would be present the following evening at Brisbane Road to hopefully see history made for the Orient and a place in the semi-final.

Entering the ground that Tuesday evening I was still a little down and knew that I needed a positive result to get my footy fix back on track. Well a positive result was for sure something I got – by 9.40pm, that day spent in the North East if not forgotten had been relegated to the back of the mind after witnessing one of the classic O's evenings.

The first game at Ayresome Park had seen a ninety-minute rear guard action by our lads, yet quite remarkably the replay at Brisbane Road was a totally different kettle of fish. Our boys came out all guns blazing from the kick-off and their positive approach totally stunned the northerners. Unbelievably after just fifteen minutes we were two goals up. And initially it was Kitch again. It may not have come as a surprise that he scored the all-important first goal, but what was remarkable was the manner in which it came. A hooked-shot-come-bicycle-kick from twenty-five yards cannot have been said to have been a trademark Peter Kitchen goal. It was a well-known fact that he never scored from further than about two yards out. I liked to think at the time that the great man had heard of our rough time the previous Saturday and had decided that he had to do something special for us because of it. Indeed news of our plight three days earlier must have filtered through to Boro custodian Jim Platt. I'm sure the 'keeper must have felt sorry for us and he thus let a weak Joe Mayo shot slip through his grasp just minutes after Kitch's effort to give us an unbelievable two goal cushion. This goal in many ways was as unthinkable, as Kitchen's twenty-five yarder, in that Big Joe's goals were almost always headers – he very rarely netted with his feet.

Half time came and it was still 2–0. We were in semi-heaven, but then we knew that we were the Orient and there was still plenty of time for things to go wrong. Early in the second half Kitch was put through and had a golden chance to put the tie to bed, right in front of us on the North Terrace. Alas he missed, thus guaranteeing a more than nervous last thirty-five minutes. Boro predictably then got one back, and all the action was at the far end of the ground to us as the end neared. It seemed like three hours of injury time were played but incredibly we managed to hang on for a famous victory. The final whistle blew and we all went mad.

We had done it. An FA Cup semi-final appearance for the little team from east London. After the debacle at the weekend I felt that justice had been done. Mike, Tinks, Malcolm, Kevin and myself stopped off at The Bell in Walthamstow on the way home for a pint or six to celebrate one of the great days in the history

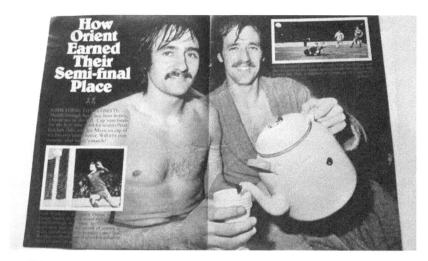

Earth's best partnership since Adam and Eve.

of the universe. It was for sure a victory that was made all the sweeter following the events of the previous Saturday.

As I was off work for the week I had had the pleasure of being able to listen to the *Jimmy Young Show* on Radio Two at 12.30pm the day before the replay for the semi-final draw. It had paired the winners of our game with Arsenal at Villa Park. This in fact was a little disappointing. The other two sides who we could have got drawn against were Ipswich or West Bromwich Albion, who on paper were not as strong as the Gunners. At the time however for us just to be there in the last four was good enough. An FA Cup semi-final appearance against anybody was something to behold.

I started work at the ANZ bank the following Monday and my life was on a real high. By changing jobs I had got a 45% pay rise but more importantly my beloved O's were in the last four of the FA Cup. Orient were just one match away from appearing on *It's a Cup Final Knockout* on the television. A trip to the church was beckoning to check out the words to *Abide With Me* in the hymnbook, in anticipation of a possible big day out at the twin towers.

Despite the fact that I only planned to be at the bank a few months before I started my time at University, I was keen to create a good impression at my new place of employment and I was given an early boost. I soon found out that the ANZ was awash with Gooners, many of them keen to obtain tickets for their big match with us. Whilst it was no problem for me to get tickets through the Orient, to obtain them through official Arsenal sources was much harder for my new work colleagues. Straight away I became a hero with four of my fellow workers (a couple of them senior managers) as thanks to me being able to get them tickets they were able to go to the big game, which had been moved to Stamford Bridge because of the involvement of two London clubs. It felt like I had scored a hat-trick on my debut for a new club, by doing some of my new colleagues such a big favour.

It was a useful job I had at the ANZ working in foreign exchange. The bank itself was a good employer, although I was only due to be there a few months. The plan was to really secure a good future for myself by going to university for four years in September. By the time I had finished my course in business management I would have it made career wise; a degree with letters after my name. I would be set up for life. Sure I would have to sacrifice not watching the O's for a few seasons, but it would be silly not to get a degree just to stay down south and watch Orient every week. Well that's what most sane nineteen year olds would have thought, but at the time my addiction to my football team was growing rapidly, buoyed by the fact that we had made it to the FA Cup semi-final and I was watching the deadliest striker in the country playing for us.

No, I really could not bring myself to stay away from the piece of heaven that was Leyton Stadium in E10 for any length of time. I still remembered my calamitous decision not to watch the O's in 75–76 and 76–77 and the Anglo-Scottish Cup Final was still very much a skeleton in my Orient closet. I therefore made the momentous decision at the time, to carry on working at the bank and thus give Aston University a miss. The subsequent result was that I ended up staying at the ANZ for thirty-one years until I was pensioned off in 2009.

Because of the Orient, I never got to sample university life. Maybe if Birmingham, Villa, Wolves and Walsall had been in Division Two at the time I may have decided to go, but the second tier was devoid of any Midlands clubs at the time, and I figured that my grant would have been too small to enable me to travel down to Leyton for all the home matches. I would have had no local papers up there to keep me abreast of any Orient news, and I would not have had any programmes either. Ok so I could have had them sent to me but I figured that that would just have made me homesick for the boys. (And heaven forbid, they may well have reached me in a bad condition.) These were pre Internet days, of course and I would have been totally cut off from my team in east London. It was something that I just could not contemplate back in 1978, so I decided against further education.

Nearly four decades on and how does that life-changing decision for me to put the Orient ahead of getting a degree look now? In staying down south and therefore missing just a small handful of home games since then, I've seen just two promotion seasons out of a possible thirty-eight. We've gone from being a half-decent Second Division side in the early eighties, to being an average team two leagues lower in 2016. The highest position we've ended any season in any league has been third in 2006. There have been four relegations and in two of those we have ended up as the bottom club. As yet we have not made it to the FA Cup semi-final again, and I've lost count of all the financial crisis I've seen at the club over the years. That has been the joy of being a Leyton Orient supporter for almost forty years without any letters after your name.

Exactly where Martin Strong BA would have ended up had I carried on studying is anybody's guess. Business Manager at one of the top companies in the country, maybe? But would I have been able to boost one of the best collections of Leyton Orient programmes in the land? (3,000 strong now and still counting) – I somehow doubt it. I made the right decision.

The semi-final back in 1978 was, looking back now, a weird experience. Along with the day we won promotion to the First Division in 1962, it was in many ways the greatest day in the club's history. Yet we lost 3–0 and gave one of the most inept performances anyone could remember seeing from any O's team. Ignoring the ninety minutes football played on the afternoon however, the rest of the day for me both before and after the match was wonderful. It seems hard to believe now, and these days something similar would never happen, but on the day there were three massive games in London all being played at the same time. Ours at Stamford Bridge, the other semi-final at Highbury featuring Ipswich and West Bromwich Albion and, attracting the biggest crowd of them all, Tottenham versus Bolton Wanderers, which was first against second in the Second Division. The police, and of course more importantly Sky and BT, would never allow it to happen these days, but happen it did back in 1978.

We set off really early that Saturday morning with Mike driving us there. Every car was heading towards west London, 90% of them had at least one red and white scarf hanging out of the window. Normally a pint or two would have been the norm before a game, but this was no normal game it was an FA Cup semi-final. One had to be inside the ground really early to capture the complete atmosphere of the occasion. After all, as an Orient fan you knew that we might have to wait a few years before we saw our heroes play in an FA Cup semi-final again (!) The atmosphere amongst the O's contingent pre-kick off was truly magnificent. We were situated in the same area behind the goal where we had seen our boys defeat Chelsea some two months earlier. There was lots of singing encouraged by some wonderful banners such as 'Kitchen fries Rice', a reference to Arsenal full-back Pat Rice. In hindsight it was just a shame that the match had to start. There were rumours afterwards that the size of the occasion just got to the players, and that half of the team froze in the dressing room before the game. Winger Kevin Godfrey, who had been a key member of the team in the weeks preceding the match was apparently the worst affected and had to be replaced very late on by Derek Clarke.

For the O's the high point of the game came after eight minutes when we got a corner. I can remember big Joe Mayo getting his head to it but the ball landed tamely in the hands of Pat Jennings. It proved to be the nearest our boys came to scoring all afternoon. Malcolm MacDonald hit two shots before half-time; both of which took dreadful deflections to give the Arsenal a 2–0 lead. Effectively they were own-goals, but MacDonald was credited with them both. It has indeed become a standard Leyton Orient joke to this very day, that whenever a goal goes against us, and the scorer is disputed, a veteran wag in the crowd will chirp up that Malcolm MacDonald's claiming it.

Rix added a third for the Gunners in the second period but the whole match was a massive anti-climax. We simply never got going. Arsenal scored three, but their display that afternoon was also pretty uninspiring. Still at least all their goals on the day were scored (or at least claimed) by Englishmen; something that would never happen these days in the matches they play now. Leyton Orient did of course eventually get their revenge on Arsenal for that infamous occasion in 1978. Just roll the clock on thirty-three years and think Johnathan Tehoue, 2011 – 88th minute at Brisbane Road. Now that's another story.

At Stamford Bridge, sadly many an Orient fan filed out long before the end, with the game well gone for us. I can remember there being pockets of West Ham supporters amongst the O's and they started celebrating just before the end as news came of a Hammers winner at Leeds to ease their clubs relegation worries at the time. This I found extremely annoying. The Arsenal fans at the other end of the ground were even getting a bit bored with proceedings on the pitch and I remember them starting to sing 'this is worse than White Hart Lane' in reference to Chelsea's ground, which was certainly pretty run down at the time.

Middlesbrough Football & Athletic Co. Ltd.
Ayresome Park, Middlesbrough.

F.A. CUP TIE

at AYRESOME PARK

For Date and Kick-off Time
See Press

£1.00 (Inc. VAT)

AYRESOME
PARK ROAD
CLIVE ROAD
ENTRANCE
Block
4
Turnstiles
36

YOU ARE ADVISED TO BE IN YOUR POSITION
AT LEAST 30 MINUTES BEFORE KICK-OFF
THIS PORTION TO BE RETAINED

J.H.C. Green
SECRETARY

THIS TICKET IS ISSUED SUBJECT TO THE RULES, REGULATIONS AND BYE-LAWS OF THE FOOTBALL ASSOCIATION.

ORIENT FOOTBALL CLUB

TICKET VOUCHER
FA CUP FINAL 1978

If we are successful in reaching the FA Cup
Final an announcement will be made at our
match with Burnley on Tuesday, 18th April
and in the Press regarding the validity of this
Voucher.

Name_____

Address_____
_____

FOR OFFICE USE
ONLY

Entrance_____

Turnstile_____

Row_____

Seat_____

No._____

No. of Tickets
Issued

_____

Date

Quarter-final ticket from an infamous day and cup-final voucher sadly never used.

Me and the other four lads were all pretty despondent at 4.45pm. Alas the 'Road to Wembley' for the Orient, which had began in 1967 was not ending some eleven years later. Knowing that the traffic all the way home would be dire travelling back east, a decision was made to stop off at a pub-boat on the Thames called the Princess Louise to unwind. It turned out to be a wonderful move resulting in what turned out to be the best part of the day. Many supporters had the same idea as us and the pub was full of not only O's and Gooners, but also of Ipswich and West Brom boys, all of whom happily mingled together, many a story being relayed amongst fellow fans. By eleven o'clock, some eight pints later, the disappointment of the afternoon's ninety minutes was just a distant memory. Indeed after the Middlesbrough experience I at last finally felt at the end of the evening that my faith in football supporters had once and for all been fully restored.

The game was shown the following day on ITV's, *The Big Match*. This I decided at the time was why we had lost. Had it been on *Match of the Day*, with Barry Davies commentating we would have triumphed that afternoon and been looking forward to *Abide With Me* come May. As it was we were left with just a relegation fight to look forward to for the rest of the season. Kitch was still scoring, of course (he got another hat-trick on Easter Monday, at home to Sheffield United) but we remained in deep trouble at the wrong end of the Second Division.

In a tight struggle it all came down to the last game of the season away to Cardiff City. A win would keep us up. With only one league victory away from Brisbane Road all season however, the chances of watching Second Division football at the Orient in 78–79 at the time seemed remote. The game was mid-week and I could not get the time off work, but I was 99% certain that we would not win. In those pre Internet and teletext days it was near on impossible to keep up with a games progress if you were not there, which made for an agonizing evening, waiting for the result.

I waited nervously all night for the Radio Two *Sportsdesk* at ten o'clock. Then came the amazing scoreline : Cardiff City 0 Orient 1. I leaped ten feet in the air. My jump of delight not for the last time in my life accounted for a lampshade, but it was for sure a small price to pay for securing Second Division football. I knew then that I would be able, in years to come, to look back at the 77–78 season as the one where we got to the FA Cup semi-final, not the one where we got relegated, but also got to the semi-final of the FA Cup. The most unsurprising news of the entire football season was that the life-saving goal at Ninian Park that night was scored by Lord Peter Kitchen.

Just to round off a fine finish to the season Ipswich defied the odds and defeated heavy favourites Arsenal in the FA Cup final. And they also won *It's a Cup Final Knockout.* Indeed that 1978 Final is up there with the 1973 Final as one of my all-time favourite football games I've seen, where Leyton Orient have not been involved. After the Stamford Bridge shambles, it was great to see Arsenal totally outplayed and well beaten by the Suffolk side. And just to make the afternoon even sweeter Malcolm MacDonald had a stinker, just as he had done there for Newcastle in 1974.

Thirty-eight years may have passed but to this very day, just as Orient versus Chelsea FA Cup 1972 remains my fav game of all time, so 77–78 is still the number one season for me. The prospect of Leyton Orient ever again getting to an FA Cup semi-final would nowadays seem about as remote as the possibility of seeing Fabio Liverani become the next England manager. Looking back now, as an achievement the O's making it to the last four of the premier cup competition, even in those long lost days of the Second Division was a truly remarkable feat.

With lucky draws, many a team from the second tier has made it through to an FA Cup semi-final over the years, yet by the time we encountered Arsenal we had played six games against three of the better clubs in the top division, winning three and drawing three. Even Blackburn were well above us in the second when we faced them. We certainly did not have an easy draw and these were days of course when everybody always picked their best team for all games. All clubs wanted to do well in the FA Cup; the thought of resting players was rightly unheard of in the seventies.

Indeed our team that season, despite only avoiding relegation at the death, was not as bad as our final league position of fourteenth suggested. Manager Jimmy Bloomfield was starting to experience problems with his health and so missed some of the matches, but he had started to blend together a nice mixture of youth and experience in a settled side. Glenn Roeder, Tony Grealish and Phil Hoadley were all fine young prospects, while the likes of Jacko, Joe Mayo and Peter Bennett had all been around for some time. And then of course there was Kitch. He ended up with a remarkable twenty-nine goals in all games that season. Thanks to his twenty-one in the league we actually managed to average more than a goal a game – 43 nettings in 42 matches. Remarkably it was the first time this feat had been achieved since our promotion near miss campaign of 73–74. It would be unfair to the rest of the team of course – particularly Big

Orient awaydays 78. Me, Malcolm, Tinks and Kev returning from a 1–1 at Mansfield.

Joe and Jacko – to say that he was 100% responsible for getting us to the last four of the cup, but in scoring seven out of our nine on the way there, he could possibly lay claim to being at least seven-ninths responsible. It was the first time I had known an Orient player to notch twenty league goals in a season, indeed little did I know it at the time but I would have to wait another thirty-eight years before anyone else – ie Jay Simpson – did it for us again. Kitchen remains to this day my all-time Orient hero.

A further indication as to how big a season it was to me is that even now, the clock having moved on nearly forty years, I can still narrate the O's team from many a match that campaign. For example: Jackson, Fisher, Roffey, Grealish, Hoadley, Roeder, Godfrey, Gray, Mayo, Kitchen, Payne for the Boro replay. Same team except Allen for Payne for the second Chelsea match.

Another reason to look back and love that season was the kit. It had changed at the start of the season from all red shirts to all white with two red braces down the front. It was unique to the Orient and it was magnificent. Even Subbuteo started to produce it. Wonderfully in 2015 the club started producing that replica braces shirt from 1978, and selling it in our club shop – sorry 'superstore'. Needless to say an 'extra-large' now sits proudly in my wardrobe, a beautiful reminder of that glory season. Even the ridiculous shape of the programme cannot hide the fact that 77–78 was for me the greatest Orient season ever. Yes after the minor set-backs that were 75–76 and 76–77, I was well and truly back as a football and O's obsessive by the summer of 1978.

CHAPTER 14

1978-79 – A STUNNING DEBUT

In what some might see as an ideal world, the summer of 78 would have seen me cheering on England at the World Cup Finals, whilst getting ready to go to Birmingham on a four year university course. As it turned out the close season saw the entire nation laughing at the Scots making fools of themselves in Argentina, and instead of preparing for some serious studying, I was looking forward to going to as many Orient games, home and away as I could in 78–79.

After the momentous campaign that was 77–78 I really could not wait for August to come around. I decided that I was going to start collecting match reports from newspapers of all O's games and put them in scrapbooks. Sure they had reports of our games in our programmes, but I found these were too biased in Orient's favour and I wanted to keep a true reflection of the season. When I started to do this the initial reaction of my mum was that it was a bit of a childish thing for a nineteen-year-old to do. I think she thought that I would soon grow out of it. I'm fifty-seven now, and have just completed my 100th volume of Leyton Orient scrapbooks. Thursday became 'cuttings day'. Traditionally it was and indeed still is, a low key day football wise with few matches on and as it was the day the local paper came out it was the natural thing to do to make it the 'cut and paste' day.

The first league game of the season paired us away to Sheffield United. My lads, Mike, Tinks, Malcolm and Kevin were not as dedicated as me and did not want to go to the game but I certainly did, so I decided to make my debut on the official supporter's club coach. This, I knew was to be my first proper encounter with the 'real fans'. I was getting on board the Orient Express with folk who claimed that they had not missed an O's game, home or away, for years. Some of them said that they routinely took time off work mid-week, so using up all their annual leave, to go to away games all over the country. Travelling up on the coach that day, I felt in awe, I wanted to be like them and become a proper fan.

The trip turned out to be a very good one. Argentina had just won the World Cup and Spurs had welcomed two of their players, Ossie Ardiles and Ricky Villa to White Hart Lane. Sheffield United had also bought an Argentinian however in Alex Sabella, who was to make his debut against us on the day. His presence boosted the attendance to nearly nineteen thousand at Bramall Lane, which included just one coach load of O's, plus a few fans who had made their own way up, encompassing the away support.

After just six minutes Sabella took the corner from which United took the lead. The crowd, or 98% of them, went wild. At this point most people present would have backed the northerners to have gone on to win the game easily. The O's did not conform to the script however. The old faithful of Joe Mayo and Peter Kitchen both scored to give us a totally unexpected, yet lovely win.

After the Middlesbrough fiasco one of the prime reasons for choosing the official coach as a way of getting to the game was the safety aspect. I figured that the police would look after the coach travellers better than they would have looked after the cockneys walking back to the station after the game. Our vehicle had been parked outside the main stand at Sheffield. I'd slipped into my seat before the match convinced that this was going to be an easy trip without any fears of aggravation.

All was going well until ten minutes before the final whistle was due. With our boys leading 2–1 an announcement was made over the Tannoy: the Orient supporter's coach had been moved to the Bramall Lane End of the ground. The end of the home kop. Oh dear. These were the dark days of football hooliganism of course, as I'd found out to my cost at Ayresome Park earlier in the year. The decision made by United was to say the least an interesting one. We were going to be made to walk to the other end of the ground against the general flow of the crowd to reach our means of getting home. If the Sheffield authorities thought that the visiting supporters had a sense of adventure, they were most certainly wrong. At the end of the game I sneaked out, tried to hide myself amongst the home contingent and tried to look glum. I walked towards the kop end and managed to creep back onto the coach safely.

The fans from Yorkshire looked a pretty rough lot. I thought that more than one or two of our boys might have got 'done' trying to negotiate their way back to our vehicle. The Middlesbrough experience had only been five months before and was still fresh in the mind. I need not have worried, however. Unlike our cup trip up north the away support this time was made up of seasoned away-dayers, folk who had seen it all before. They knew all the 'do's' and 'dont's' of away travel. Talking to them on the way back to London, they knew not to show your scarf, not to smile if the home side had got beaten and not to open your mouth until the coach had been safely boarded, especially if up north.

I started to go to a lot of the aways that season, as well as all the homes, but as the year progressed it became obvious that after the highs of the previous campaign, 78–79 was going to be a pretty average season. A major disappointment was Peter Kitchen. His form was nothing like it had been in 77–78 and he made it known publicly that he wanted to leave to seek First Division football. Jimmy Bloomfield started to leave him out of the team and bought a replacement, Ian Moores from Tottenham. I knew Moores from the few times I had seen him play at White Hart Lane. It's fair to say that the Spurs faithful did not take to him. As an often unused substitute I'd heard them relentlessly boo the poor chap for just running up and down the touchline. I'd even seen him score a hat-trick in a testimonial against Arsenal and still get jeered.

We'd signed him for £60,000 and his debut at Charlton on 6 October 1978 remains to this day, one of the most memorable for any O's player. Leading up to the game we had gone six league matches without a goal. Yet within twenty-five minutes of the start we were 2–0 up and Moores had got them both. In fact the whole game was remarkable. For the remaining sixty-five minutes the entire Charlton team seemed to want to pass to our debutant to give him every opportunity to score as many as he wanted. Chance after chance he had to get his hat-trick but in the end he missed them all and at the end of the day he had to settle for the brace. He had been the match-winner, yet for the rest of the game he had given us a taste of the Ian Moores we were to see many a time over the next four seasons. Although in the end I got to quite like him because he always gave everything in an Orient shirt, I could never fully relate to him, probably because he was bought as a replacement to my all-time hero Kitch.

Looking back now Moores was not actually a bad player but he just looked a bad player. He was six foot three, weighed fourteen stone and had legs that looked like great big oak trees. His shorts always seemed two sizes too small and he had a silly beard that could have been stolen from a goat or Francesco Becchetti. He looked like one of those ridiculous models that used to appear at the time on the television every week in *It's a Knock-out*. I met the big man a few times in the O's clubhouse however, and he was a nice fellow, a real gentle giant. It gave me great sadness when I heard that he had died of cancer at the end of the nineties, still only in his forties.

Although our form was not great it at least became clear that there were to be no relegation worries in 78–79. I started to become a regular on the official supporter's coach as the seeds were well and truly sewn for my mad years as a fan, when I never missed a single game home or away. I got to know well the boys who travelled everywhere, lovely blokes like Dave Staplehurst, Peter Collins and Glenn Strongitharm who had all gone years as ever presents following the Orient. I started to look up to these lads who could boast seeing every game for god knows how long and I decided that I wanted to be like them. I used to listen in awe to stories of away days at Anglo-Scottish trips to Aberdeen and Patrick in 1976. At this point I would keep my head down, feeling ashamed that I'd actually gone two seasons when I barely watched the Orient at all.

It was getting to the point when I did not want to be one of those pansy fans, supporters who only went to thirty-five games a season. I wanted to be right up there with the top boys. The 'real fans' who went everywhere. Ok it was too late to do it in 78–79 but starting in the next campaign, I was going to try to be there at every single match. The results were important, of course but the main thing would be that I was there in attendance, even if they lost.

The season finished with us in eleventh place. The highlight was an away draw in the FA Cup with holders Ipswich Town. They were the team of course, who we could have played in the 1978 Final had we beaten Arsenal. Jacko had a blinder in the goal-less draw at Portman Road, though we lost the replay 2–0 at Brizzy.

Kitchen, alas was transferred to Fulham in February for a then club record fee of £150,000. I still loved the man. No one could ever take away what he had done for us the season before. Indeed to this very day no one who has ever had the honour to wear the shirt of Leyton Orient has come close to him in my popularity stakes. We had to wait thirty-eight years for someone else to score twenty league goals in a season and we're still waiting for anyone to have such a silly moustache. Yet when he left I can remember feeling strangely not too unhappy at the time. For some reason I had a hunch that we had not seen the last of him at Brisbane Road and that someday he would return. It was indeed a feeling of mine that was indeed to prove correct.

CHAPTER 15

1979–80 – WHERE WERE YOU AT WREXHAM?

I had missed just seven away games in 1978–79 and for the first time had been to every match played at Brisbane Road. Yet any notion I might have had about attending every encounter in 79–80 went down the pan as early as September. The O's were away to Wrexham on the 15th of the month, which was my parent's silver wedding anniversary. We arranged to go out for a celebration as a family in the evening, so that I had to miss the game. It actually did not bother me too much at the time. After all it was for my dad, who was the great man who had started to take me to Brisbane Road in the first place and my mum who had tried her hardest to console me in 74 by telling me the 1–1 draw with Villa in May was not such a bad result.

Despite this small aberration though, it's fair to say that for me the obsessive years of watching my club had begun. Wrexham was to be the last Orient game I was too miss home or away for fifteen days short of five years. For the record we lost that day in north Wales 2–1. I had a good reason to not be present that day, yet for years afterwards whenever we played them I tried to keep my head down. I imagined there were Welsh boys present looking around, eager to taunt me with 'where were you in seventy-nine?'

Between my bonkers supporting years of 1979 and 1984 I used to think of my occupation as 'professional Orient supporter' and 'part-time bank clerk'. As a footballing anorak at the time, I started to do some pretty sad things. I started to collect lapel badges at all the new grounds that I visited. I felt really gutted if I went to a new venue but did not acquire a badge in the club shop before the game. And of course in those lovely days most clubs had programme shops where I could delve through their stock hoping to find that old missing O's match-day magazine.

I started hording anything that was related to the O's and even starting an Orient car-sticker collection. This may not have been such a weird thing to do, but for the fact that at the time, I didn't have a car. I also used to purchase Orient key rings from our club shop which they produced from time to time, and got up to having eight of the buggers, even though I only had one front door key that I could put them on.

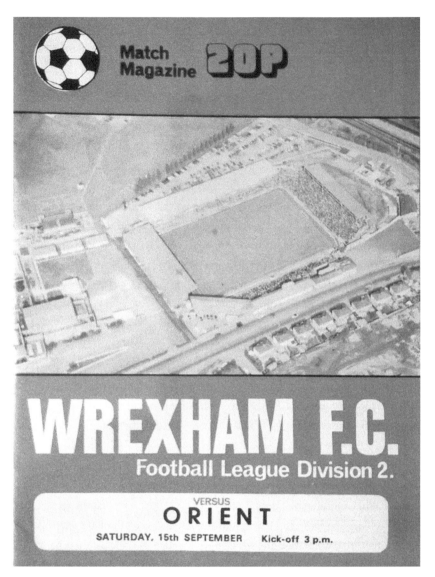

Best game of the season?

I suppose my keenness may have been more understandable had I been supporting a half-decent side at the time, but I was supporting Leyton Orient. The footy being played by our boys at the time was not very good. It was not until 9 October that we won our first home game in 79–80 against Fulham. 10 November saw us lose 7–3 at home to Chelsea in an amazing game that could have ended up ten all. Those cup classics with the Blues back in 1972 and 1978 seemed a million miles away at the time.

I went to a lot of the aways on the official supporter's coach, though I was still going to a few games with Mike, Malcolm, Tinks and Kevin, with Mike usually behind the wheel. They were not as keen as me, but I often convinced them that the best way to spend a Saturday was to travel two hundred miles to watch a crap Second Division side usually lose to a not quite so crap Second Division team, and then spend hours driving home, getting stuck in a large traffic jam on the M1. When we finally arrived home I'd then tell them what a great day out they'd all had.

On 21 December 1979 we had a memorable trip. It was a snowy Friday night just before Christmas, and Mike drove us down to Swansea to see, quite remarkably, a 1–0 Orient win. The snow got progressively worse as the evening wore on, so that by the time the final whistle was blown Mike made it clear that there was no way he would be able to drive all the way home.

We started on the return journey however, and got as far as Cardiff where a decision was made that we would stop off at a fish and chip shop, and then stay the night in the car. Our driver stopped at one in the city centre and we all got out to order our food. Then a chap came in behind us and ordered twenty-six portions of fish and chips. We recognized him immediately as Orient Director Adrian Harding, and looking outside we saw the team coach parked outside. We had a bit of a chat with him, he told us how happy everyone was on the coach and thanked us for our support. He then insisted on paying for our food, which was a lovely bonus for us, before he departed back to the bus with all of their food. A nice way indeed to finish off the evening, we thought.

As we saw the coach move away however, the talk we had with him was beginning to suddenly look like a bit of a bad tactical move. A group of locals had gathered outside. Word appeared to have got out that there were a group of cockneys in the local chippie. With about twenty meaty looking Welsh lads looking in at us, my mind was taken back some twenty months. Middlesbrough was being revisited within my brain. Our car was parked about thirty yards down the road. Something inside of me was telling me that Cardiff hospital was calling for me that night. We heard them all mumbling in Welsh and feared the worst. Then suddenly they all broke into a round of applause. We were at first bemused, but then flabbergasted as we suddenly realized that it was actually being directed at us. They then all broke into a chorus of, 'we hate Swansea', and after that the penny dropped. The lads did not care much for Londoners, but they cared even less for Swansea. We had defeated their bitterest enemies 1–0, so that for that evening at least we were their heroes. We got nice handshakes from them as we offered them chips, and they bade us goodbye, wishing us a safe journey home. A highly uncomfortable night in the car followed, but we figured that that was better than the Cardiff hospital bed that we had all feared earlier in the evening.

A few days later in the New Year's Honours list my Uncle Roy became Uncle Sir Roy as he won a Knighthood for services to the arts. It was a nice feeling to have a knight as an uncle, although naturally I would have preferred it if my relative had been a footballing one, such as Sir Alf Ramsey or possibly Sir Stanley Matthews. (Not Sir Alex Ferguson, though.)

What it did give me however was a talking point when I had to entertain other businessmen at work, which I had to do on a regular basis at the ANZ. Football anoraks are generally boring people. I was no exception. At the time, I could twitter on about the great game for hours, indeed rant about the O's for days, but I actually knew very little about anything else. Regrettably, for some unknown reason, the other bankers that I was meeting were never too interested in hearing about my collections of Orient car-stickers or newspaper cuttings. If they wanted to know the result of any O's game since 1970 then I was their man, but generally they didn't. From Christmas 1979 onwards however, I could now throw into the ring that my uncle was indeed a knight and this tended to keep the conversation going, at least for a while.

Indeed it may have assisted me as a chat-up line, if I had had any interest in women at the time. I reckon girls would have taken a lot more kindly to 'hello, did you know that my uncle has been knighted?' rather than 'hi, do you fancy going to Orient versus Oldham on Saturday?' The truth was that I was more than happy to have a football club as my best friend. I was content to stay in on a Saturday night and read over that Orient versus Burnley programme from 1971, rather than go out with the lads and try to 'pull a woman'. Yes it's probably fair to say that as sad blokes go, at the time I was right up there in the Champions League of saddos.

When I travelled away on the coach trips I was beginning to feel really at home. I felt I was truly becoming 'a real fan'. Ok, so I had blown my chance to go to every game that 79–80 season, but I would be all geared up to do it in 80–81.

On 5 February 1980 there was another effort by me to try to show the world that I was indeed a top Orient supporter. The O's had defeated Wrexham 4–0 the day before in a rare very good performance, and manager Jimmy Bloomfield was to appear on a BBC Radio London football phone in, answering questions from Orient fans. The programme started at 11 in the morning, but I started ringing the number at 10.30 in an attempt to be the first caller on air. As a result I asked our manager the first question at a minute past eleven: 'Why is it Jimmy,' I said, 'that we can never defeat West Ham or Chelsea in the league?'

Actually it was a bit of a daft thing to ask, as we had in fact beaten the Hammers just a year before, and our 7–3 defeat to Chelsea was our first set-back against them for years. Dear Jimmy pointed this out to me, and I went a bit quiet for a few moments. I then congratulated him on the win the previous day, and wished him luck for the rest of the season. Any normal person might have felt a bit of an idiot asking such a ridiculous question but not me. I was really chuffed at the time that I had been the first O's fan on air that morning. I even recorded it, so that I could add it to my portfolio of anything Orient related.

For the record we finished another pretty boring season 14th in Division Two. Not too many games lived in the memory for too long, apart from the Chelsea fiasco, the Wrexham 4–0 thrashing and a 3–0 victory at Watford, which was our biggest away win for a few years. It became a standard joke among my friends that the best game of the season was Wrexham away, the only game that I missed. For some years afterwards they used to taunt me by saying that Big Joe Mayo's goal in our 2–1 loss that day was the best goal they had seen for years from an Orient player, and did I agree?

In true O's fashion we ended the season going ten games without a win, but the main thing as far as I was concerned, was that I had seen forty-one consecutive home and aways at the end of it, and I was all set to continue that sequence come August.

CHAPTER 16

1980–81 – THE ANGLO-SCOTTISH DREAM FADES

I really could not wait for the new season to start. Not because I thought we had a really wonderful squad and that we had a great chance to go up to the First Division, but because I saw no obstacles to me being there at every Orient game in 1980–81.

The first fixture was to be Notts County away in the Anglo-Scottish Cup on 2 August. To my dismay we had not entered this magnificent competition the year before, thus thwarting any chance there may have been of me going to places such as Morton or Dundee later in the year. I was desperate to make up for the two Scottish trips that I had missed out on in 1976, during our wonderful run to the Final that year. Thus I saw this fixture at Meadow Lane as one of the most important games of the season. It would give us the chance to progress beyond the group stage and into the knockout phase of the competition, which would include the Scottish teams.

For some strange reason however, the rest of the world had failed to see the significance of the game. A mere 2,450 entered the turnstiles that afternoon, twenty-one of whom had accompanied me on the official Orient supporter's coach up to Meadow Lane. It was the second day of August, yet at the time I liked to think that it was the kind of trip that sorted out the proper fans from the part-time supporters. There were about forty O's followers there in all, and I felt really proud that I was one of them. I knew that for the next

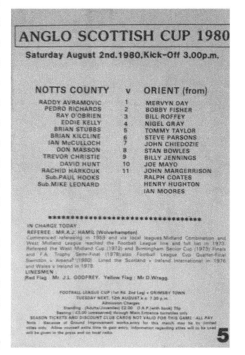

Biggest game of the season?

ten months whenever any fellow Orient supporter would say something that annoyed me at a home game, I could turn to them and say: 'call yourself a fan – where were you on 2 August, then?'

These people with wives and two kids with big mortgages, who only went to home games plus a few aways were, in my eyes, just 'glory hunters', not in the same class as myself. I looked down at them. Little did I know then but some years later I in fact would be married with two kids and a large mortgage and would be going only to all the homes plus a few aways.

We drew with County that day 2–2 in what, for what it was worth, was a very entertaining game. There was much sadness just three days later however, as a home defeat by Fulham meant alas, that there would be no chance to progress beyond the group stage of the Anglo-Scottish Cup that year. Much to my dismay I would not be going north of the boarder to watch the O's that campaign. It was only 5 August, yet to a certain degree I felt that the season was already over. I would just have to let certain of the coach regulars twitter on about the Aberdeen and Partick trips of 1976, and hope that we would have better luck in the competition in 1981.

When what most sane people considered the proper season started with the first league games, it quite unbelievably seemed that the O's had really sorted themselves out on the park. Manager Jimmy Bloomfield had signed former England international Stanley Bowles pre-season for £100,000. Although past his best, Stanley was still a more than useful player. He linked well for us with young black winger John Chiedozie, who had a fine season. The defence of Mervyn Day, Bill Roffey, Tommy Taylor and Nigel Gray remained virtually unchanged, and up until Christmas at least was really secure. Steve Parsons and John Margerrison were the ball winners in midfield, the perfect foil for Bowles.

As is so often the case with the O's over the years though, it was up front where we lacked a real cutting edge. With Kitchen gone a sense of normality returned to Brisbane Road, striker wise. In 1980–81 no one made it into double figures for the season.

Despite this however, there were still some marvellous performances from the boys. On 4 October we defeated Preston 4–0 with what I still consider to be, to this very day, one of the best all round team showings I've ever seen from us. Bowles was quite magnificent for the entire ninety minutes, scoring the last and making goals for Parsons and Chiedozie that day. Even Ian Moores made it onto the score sheet. Stanley just seemed to stand in the centre of the park all afternoon, spaying passes to all corners of Brisbane Road, all of them finding an Orient shirt.

And this was not an isolated game. November brought two fine away wins at Oldham and Swansea, as promotion to the First was beginning to look a real possibility. Even I was enjoying the football, though of just as much importance to me was the fact that I was present at all the matches to keep up my consecutive run of games. To give us that final push towards top division football another ex-England international, Peter Taylor, was signed from Spurs in the late autumn. It can be said that the season – indeed looking back now the entire eighties – peaked on 20 December 1980. An away victory at Chelsea took us to the dizzy heights of fifth in the Second Division.

In parallel to the fortunes of the O's, work wise things were really going well for me too. In October I got moved from foreign exchange 'back-up' at the ANZ into the money market dealing room. This was the equivalent in international banking terms, of a transfer from the youth team into the first team squad. It meant a nice little pay rise for me. I was still living at home with mum and dad, which basically meant that I was quite flushed with money.

With my surplus of funds I decided to invest in a video cassette recorder. These were brand new gadgets at the time and they were very expensive at around £500, but think of it – I could actually record the O's whenever they were on television, and watch them over and over again. It was for sure at the time, a dream come true for me. I could start to build an Orient video cassette collection to go alongside my car-sticker and key-ring collections. Being in the Second Division generally meant that we were on *The Big Match* or *Match of the Day* a few times during the season in those days. Now that I had my new toy it was just a question of being patient and waiting for our lads to appear on one of those programmes.

The big day finally came on 28 March 1981. Upon arriving at Brisbane Road I saw BBC vans everywhere. That could only mean one thing of course: *Match of the Day*. There was a tinge of disappointment at two-thirty as I saw the commentator climb the steps onto the gantry in the west-side. Our lucky man, Barry Davies, hero of the Chelsea cup clash in 1972, it was not. Instead it was a young chap with the silliest moustache I'd seen at Leyton Stadium since Peter Kitchen. A chap named Desmond Lynham, who I heard was new to television having just been promoted from BBC Radio. With such a silly moustache I could not see him having much of a future in the sports commentating game.

Was I desperate to see an O's win that day. Boy would I be in seventh heaven being able to watch an Orient victory over and over again at home on my new machine in the comfort of my own home. Fortunately the lads did not let me down, defeating Sheffield Wednesday 2–0 that afternoon. In a strange move that season *Match of the Day* had been moved from its customary position on a Saturday night to four o'clock on a Sunday afternoon, while *The Big Match* was being shown on a Saturday night. This meant that I had to wait until the next day before I was able to record our match for posterity. At four o'clock however Jimmy Hill and Bob Wilson, *MOTD* presenters arrived on screen, and the record button was pressed on my video recorder. The brief highlights were duly recorded, along with a short interview Lynham did with Wednesday manager Jackie Charlton after the game, who was not happy with his team at all that afternoon. I stopped the recording after our game had been shown and immediately played it back. Indeed by seven o'clock I had played it back some six or seven times, much to the dismay of my dad who wanted to watch *Songs of Praise* on the one television we had. By the end of the evening I could narrate Lynham's commentary word for word. To my great joy, my Orient video recording collection was up and running. Nowadays, of course you can watch that Wednesday game from 1981, and the original BBC recording on YouTube whenever you want, though I have to say that for sentimental reasons I've still kept that original video cassette, bringing back as it does such wonderful memories of my life in the early eighties.

Despite *Match of the Day* for an hour, Sundays were pretty desperate affairs for all us football buffs in those days. It really is hard to believe now, but back then there were no games played at all on the Sabbath. All you did have however on that day to keep your mind football occupied, were the programme fairs. It's all so different these days of course, if you are a collector of the match-day magazines. Now you have got the Internet, with dealers having their own sites on-line and there's e-bay as well to satisfy you needs. The fairs still happen, but there are a lot less of them now. It was so different some thirty-five years ago though. If you were a collector, then the fairs were really important events. I'd travel miles on a Sunday morning to the various fairs, hoping to get those missing Orient programmes from the fifties, sixties and seventies. I can remember getting up early and queuing up at places such as Walthamstow Avenue Football Club around nine-thirty in the morning, waiting for the doors to open at ten. I would spend a couple of hours delving around the dealer's tables, on the lookout to fill those gaps in my Orient portfolio.

After going to a few of these affairs you got to recognize many of the other punters. There would be about thirty regulars. You'd always see the same faces usually middle age blokes who you thought were still single living at home with mum and dad, always armed with their precious little books which listed the ones they were missing from their club's collection. They usually wore a not too clean coat or rain-mac, the likes of which you saw at the time worn by TV detective *Columbo* on the television every week. These guys may have seen their team lose the day before but if they had managed to pick up an obscure programme or two of their club at the fair on the Sunday, then it hadn't been too bad a weekend for them after all. I suppose we were all a little bit sad, but looking back now they were in many ways good times for me. Instead of worrying about where the money was to pay for that big mortgage, which was what was to happen to me in the years to follow, my biggest concern at the time was wondering where you could find those two missing homes from the 61–62 promotion season.

Back at Brisbane Road, after the fine start to the season, things unfortunately started to go somewhat pear shaped. 1980–81 saw a vintage second half of the season Orient collapse, the likes of which we have seen so many times over the years at Brisbane Road. Fifth at Christmas, we proceeded to win just three more games, to go sliding down the table, in the end finishing seventeenth. It was all actually a bit strange as to why it happened. The team remained the same – if anything we should have been stronger, with the arrival of Taylor – yet we lost our way totally. At one time, talk on the terraces was of the possibility of playing Manchester United, Arsenal and Liverpool the following season. In the end we had to scramble a draw in our penultimate game against Bolton to secure our place in the Second Division.

That draw just left the final fixture of the campaign, away to Newcastle. Although a meaningless match, the day turned into one of the more memorable away trips that season. There were just twenty-nine of us in the official supporter's club party, though with the distance involved the travel was by train as opposed to the normal coach. I would imagine a few Orient supporters made their own way independently, though I don't remember seeing any on the day, but there can't have been more than about fifty O's there.

The train arrived at Newcastle station around 1.30 and the twenty-nine of us were amazed to be greeted by about two hundred of the boys in blue. We were told by the policeman in charge that we were to be given an escort all the way to the ground, so off we went, our small group flanked by about sixty to seventy police all the way to St James' Park.

One of them asked me when the rest of our supporters would be arriving. I told him that there were two football specials coming, which were due to arrive at the station shortly. It was hard to know if he knew that I was only joking. He did not laugh, but then as I knew from my trip to Middlesbrough, police in the North East did not laugh anyway. We got to the ground some fifteen minutes later. The route had been awash with bobbies. We were escorted into the away end, which in those days was a small standing enclosure in one of the corners of St James' Park. Not a particularly wonderful view, but bearing in mind what had happened at Ayresome Park in 1978, we knew that it was nice and safe. I may have been tempted to keep my mouth shut and go alone into the Gallowgate End with the other Geordies, but the local constabulary gave me little option but to enter St James' with the other twenty-eight O's fans.

To more utter amazement after we had paid our money and entered the ground, we found ourselves surrounded by about one hundred more of the boys in blue. A big cheer went up from all sides of the ground as they saw the sight of the away end. Three policemen for every cockney. It was standard procedure, of course to taunt and abuse the opposition contingent at most grounds up and down the country, but this was something different. We could not really be taken seriously. The massive police overkill just had everyone in stitches.

At the time there were often too many coppers at our home games, though I knew this was because the policemen wanted the overtime and there was easy money to be made for them through working an afternoon or an evening at Brisbane Road. I had never seen anything like that day at Newcastle, though. Having questioned one of the friendlier North Eastern policemen however, things became a lot clearer.

The last team to visit St James' Park had been Chelsea. It had all gone off apparently in the city centre before and after the match. The police chief, I was told, had got a severe reprimand from his bosses, for not having had enough men on duty to cope with all the trouble. Before the Orient game he had obviously looked at the fixture list, seen a game with another London team and feared the worst. As a result most police leave had apparently been cancelled that Saturday to control the twenty-nine known football thugs who had come up from E10 that day.

The man may not have had much idea about football fans in the capital, but at least he gave everybody present at Newcastle much amusement that afternoon.

To compare Orient fans with those from Chelsea in those days was like comparing Liverani to Bloomfield when talking about Leyton Orient managers. We lost the match 3–1 and after the game we were all heralded into a police van, and they very kindly drove us back to the station. It was the second of my four visits to date to Newcastle to see the O's play and so far we've lost every time. Indeed Big Joe's goal for us up there that day was the only one I've ever seen us score up there. Lucky ground for us it is not. But then again how many grounds have been lucky for the Orient over the years? Not many, to be honest.

So the season ended disappointedly for the O's. Many fans were very disappointed that we had not pushed on at Christmas, and had a good stab at getting into the top flight. I shared their sentiments, though I felt very proud that for the first time I had seen every game home and away during the season. I at last felt that I could truly classify myself as a proper fan. I had got every programme, of course, cuttings from every match and a few new lapel badges on my travels.

CHAPTER 17

1981–82 – RELEGATION, BUT ORIENTS, ORIENTS NUMBER ONE

Around this time, I was very vainly and quite wrongly starting to think of myself as the O's number one fan. Ok, so my Orient car-sticker collection was I'm sure, better than anyone else's, but there were folk around who had seen many more consecutive games than I had, fans who had far greater claim to that title than I did. Many folk had been going a lot longer than I had. I decided though that I had to try to get season ticket number one, which I felt would really enhance my credentials to being the 'number one' supporter. As a result the club was rang at the beginning of April to try to find out what the prices for the new season would be. This was a few weeks before they would put them in the programme. As it turned out, my quest was successful. By the second week in April the club had already cashed my cheque and sure enough I managed to acquire season ticket number one for the 1981–82 season. Opening the SAE (that's a stamped addressed envelope, for anyone under thirty) that I had sent to the club, I was naturally thrilled when I saw the number. It felt almost as good as if I'd seen Orient win the Anglo Scottish Cup. I liked to think at the time, that for the forthcoming campaign, I was the 'numero uno' supporter at Brisbane Road.

Having watched Orient verses Sheffield Wednesday on my video cassette recorder on more than the odd occasion over the summer, I was itching for the real action to begin again. Not least of all, because I wanted my run of consecutive games to continue to grow.

At the club however, there were strong rumblings of discontent. The rumour was that cash was in short supply, after the big name signings of players such as Mervyn Day, Stanley Bowles and Billy Jennings. The gamble of purchasing Peter Taylor for one last push to achieve First

Note the season ticket number.

Division Football had not come off. At the start of the new campaign the board forced manager Bloomfield to sell our best young player John Chiedozie to Notts County for £600,000 against Jimmy's wishes. As a result of this Bloomfield left the club, ending his second spell in charge of the O's. He had suffered major health problems and sadly died of cancer at just forty-nine, a few years later. He certainly goes down as one of the better managers Leyton Orient have had over the years. Under him the club achieved what was a remarkable Third Division Championship win in 1970, and we had an even more unbelievable FA Cup semi-final appearance in 1978.

There was a major disappointment at the beginning of the season, when it was announced that the Anglo-Scottish Cup was to be discontinued. I was gutted. Any thoughts I might have had about trips to Scotland to make up for the Aberdeen and Patrick Thistle non-showings in 1976 were thus thrown out of the window. The Football League in their wisdom came up with a replacement that they imaginatively called 'The Group Cup.' As with the Anglo-Scottish in previous years, teams from the lower reaches of the League played three pre-season matches before the most successful sides progressed into the knockout stage of the competition. As with the Anglo-Scottish Cup nobody went to watch these games. In those days there was not even a Final at Wembley to look forward to if your team did well. Orient's two homes at Brisbane Road attracted gates of 1,806 and 1,777 for games against Southend and Wimbledon respectively. The away game against Gillingham saw 2,234 pack the Priestfield Stadium to see a 1–1 draw. I of course was present at all three encounters, but for me our participation in the competition that year will always be remembered for the disgusting behaviour of Gillingham in their home game with us. When I turned up at their place that day, I was fuming. This was because the home club had not had the decency of producing a proper programme for our match with them. We were forced instead to make do with what they called a 'triple issue' – a combined effort for their home games with ourselves and Southend in the Group Cup, as well as a friendly against West Ham. I was forced to read articles in it about the Hammers and Shrimpers team, as well as our own. I thought it absolutely outrageous at the time. Had my programme collection been increased by three, or was it not a proper programme at all? Either way the whole sordid affair left a bitter taste. Gillingham I strongly felt should have been charged by the FA for bringing the game into disrepute, such was the seriousness of their misdemeanour. For the record Wimbledon defeated us at Leyton Stadium and we did not progress out of the group stages of the Group Cup.

There was however better news on the programme front concerning the home games in 1981–82. After the ridiculous oblong-shaped efforts of 77–78 and 78–79, the size had improved marginally to a longer version for the next two seasons. In 81–82 though it was revamped totally to a more manageable and much smaller size. I actually had a jacket where the new model could be placed in the pocket without creasing it at all. Alright, so we ended the season bottom of the Second Division and were relegated in 81–82, but at least all my homes ended the year in mint condition. After all of the headaches I'd had with the things since the late sixties, I felt that the club had finally come to its senses with regards to the size of the match-day magazine.

The supporters to feel really sorry for at the time, of course were those who followed Preston North End and Plymouth Argyle. Their clubs did not even have the decency to produce a programme for each match, but of all things a big club newspaper. Disgraceful. How the hell were you supposed to keep that in any kind of decent state during the afternoon? Christ it must have been grim supporting those two teams at the time. Looking back at my old *Rothman's Yearbooks*, it still amazes me now when I see the league tables for the 81–82 season, that Preston, Plymouth and indeed Gillingham were not given any points deduction for their misdemeanours, at the time. At the time I was always baffled by football matches played in Italy. I had been told that programmes were not produced for any matches in that country. So why on earth did anybody go to watch any games that were being played there? It was for sure a funny world we lived in, in the early eighties.

On the pitch 1981–82 was a really desperate affair for the Orient. Paul Went replaced Bloomfield and lasted all of twenty-one days after a wretched spell in charge. Ken Knighton and Frank Clark replaced Went but things did not improve much. One novelty about the season was that we started to play a few home matches on a Sunday. As said, the club were not looking good financially and chairman Brian Winston was keen to try anything to bring in more cash. It really does beggar belief just how different Sundays were in those days. Absolutely nothing happened anywhere in those days on the Sabbath, except programme fairs of course. Practically all of the shops were shut, pubs only opened from 12 till two and then from seven till 10.30pm and there was practically no professional sport played on the day at all. You were just expected to go to church and then go home and watch *Songs of Praise* and *Stars on Sunday,* on the television. There were strict laws at the time prohibiting virtually anything taking place on a Sunday.

These laws made Orient's Sunday matches in many ways strange events. Officially you were not allowed to charge to watch games. We got round that by charging for a team sheet, which you got when you entered the ground that was priced at the normal cost of admission. No music was allowed to be played over the Tannoy before the kick-off, but the most bizarre thing was the 'free gate.' By law all clubs staging matches on the holy day, had to have one entrance where you could get in without paying. I can remember the Orient had their 'free gate' at an obscure turnstile at the Coronation Gardens end of the ground, which was never usually used. It was obviously hoped that nobody would notice it was there, with few people aware of the little known 'free gate' law. At first they succeeded with these tactics, but after a couple of matches word got out, so that I remember there being quite a queue to use it when it came to about the third Sunday game. Folk were quite happy to miss a few minutes of the game, if it meant not having to pay to get in. It was all a bit bizarre. It really is incredible now to look back and remember just how different things were in those long, lost days of the early eighties.

Nowadays I like to think of myself as a pretty good supporter of Leyton Orient Football Club. I'm there at every home game, and try to go to as many as I can on the road. The programme collection is still going strong of course, and I do a bit of writing about the team in the local *Guardian* and in the *Leyton Orient fanzine*. I don't however pretend to be anywhere near the top of the pile when it comes to being the number one O's fan, as I once tried to. Around this 81–82 season, looking back now I think that my total obsession with the O's peaked at about this time. My good mates, Mike, Malcolm, Kevin and Tinks remained Orient fans and came to the home games whenever they could, but they had all finally decided that four hundred mile round trips to places such as Rotherham, Barnsley and Bolton to see the inevitable defeat, was not for them. As they were the ones with the cars (though I had the stickers to go on them) I now started to go to every away game on the official supporter's club coach.

Becoming a regular I got to know all of the lads well – many remain good friends now, the likes of Peter Collins, Dave Staplehurst, Glenn Strongitharm and Bob Seaman, all of whom still suffer pain of the O's to this very day. Having gone to all of our games back then, I could readily join in all the conversations about Orient matches at the time. Yet when a few of the boys started to talk about the reserve games that they went to, that were being played on a Tuesday afternoon in the Football Combination, I felt a bit lost. Yes, this was another gap in my quest to be the ultimate Orient supporter that I felt had to be filled.

As well as trying to develop my career as an O's fan, I was also at the time trying to build a future at the ANZ bank. I was getting on well, but I knew that the management looked upon me as a bit of an odd one. For some reason they believed that normal foreign-exchange bank clerks did not book up a days leave to travel up north on a Tuesday night to see some useless team lose, arriving home at two in the morning, and be back at work some five hours later. I figured that if I told them that I wanted a half-day off on a Tuesday to see the second team play they would have thought me completely bonkers. I therefore made up a story that one of my aunts was ill in hospital and for one afternoon in the week I had to take time off to visit her. I just hoped that no one in the bank looked at the Football Combination results in the paper the next day and blew my cover.

Those afternoons at Brisbane Road were for sure weird experiences. Apart from the O's and a few other teams, most of the clubs in the Combination came from the First Division. Our team was usually a (not very good) mix of youngsters and trialists, together with the odd first teamer who was on his way back from injury, or who was someone who had had a row with the manager and was named in the second team as way of a punishment. The First Division sides always beat us. At the end of the season, we nearly always ended up bottom of the reserve league.

For our home games it was normally only the Main East Stand that was open. Managers would fill the Directors box, usually looking at opposition players who were unable to make their clubs first team at the time. You could often catch the odd Orient first team regular there watching, someone who was on a bad run either at the bookies, or in the Leyton snooker hall which was across the road. The rest of the stand would be occupied by one hundred or so punters. The numbers would be made up of pensioners, school kids if there was a school holiday, or plain nutters like myself.

It was often the norm in the games for the opposition to score a couple of quick goals to kill the game off so that they could stroll through the rest of the afternoon. From time to time you saw the odd old pro in the opposition who was seeing out his contract in the stiffs before sloping off to retirement. He had played in these kind of affairs many a time and he knew the ropes. He knew that a boot into the west-side would mean a nice two to three minute breather, while some poor Orient youth team lad was sent up to the empty stand to retrieve the ball.

The biggest cheer of the afternoon would inevitably go up if the O's managed a goal, though this was rare and if it did come more often than not it was usually just a token consolation. One extraordinary second team game sticks out from this period. It was from this 81–82 season when our boys entertained Arsenal reserves in February. Word had got out that the Gunner's 'keeper Pat Jennings, who had been side-lined for weeks with an injury, was due to make his long awaited comeback that afternoon for the north Londoners. It was of great interest to the football world as the great man was fighting to get fit for Northern Ireland's World Cup campaign in Spain later that year.

With my Aunt apparently still ill in hospital, I can remember entering the ground at around five to two and being amazed at the sight of a full press box next to me. There were also about thirty or so photographers, plus two camera crews camped behind the goal that Jennings was about to defend. To us fifty or so regular Brisbane Road reserve punters this was hilarious. The snappers who were there to see Jennings make some magnificent saves on his return to football, had clearly not seen Orient reserves play before. If the first team during 81–82 were poor, they were positively Brazilian-like, compared to our second team at the time. Jennings and the photographers remained unemployed for most of the afternoon, while the other twenty-one players spent most of the ninety-minutes camped in the other half of the pitch.

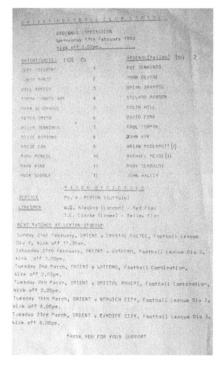

The Jennings game.

By the time our boys got their one and only corner deep into the second half many of those gathered behind the goal had long since departed, having realized the mistake they had made hoping for some action shots. As the ball came over from the corner Jennings I remember came off his line and caught the ball one handed, to ironic cheers from the crowd. It was all he had to do all afternoon. The ref blew the final whistle a few minutes later, to signal the end of hospital visiting hours for me, with Arsenal having cantered to a comfortable 2–0 victory. Most of the photographers must have gone home with a full film still in their cameras. The local news programmes showed about five seconds of action between them on the television that evening.

Jennings went on to have a magnificent World Cup that summer for the Northern Irish in Spain. The great man more than played his part in their great campaign, highlighted by their incredible 1–0 victory against the hosts. It would be nice to think that our club played some part in his return to fitness by giving him a nice little warm up in that February fixture. The reality was though, that he wasn't tested at all and we played no part at all.

Despite the fact that we nearly always lost, highlighting again what a bit of a saddo I was at the time, I really enjoyed those reserve afternoons. They made me look down even more at the ordinary fans who only went to first team fixtures. Part timers, them I thought. In deed it came as a great disappointment to me when a decision was taken to leave the Combination at the end of the 81–82 season. Officially it had become too expensive to run our second team in it, so we joined the Capital League, a more local competition, where all of the games were played in the evening. It was just not the same. When I found out about the new league we were to be playing in, there was much sympathy for me at work as news broke that my sick aunt had died and that I did not need to have any more afternoons off to visit her.

As far as the first team were concerned, to say that we were struggling a little would be a mighty understatement. After amazingly winning the opening game of the season 2–1 at Derby, we went thirteen without a victory and found ourselves well and truly stuck at the bottom of the league. Although most games during the campaign gave us little to cheer about, there was one encounter at Leicester however, which remains vividly in the memory.

As per normal our boys were being totally outclassed during that November fixture in the midlands. You had to feel a little sorry, however for the home team's young centre-forward who fluffed a string of chances and was getting a lot of stick from the crowd. Mostly as a result of his many misses the score remained 0–0 until well into the second half. Then with just seventeen minutes left on the clock, the O's young striker Mark McNeill led a rare Orient attack, leaving the Leicester defence for dead before he hammered the ball past the City 'keeper. It proved to be the only goal of the game, as we won 1–0. McNeill had been running around bravely for us all afternoon and in scoring the winner had given the home side's number nine a nice lesson in the art of finishing. It would have been crystal clear to anyone present at the game that day that our lad, given some proper coaching and a decent club, could look forward to a great future in the game. Alas, you could also see that his Leicester equivalent simply did not have it in him to become a top player.

The point was reiterated again in the return fixture at Leyton Stadium in May. Whilst McNeill scored once more for us in a 3–0 win, the City centre-forward from the first game did not even make the starting line-up for the opposition on the day. So what did become of the opposing strikers who had had such contrasting afternoons back in November 1981? Four years later Mark McNeill was plying his trade playing for Aldershot reserves, while the Leicester no-hoper, a chap named Gary Lineker was busy scoring hat-tricks for England. Didn't somebody once say about football, that it's a funny old game?

The double over Leicester was a rare bright spot in an otherwise totally depressing season for us results wise. From February onwards we won just twice in the league. The big name players such as Jennings, Bowles and Peter Taylor disappeared completely from the team. It was said that they did not get on with hard-man boss Ken Knighton. There was a useful FA Cup run as we got to the Fifth Round before being defeated at home by Crystal Palace, but there was little

Orient awayday 82 – Me, Dave, Malcolm, Paul and Mike.

else to cheer about. Towards the end of the campaign, the official supporter's club coach was barely half full.

Leyton Orient's support over the all but fifty years that I've known it, I've always found an interesting phenomenon. There we were some thirty-five years ago playing two divisions higher than we are now in 2016, yet our support both at home and particularly away then was actually much lower than it is today. Ok so we were having a bad season in 81–82, but even before that attendances at Brisbane Road were below what they are now. And as for our away following although there were no official figures kept in those times unlike today, I can remember games when we'd struggle to get our numbers into three figures even if we were playing not too far away. Yet in 2016 with our team hardly setting the world on fire, we have taken nearly 1,200 to Stevenage, 800 to Wycombe and 650 to York. These are numbers that would have been unthinkable for any run of the mill non-local games back in the eighties. The mysteries of Leyton Orient fans. I just find it all very strange but then again in many ways I suppose, we have always been a strange club.

Going back in time, in the early eighties, some teams in our division such as Sheffield Wednesday, Chelsea and Newcastle were regularly taking three to four thousand to away grounds. Following on from the Newcastle fiasco the season before however, police forces up and down the country could not get to grips with the reality that there was one club in the division that barely took one hundred to games.

I used to sit in my regular place at the front of the supporter's coach and Glen Strongitharm, our steward would have received instructions from the local constabulary on where we were to be met. It was usually just off the motorway and we were then given an escort by the police all the way to the ground. Sometimes the thirty or so of us who had travelled up from east London were met by three or four police cars as well as a back-up of motorcyclists to see us safely to the stadia.

Although nothing could compare with the Newcastle experience, the constant overkill at least always managed to give us all a good chuckle, which was more than we were getting from the actual match itself. Indeed at some venues the abundance of uniformed men, just as had been the case at St James' Park, would continue even inside the ground. If my memory serves me right Rotherham held the record for overkill in 81–82 with three policemen and one and a half police dogs for every away supporter present inside Millmoor when we played them.

When May came, predictably enough the O's were in twenty-second place out of twenty-two teams. We waived goodbye to the Second Division, alas to this day, never to return. Support had dropped off even for the home games. Just two thousand witnessed both our last two matches at Brisbane Road against Oldham and Leicester. Interest started to wane even amongst the regulars, some of whom stopped going having supported the club for years. I however, was as keen as ever and went to every game once more both home and away. I was upset at where we had finished in the league, yet in a perverse kind of way something inside of me was happy that we had come bottom. The fact that we had been so bad yet I had seen not missed a single game, I felt had made me a better supporter and had given me yet more reason to look down on everyone else who followed us at the time.

I was really proud of myself. Indeed it was a view enhanced by manager Ken Knighton's decision to give to the club's top supporters all of the FA Cup Final tickets that the FA had given to the club for the players that season. He said at the time that the players did not deserve to get them after their performances that season, and that the forty-five he had would go to the most deserving fans who had followed the club everywhere. I of course was one of them. As a wonderful gesture by the club, I felt it was almost on a par with the decision to

make the programme a decent size that year. Knighton's deed made national headlines, a picture of him handing over the tickets to Frank Woolf of the supporter's club made the back page of the *Daily Express*. Thanks to the Orient then I finally made it to the twin towers, though unfortunately not to see my team play there, but Spurs and Queens Park Rangers battle it out in the FA Cup Final. The road to Wembley with the Orient, was alas, not yet over for me.

My O's video cassette collection ended the season numbering four. The FA Cup tie against Crystal

Palace, which we lost 1–0 at Brizzy was on *Midweek Sports Special*. Our away defeats at Sheffield Wednesday and Norwich were also on the box so that by the summer of 1982 the record as far as the video cassette collection went was:

Played 4 Won 1 Lost 3

It was a pretty poor return for the £500 that I had spent on the thing some eighteen months earlier. It worked out £250 for every Orient goal that I had recorded on it. As spending cock-ups went this was pretty much on a par with the sock-tags and silk scarf that I had bought some eight years earlier in the club shop.

If my life had taken a different path, the one that it was meant to go on at one point, the summer of 1982 would have seen me celebrating at the end of my four year University course and I would have had letters after my name. As it was I was celebrating having seen 139 consecutive Orient matches home and away.

CHAPTER 18

1982–83 – A CONTINUED DISLIKE OF NEWPORT COUNTY

The World Cup in the summer filled a gap – at least this time you could watch England participate after their non-appearances in 1974 and 1978 – but as ever I could not wait for the new season to start. Despite the disaster that was 81–82 for the Orient, I had once more sent off for my season ticket really early thus securing 'number one' again. Alas though, relegation meant that my lifelong ambition of watching the O's at Wembley was made even harder, as there were now two more FA Cup rounds now to negotiate. Still at least there was the prospect of plenty of new grounds in the new division to go to, which I always enjoyed, and at long last there was a chance for revenge on Newport County, who were in the Third Division.

The close season saw me do what I still consider to be the daftest thing that I've ever done in my capacity as an O's fan. A good friend of mine Kerry, who often went to our home games was twenty-one and she decided to celebrate by holding her party in our supporter's club, which was then on the corner of Brisbane Road. There were plenty of her female mates there that evening and there was a fine disco. With the many young ladies there making the most of the free bar, any normal heterosexual twenty-three year old like myself, would have spent the evening trying to 'pair-up' with one of the many young females present.

Not me. At around nine o'clock, just as things were beginning to warm up, I ordered eight pints on a tray, sneaked out the back and spent the rest of the evening sitting alone on the Coronation Gardens terrace. I plonked myself down and spent the remaining hours reminiscing alone about Chelsea in 1972, together with some of the other great ninety-minutes football that I had seen on the pitch in front of me over the years. In fact, what made the sorry affair all the more pathetic was that it was the middle of June, the goal posts had long since been taken down, the pitch markings were no more and I was just staring at grass all night. Having got really drunk, predictably enough I don't remember going home that evening. Apparently Mike drove me back to Chingford much the worse for wear having downed the eight pints of lager. The next time I saw Kerry she told me that at the end of the evening I had informed her what a wonderful night I had had, and I thanked her for inviting Barrie Fairbrother to her party. Martin Strong circa 1982 was for sure, a sad man.

After the 81–82 shambles, general opinion at Brisbane Road was that the team for the next season could not get any worse. It did. Looking back – and I've had many an argument with O's fans over the years about this – I still consider the 82–83 team to be one, if not the poorest I've ever seen at the Orient. Ian Moores had gone, to be replaced by an even more inept centre-forward in the shape of the home grown Mark Blackhall. There were players in the side like Peter Smith and Nigel Donn who would, in my opinion, walk into any all-time Orient useless eleven. An example of the mess we were in was highlighted by a chap by the name of Robbie Vincent. Manager Knighton had brought him down from the North East, yet within a couple of months he had packed his bags and was heading back up to Tyneside, unable to settle in the south. Mind you, he too was useless.

On 16 October there was a massive game for us. Newport County at home. It was to be the first time I had ever seen us play them. Thoughts went back to the sixties. I had not forgotten those incomplete programmes in the wardrobe, those 3.15pm kick-offs. I had waited thirteen years for some kind of revenge. We just had to beat them. So what happened? We lost 5–1. Five-bloody-one they beat us on our patch. They murdered us in fact, with a young striker of theirs called John Aldridge having a blinder. I left Brisbane Road that afternoon absolutely gutted. I'd seen us lose heavily before to good sides but Newport County? Nobody lost 5–1 at home to Newport bloody County.

I just hoped at the time that it would be a long, long time before I saw us get defeated so heavily to such a poor side. In fact after the Newport debacle, of the next four matches played at Brisbane Road, we lost two of them by the identical score line of 5–1. Bristol Rovers and Oxford were the teams lucky enough to have been playing us. By the beginning of December we were well and truly established in the bottom four of the Third Division.

Still there was always the old faithful of the FA Cup to cheers us up though, wasn't there? We had somehow managed to secure a fine 4–1 First Round victory against Bristol City. Surely the Gods would be kind to us and give us a nice easy home tie in the Second, so setting us up for the Third Round draw with the big boys. So who did we get? Yes, Newport County. We got Newport flipping County away. A tougher game we could not have been given. As it turned out our lads actually put in one of their best displays of the season in down in Wales.

Keith Houchen, one of our better signings who had come from Hartlepool earlier in the year, hit the post twice and with the game entering its final stages, a highly creditable 0–0 looked on the cards. With under ten minutes remaining I was looking forward to hearing our name in the Third Round draw – which was to be broadcast live on the radio at 5.30pm – on the supporter's coach on the way home. Now that we were in the Third Division, we of course had the chance to be even bigger giant-killers than we had been in 1972 and 1978. But then disaster struck. Full-back Bill Roffey brought down their substitute Kevin Moore inside our area. County scored the penalty, and we were out of the FA Cup for another year.

We had been just six minutes away from having our name in the draw but it was not to be. For the first time in years we would not be in the FA Cup Third Round. I would have been distraught no matter who we had been playing that afternoon had we lost, but with the opposition being Newport County, it somehow seemed ten times worse. Walking back to the coach after the game knowing that we were going to have to go through the pain of hearing the draw on the way home, I just prayed that they did not land a big team. They got Everton at home. A golden tie for them. It really did make the journey home even more horrible.

Back in the league, if the home games were generally dire, then the aways were usually worse. Huddersfield on 28 September was one of those infamous Orient awaydays. A Tuesday evening journey up to Yorkshire, I arrived at Brisbane Road at around one o'clock having booked a days leave to go to the game. Upon boarding the official supporter's club coach it started to rain. As the coach departed from our Leyton theatre of dreams, it continued to rain. In fact it carried on raining for the whole journey, slowing us down considerably so that we did not arrive at the ground until 7.20pm, just ten minutes before kick-off. Though none of us were too optimistic about our chances, we hoped that the O's might give us something to cheer us up that evening. Six minutes into the game we were already 2–0 down however, and as a contest the game was effectively over.

In those days I had found a nice little way of making a few bob on our away days. There was – and indeed still is – a sweep on the supporter's coach to predict the score of the match. Many would optimistically go for an Orient win – 2–1 was usually the favourite score. A few of us wise old heads would always go for Orient to lose, however. I never even had them down to score and as a result could end up between fifteen to twenty pounds richer after the game. I always wanted the O's to do well of course, but if they were defeated I could often have the consolation of a small windfall to ease the pain, having won the sweep.

My favourite scorelines were 0–2 or 0–3, depending on who we were playing and the team we were likely to be putting out on the day. For the Huddersfield game however I went for 0–5. My logic was that our defence would normally have conceded three, but I added a couple that night due to the adverse weather conditions. Without a car and, unusually for me at the time, being a bit short on money, I was particularly keen to scoop the jackpot on this occasion to pay for a cab back to Chingford after the coach had dropped us back to Leyton.

At half-time it was 0–3, we had been predictably awful and I was reasonably confident that there would be a good chance the game would end 0–5, and that I would not have to walk home. There was a small group of travelling fans – about twenty of us – sat high in the main stand disappointed, but not at all surprised, at our teams first half performance. The big open bank for away supporters behind the goal was housing just five punters from the East End of London, though there probably would have been double that – including myself – had it not been raining. My late seventies and early eighties policy of often mingling in with home supporters had by now been abandoned.

The game progressed, not getting any better as we conceded a fourth. The home punters then looked amazed to see one of the away supporters celebrating wildly as a fifth goal went in. It was me of course. There was just twelve minutes to go. Could our boys hang on for the remainder of the match so that I could collect the money?

Predictably enough the answer was no. In fact we held out for a mere sixty seconds before the sixth was added. At that point Huddersfield decided to declare and 6–0 was the final score. I ended up walking back to Chingford after we had got dropped off at Brisbane Road, having not won the money. It was the first time that I had done this since the infamous Villa game back in 1974. And it was still raining all the way home.

Indeed even the walk back to Old Church Road in Chingford was not entirely smooth. About half way towards my destination I was stopped by two policemen. They enquired as to where I had got the portable cassette from that I was listening to while walking along. Apparently a gang of youths had smashed into a hi-fi shop in Walthamstow a few hours before and ran off with lots of expensive equipment. The two boys in blue who questioned me were not very pleasant. (I thought at the time that they must have got a transfer down from Middlesbrough) It appeared that my name was in the frame for being involved in the smash and grab. They asked me where I had been that evening.

'I've been to Yorkshire to see my team lose 6–0.' I said. 'You trying to be funny, son' was the reply, 'if so, we'll take you to the station.' Neither of them it appeared, believed me. One of them then went away and I think may have rang the station to confirm the scoreline from Leeds Road that night. Finally after about ten minutes they let me continue my journey home. I arrived home at three in the morning that night, and it was still raining. I was wetter than even my dad had been after the World Cup Final in 1966.

There were some other infamous away trips that season. Many things in our game have changed dramatically over the past thirty years or so, but one thing that has remained as constant as ever has been the incompetence of the football league fixture planners. In the recent 2015–16 season the O's had midweek away games at our two furthest venues to get to, Plymouth and Carlisle. Yet our six matches against London sides were all played during the season on a Saturday. Back in 1982, amongst other things, we had the Huddersfield game on a Tuesday night and they also contrived to give us Sheffield United away on New Year's Day. I went, of course on an 85% hung-over coach (the other 15% had not bothered to turn up) to see a 3–0 reverse. On the day it looked as if our players, as well as all of us supporters, had been on the beers on New Year's Eve, the night before.

With a drop into the lower division, there was a definite change in atmosphere on the away trips, though. In those days of football hooliganism, as mentioned before, we had often endured a massive police overkill in the Second Division. This had all changed now though. In the Third, we were often escorted to the ground by a single policeman. And in 82–83 I did not see a single police dog all season.

As we entered December events in the league were looking extremely grim. The Fourth Division beckoned for the first time in our history. Then came a dramatic happening that was to put an entirely new complexion on the rest of the season. Peter Kitchen came home. It's fair to say that the great man's career had never really taken off as he had wished after he left Brisbane Road in 1979. He had signed for Fulham for £150,000 hoping eventually to play First Division football for them. Kitch was very unlucky with the timing of his move, however. At around the same time the Cottagers had signed a young forward called

Gordon Davies from Merthyr for just £2,000. He was initially meant to be purely a back-up player to Kitchen. Davies however soon proved to be some signing, scoring plenty, and to this day is seen by many fans as something of a legend at Fulham. He is still thought of as being one of the clubs best ever signings. Unfortunately though, as a player he was very similar to our Kitch, so that the Brisbane Road legend never got a look in at his new club, as Davies established himself. Our legend was often made substitute. The great man moved on to Cardiff, and eventually ended up in Hong Kong, of all places. But around the middle of December in 1982, with the O's stuck in the bottom four, he returned to his real home in E10. Funnily enough, when he originally left our club, gutted as I was at the time, for some strange reason I always felt we had not seen the last of him at the Orient, and so it proved.

His debut was to be a home game against Preston on a Friday night. The crowd – and there were 1,668 of us – cheered wildly, welcoming back the messiah, as the teams took to the field. The match was locked at 1–1 with just five minutes remaining when the inevitable happened. A long through ball from Kevin Godfrey left the returning messiah one one-on-one with the Preston 'keeper. No contest. A little dummy, a side-step past the custodian and a nice finish into the empty net. 2–1. We all went crazy. We had had nothing at all to get excited about for a few years at our east London home of football, so to see this was just wonderful. The goal proved to be the winner, of course. Oh, how I still loved the man.

ROOM FOR KITCHEN

ORIENT completed the signing of Peter Kitchen this week and will throw him straight into first team action.

Kitchen, who left the club three years ago, makes his comeback against Preston tonight (Friday) to the delight of manager Ken Knighton.

He said: "I'm absolutely thrilled. Kitch has a proven goalscoring record and could prove a very valuable asset. His general fitness is very good and he's raring to go."

Knighton also hopes that his new striker will help the younger members of the team, in particular Keith Houchen and Kevin Godfrey.

"Just his presence will be good for the side," added Knighton.

The O's boss failed to sign the 'mystery' player he has been watching, but the talent spotting continues.

He said: "There's nothing happening at all with that player. I'll be at a game on Saturday though, as we're not playing."

Knighton also visited Sheffield on Tuesday night to watch United play Boston in the FA Cup. Orient play "The Blades" on New Year's Day.

The Kitchen signing served as a morale booster for the club after their cup exit on Saturday.

Said Knighton: "We were desperately unlucky at Newport. We created a number of chances and really battled away. I've no complaints."

"We must put that game behind us now. It's vitally important that we carry on the way we did then."

Preston had a good Cup win against Blackpool on Saturday and their confidence will be high.

Tim Elmes is still training with the side and the only injury worry is Keith Osgood, who hasn't been able to train all week.

A legend returns.   ● Ken Knighton welcomes back Peter Kitchen.

The statistics for the 82–83 campaign tell their own story. With the truly awful side we had before Peter Kitchen returned, we had won just five all season. Then, when Kitchen then came back, we proceeded to win six out of the next seven, with Kitch netting in four of them. Then disaster struck, however. Our saviour broke his toe in the game against Portsmouth. Without him we failed to win any of our next six. The last of these was the return fixture with Newport County in the league. Surely we could get some kind of redemption for the home humiliation, the cup defeat and my programme collection, couldn't we? Alas no. By half-time we were 4–0 down. Barry Silkman managed a consolation for us after the break, but it was too little too late, and we went down 4–1. They had done us again. O how I loathed the team from Wales.

Our best player that afternoon was keeper Mervyn Day, who kept the score down to four. Indeed it shows just how bad we were at the time that our ever present custodian was probably our best player over the season. The continued struggles meant that we entered the last league game fourth from bottom in a relegation place. A win at home to Sheffield United however would keep us up providing that Wrexham did not win at Reading.

Predictably the game was very tense, but at least with Kitchen now back playing we knew we had a chance. Keith Houchen broke the deadlock after half an hour and then the mighty Kitch played his part, stooping low to head home for an all-important second, thus relieving a lot of the tension. They pulled one back, but further strikes from Kevin Godfrey and Bill Roffey confirmed a 4–1 victory and celebrations ensued as we heard the news that Reading had defeated Wrexham 1–0. We were thus safe from a second successive relegation, and a drop into the Fourth Division for the first time.

There was the inevitable pitch invasion and mass hysteria ensued in front of the main stand. It brought back memories of 1977 when we all celebrated wildly when a draw with Hull had kept us up in the Second Division. Once again it summed up what being an Orient supporter was – and indeed still is – all about. Fans of other teams look back fondly on cup wins, championship successes, nights of European glory for their happiest memories when following their teams. For us though an afternoon avoiding a bottom four finish in the Third Division was a cause of ecstasy.

I can still remember now, all these years on, standing on the pitch thinking what a weird bunch we all were. Manager Ken Knighton came out onto the Director's Box in the East Stand and we were all there in front of him, cheering him wildly. We gave him an even better reception as he took to the mike and told us that he was going to give us all a season to remember in 83–84. We all chanted his name, proclaiming the man a hero for merely keeping the side up, despite the fact he had given us the worst Orient team anyone could ever remember. I thought it all a bit bizarre. Indeed, just a month later Knighton was predictably enough sacked. He still had two years of his contact left, which the club honoured financially. In a typical Orient-like move assistant manager Frank Clark was made up to take charge, thus saving the club the expense of having to pay for a new manager from outside.

Perversely, despite all the traumas that the year had brought and despite the ultimate trauma that was Newport County, I actually found 82–83 a pretty enjoyable season. The new division had meant new places to visit. Lincoln, Plymouth and Exeter were frankly more appealing than the northern outposts of the Second such as Bolton and Grimsby. The new grounds had done wonders for my collection of lapel badges and of course there was the return of Peter Kitchen. By May 1983 my run of consecutive Orient games was up to 193. I had already achieved my hat-trick of number one season tickets, and was already looking forward to the new campaign.

CHAPTER 19

1983–84 – THE ROBBIE SAVAGE OF ALL COACH COMPANIES

17 September 1983 and something was not quite right in the world. We were travelling back from Rotherham and the Orient were top of the league. Under the management of Frank Clark we had won four out of our first five and were riding high. The new man had brought in a few new guys and there was an obvious improvement on the previous season. Though we knew it would not last for the whole campaign, it was still refreshing after the disasters of the previous two seasons.

I did an unusual thing at the end of 1983 in that I took a week's leave at work during the football season. This did not mean that my addiction to the great game was on the wane, and that I had decided to go away on holiday, however. Far from it in fact, I took a week off in November and went up north for a few days to take in some games. I saw Wigan versus Orient on the Tuesday, I went to Manchester United versus Sparta Varna on the Wednesday in the Cup-Winners Cup, did Halifax against Tranmere on the Friday night, Bolton versus Orient on Saturday and rounded it all off with Liverpool versus Everton at Anfield on the Sunday. Much as I tried I could not find any fixture on the Thursday, not even in the Pontins League, which was the northern reserve league at the time.

Not a common sight in my Orient supporting career. The O's are top of the league.

We finished the season in eleventh place. It was nice not looking at the papers every Sunday and seeing us down the bottom for a change. All in all though, it was not the most exciting of campaigns. I ended it no nearer to fulfilling that life-long ambition of seeing Orient play at Wembley. That road was certainly proving to be a longer one than I had originally envisaged. How I longed at the time that someone would hurry up and invent the play-offs.

My only real lasting memory of 83–84 was the away travel that year. There had been complaints that the official supporter's coach had been too expensive for a lot of people the previous season, so a cheaper firm was hired. It is unfair to give their name, as I know they are still in business and I know they are much improved these days, but at the time they were to away travel what Robbie Savage is to sports broadcasting these days. In a nutshell they were hopeless.

The tone of the season's travel was set on the second outing. A Wednesday night trip to Lincoln City. After much aggravation and four or five stops, our vehicle finally conked out some twenty miles from Lincoln. We rang Sincil Bank and the Orient player's coach was dispatched to ferry us to the ground. After witnessing a 2-0 defeat we had to hang around in their clubhouse until after midnight while the original coach was being repaired. We finally got back to Brisbane Road at five-thirty in the morning. This was just a taster of things to come, as misdemeanours like that continued throughout the season.

Throughout most of the eighties, when watching the O's away from home there was generally one near certainty when you went. The fact that whoever we played, you would nearly always see us lose. For this one season, however there were two near certainties. One was that the O's would be defeated, and the other was that the supporter's club coach would breakdown. In fact on the couple of times when it did not breakdown on the way there, the driver got lost anyway so that we ended up missing the kick-off. In the penultimate away game at Burnley we arrived at three-fifteen, having previously been led on a tour of Lancashire by the man behind the wheel.

Upon reaching Turf Moor that afternoon, we heard a loud cheer and guessed that the home side had scored. In fact we found out that they had gone 2-0 up and that we had missed both goals. Remarkably though, most un-Orient like, we pulled it back to win 3-2 and would have gone home very happy had the driver not taken the wrong turning again on the way home. We got back to Leyton (via Oxford on the M5) at around midnight.

It was to be Kitch's last season with us. It was a patchy one for him, it has to be said, yet I still adored the man. He left us all with one last memory in 83–84, a four goal haul in April against local rivals Millwall, as we defeated them 5–3 at Brisbane Road. Just as the great man was the first O's player I'd seen score a hat-trick, he thus became the first I'd seen score four in one game. He moved to Chester on a free transfer, leaving us with a final Orient tally in his two spells of sixty goals in one hundred and twenty-seven appearances. In O's terms an unbelievable ratio for a striker. What also made him so special was the fact that practically all of his efforts were so crucial. In 77–78 his goals got us to the Cup semi-final, and then kept us up, while in 82–83 until he returned and started banging them in, it looked as if we were doomed and destined for the drop. His goals in that year once again kept us up. We had to wait thirty-eight years until another Orient player managed to notch twenty league goals in a season, through Jay Simpson in 2015–16. Great effort as it was by Simmo, another wonderful 'O', his contribution was in a division two below the one where Peter Kitchen had scored his twenty. In my eyes Kitch remains immortal, the still best finisher I've ever seen at the club and still my all-time favourite 'O'. He makes the odd appearance nowadays at Brisbane Road, and is indeed prominent in

the reflections the club make in the battle of the Somme in 1916, when all the O's signed up to fight for their country and three players lost their lives. When he comes back now, it still baffles many a younger fan when they see a bloke walking around Leyton Stadium with a halo over his head. Saint Peter Kitchen, a true Leyton Orient legend.

I went to every O's game home and away once more in 1983–84, and by the end of it had clocked up around 240 consecutive games. Domestically I was very

The ultimate Leyton Orient legend.

happy, though still woman-less. As Kerry's party had illustrated I was playing an ultra-defensive game when it came to the other sex. It was the equivalent of playing with a front line of Moores, Plasmati and Ollie Palmer. Basically you did not expect to score.

Work was going fine, I was making the bank a few bob in my role as a foreign exchange dealer at the ANZ. Though still a footy and Orient nut however, there were signs that the full-monty football obsessive that was Martin Strong in the late seventies and early eighties was beginning to show a few signs of waning. For starters I had stopped going to the programme fairs on a Sunday, though this had something to do with the fact that there were not many holes left in my Orient collection to fill. I had also stopped going to the Capital League games in the evenings. Further evidence that I was returning to the real world was that I did not bother to try to get season ticket number one for the 84–85 campaign. I was on the verge of sanity once more.

CHAPTER 20

1984–85 – OUT FOR TWO HUNDRED AND FORTY-FOUR

Season 1984–85 was for sure when I came back down to earth and once again became what you might call a 'bread and butter' supporter. A run of the mill fan I have been ever since, going to all the home games and as many of the aways as I can manage, but it has not been the end of the world if I've not been there at any game. That was not the case in the late seventies and early eighties though, when I just had to be at every game no matter what. Season 84–85 though, was when I stopped looking down at other fans, thinking that I was above them because I went everywhere to follow my team and they didn't. Basically I became a nice supporter again.

The day that changed it all was 1 September 1984. That was the day that I missed my first Orient game for two weeks short of five years. It had all started back in June. I got on very well with a young lady who I used to work with at the ANZ called Diane, who I still keep in touch with today. I went to lunch with her and she told me that she was getting married in September, and that she wanted me to be an usher on her big day. I suppose it was the close season and football was not uppermost in my mind at the time – England had not qualified for the European Championship Finals – and I agreed. A few weeks later the fixtures came out and there it was: 1 September, home to Gillingham. I was finally to miss a game. I was to go back to being a 'part-timer'. My thought then was that I had scored a massive own-goal in agreeing to go to the wedding, almost as bad an own-goal as Bill Roffey had scored at Stamford Bridge in 1978.

When the season started, I saw the first two games – the opening one was a fine 1–0 victory away at Brentford – but then the big day arrived. Even on the morning of 1 September it was tempting not to go to the church but to head to Brisbane Road instead. I was not that kind of bloke though, to let Diane and everybody else down, I had made my decision and had to stick to it.

The wedding was a three-o-clock kick-off. By five to three I had ushered everybody to their seats and taken up my position at the front of the church, waiting for *Tijuana Taxi*. It never came. Turning round to the back of the church I expected to see Tommy Cunningham leading the lads out. He was nowhere to be seen. There though was Di's dad taking his daughter down the aisle. It was all over. A run of two hundred and forty-four consecutive, competitive Orient matches, home and away had ended.

The whole afternoon was all a little unreal. The O's had had a good pre-season, and had then defeated Brentford in the league, as well as Southend in the League Cup. Nowadays of course given similar circumstances I would have sneakily been able to keep abreast of Oriental events via the mobile phone, but that was not the way of it the eighties. Instead I turned on the transistor radio at ten to five to find out that we had got beaten 4–2. I felt so guilty. I was not there and as a result the boys had gone to pieces. Indeed I found out that they had raced into a 2–0 lead early on. It had then obviously struck them that I was not there and they had fallen apart afterwards.

I put on a brave face that evening at the reception, but underneath it all I knew that I was responsible for the defeat. At the end of the evening Di thanked me for all my help that day and presented me with a tankard to mark the occasion. It had '1/9/1984' engraved on it. It was a lovely gesture, of course. Diane and Paul are still happily married today, 1 September every year will always be a big day for them. For me too though, when that day comes my mind always goes back all those years and I remember how it changed everything for me too.

Having missed one match, with the run over I decided that I would not go to every away fixture in the future, though I would still be present at all the homes. The sequence was broken but I felt that I could still be termed a pretty good fan with my new tactics. There were the lads in the programme shop in Brisbane Road, led by the admiral Dave Staplehurst, who would save all of the match-day magazines from those games that I missed, so that that was one worry that I did not have by becoming once more, a part-time fan.

The change in my style of supporting was not well received by the team, however. After the Gillingham defeat we lost the next four in the league. In fact we won only three and drew two of the remaining games up until Christmas. Crowds were barely above two thousand for the home matches and relegation again looked a distinct possibility. There was the inevitable defeat at Newport, this time 2–0, and a Robbie Savage of a match against Hull City at home, where we lost 5–4 having been 4–1 up with just twenty minutes to play.

Indeed the only bright spot on the pitch during the 84–85 campaign was another FA Cup run. The first round had us paired with Buckingham Town. It was three seasons since we had been relegated from the Second Division, yet this was our first encounter with non-league opposition in the major cup competition since we went down. An old mate of mine, a Charlton Athletic supporter, had said to me, that it would not really hit home that you were in the Third Division until you got drawn away against obscure non-leaguers in the FA Cup First Round, and he was right.

Upon arriving at Buckingham, on a wet November afternoon, you could pick instantly who the home fans were. They were the ones who had arrived at the ground wearing wellington boots. The pitch had a rope around it and there was just one stand, which seated no more than two hundred. There was no club shop, but a tent, which did not sell any lapel badges. Still, at least they weren't Gillingham, Plymouth or Preston and had the decency to produce a proper programme for the occasion.

The day summed up just how much our beloved Orient had fallen. Just six years previously we had been playing in an FA Cup semi-final in front of fifty thousand. Now here we were in the same competition plying our trade against a poor non-league outfit on a pitch that made those on Hackney marshes look like Wembley. The continued joys of being an O's fan.

We eventually saw off the part-timers 2–0, though it was hard to pick out who the professionals were that afternoon. One bonus to come out of the game however, was to get a video of the game a few weeks later. Relegation to the Third had sadly meant no television coverage at all for our boys, so that my Orient video collection had remained static for some time at just four matches. Buckingham's first appearance in the First Round proper of the FA Cup was the biggest day in the club's history however, so they decided to record the event. By this time even I was getting a little bit fed up with watching Orient verses Sheffield Wednesday from 1982 on my twenty stone, five hundred pound machine, so I jumped at the chance of doubling my number of O's victories I had on video to two.

We were presented with a lucky draw in the Second Round – Torquay United at home. The Devon side were the ninety-second team in the league. They were duly beaten 3–0 and so we were in the Third Round with the big boys for the first time since 1982. Our reward was a plumb home tie with West Bromwich Albion, who were riding high at the time in the top flight. Getting ready to go to the game on the day of the match, I saw Bob Wilson, on the Beeb's *Football Focus* programme tipping the Albion as his team to win the competition that year. Waiting for the '69' to arrive at the bus-stop shortly afterwards, I hoped our lads had watched the show as I guessed it would give them all just the incentive that they needed to go and beat the Baggies.

After all the dross we had been forced to endure watching our team for the first five years of the decade, the match turned out to be a long overdue Oriental classic. The Midlanders took the lead, but our boys defied the two clubs differing league positions, and deservedly equalized when West Brom 'keeper Tony Godden let a soft Barry Silkman shot slip underneath him. We then had the luxury of missing a penalty, Silkman's effort producing a save from Godden that, to this day, I still regard to be the finest penalty save I've ever seen at Brisbane Road. It was only a temporary set-back however, as with just seven minutes to go, our rising star Richard Caddette latched onto a through ball and duly dispatched the winner past Godden. The fact that it was scored right in front of us at the North Terrace end made it all the sweeter for us.

There were for sure some large celebrations that night. The supporter's club was just for a change a happy place after the game. I think I left there around eleven that night. A large hangover did not prevent me cutting out all the newspaper cuttings of the encounter the following day.

We were handed another good draw in the next round, this time we were paired at home to another First Division club in Southampton. The build up to the game with the Saints got us some much-needed publicity, it helped that it was the only cup game in the capital on the day. The BBC contacted the O's with a view to interviewing a few of the clubs keenest supporters on the day before the match. They were to be live on television on their South East Regional News programme. It appeared that nobody at the Beeb had been told about Di's wedding on 1 September, so that I was selected to go on the show despite the fact that I was now officially only a 'part-timer'.

We were told to go to the Sobell Sports Centre in Islington on Friday evening, where Michael Wale would ask us questions on the television, in front of live cameras. It's fair to say that I was more than a little nervous as he thrust a microphone in front of my mouth, asking:

'How do you feel when all these invaders come to your ground as they will tomorrow, when you're there through thick and thin?' (He too obviously knew nothing about the infamous wedding.)

'Well, it's all good money for the club, like, that's the way we treat it.' So went my immortal reply, muttered live to the Capital's millions. Following on from my appearance with Jimmy Bloomfield on the radio back in 1980 I now felt that I was for sure a celebrity fan. I went on to say that I thought we would win 2–1, despite the fact that in reality I could see us losing quite easily. Everybody's

A group of Orient supporters are pictured with Michael Wale of BBC TV at the Sobell Centre, Islington, when they took part in a live London Plus feature on the eve of this club's fourth round FA Cup-tie with Southampton. (Photo: Mike Childs).

meant to get their fifteen minutes of fame, of course but if you were a Leyton Orient fan it appeared at the time, that with my live appearances on both the radio and television, you could stretch that to at least an hour.

I even managed to capture on video the greatest moment on BBC television since they showed the Chelsea game back in 1972. And as an added bonus my picture appeared in the Orient programme for the next home game.

There was certainly high anticipation the next day, especially when we all saw Lord Barry Davies climbing the steps up to the television gantry in the westside. The game was going to be on *Match of the Day* with our lucky man doing the commentary. As I saw him sitting there, waiting for the teams to take to the field, I guessed that Davies' mind must have been going back to that day thirteen years before, when he sat there for the Chelsea match and had given his finest performance as a commentator. Sadly, however the game was somewhat of an anti-climax. We lost 2–0 and really did not give Peter Shilton, the Saints goalkeeper, a shot to save all afternoon. Alas the O's were out of the Cup for another year, but at least this time we had made it to the Fourth Round.

The attendance for the Southampton game of 17,622 (surely boosted by my television appearance the day before) was exactly 16,718 more than the number we managed for the previous home match at Brisbane Road some four days earlier. Just 804 had turned up to see a goalless draw against Aldershot in the Freight Rover Trophy, the new mickey mouse competition that had followed on from the Group Cup a few years before. The game had turned out to be a bit of a disaster for us in that Richard Caddette, our star of the Third Round, had got injured and so was forced to sit out the Saints encounter. Manager Frank Clark said at the time that the Freight Rover was a daft competition in that crowds were desperately low and we always seemed to pick up an injury and he was spot on.

There weren't even any games against Scottish sides to look forward to if you did well, although that was more than made up for by the fact that there was now a Wembley appearance at the end of it if you got to the Final. It was still a daft competition though, never highlighted more than by our participation in it in the 84–85 campaign. Having beaten Aldershot over two legs in the First Round and Millwall 3–2 in the Second Round, we got drawn in the Third Round at home to…Millwall??!!!! This I must admit was a bit baffling. All I could think of at the time was that the Lions, with their ever-notorious following had intimidated the Football League into letting them back into the competition. We defeated them for a second time however, to leave us remarkably just two ties away from a long overdue appearance at the twin towers. We eagerly awaited the Southern Area semi-final draw half expecting us to get paired with Millwall again. But no the draw was a disaster. We got the auld enemy. Newport County. We bloody got Newport County.

The game with them was at Brisbane Road and we took a twenty-third minute lead through Pat Corbett, but despite being well in control we were unable to add a second. As the game entered its closing stages, knowing who we were playing against we all awaited the inevitable equalizer. Four minutes from time and sure enough it came, through a twenty-five yard free-kick. Extra-time saw no more goals, so it all came down to a penalty shoot-out. For the O's then, it was a double whammy. Not only did the entire football world know that we never beat Newport bloody County, but they also knew that Orient never won any penalty shoot-out. We were still waiting at the time for our first success from a spot kick lottery. Sure enough Neil Banfield and then Barry Silkman missed to leave County 'keeper Mark Kendall to score the winning pen. Yet another chapter was therefore written in my book *Why I hate Newport County*.

For all the form shown in the cup competitions, we continued to be abysmal in the league. Seven games without a win in February and March left us on the brink of the Fourth Division for the first time in our history. As with our 82–83 vintage, it has to be said there were some not very good players in our team. Regrettably, David Stride, Neil Banfield and Pat Corbett were not really up to league standard.

There was one memorable match in March, when we defeated Bolton 4–3 at Brizzy, having been 3–1 down, but we followed this up by losing our next three. We entered our last game of the season at home to Bournemouth needing a win to have any chance of staying up. It was just one of those games however, when we seemed destined not to score, and the match sadly ended 0–0. Ian Juryeff was a forward who scored more than a few useful goals for us in his years at the club. For many an 'O' however, he will always be remembered for famously missing an open goal in the Bournemouth match which effectively cost us any chance of avoiding the drop.

Whether the fact that I had missed my first game for five years back in September had an adverse effect on the team and caused relegation I guess we shall never know. The lads had certainly played well enough in all of the cup games, when they knew that my presence was guaranteed.

After the Bournemouth game I felt really deflated. As deflation went, this was on the same scale as that when I found out that the Anglo-Scottish Cup had been scrapped. Looking back now however, there had been an air of inevitability about eventually having to suffer the Fourth Division, ever since we had got relegated from the Second back in 1982. There were also the tragic events with the fire at Bradford City, which occurred on the same day as the Bournemouth fixture, which put the deflation into some kind of perspective. Despite all of the lows that I had experienced in supporting my team, at the end of the day was not a matter of life and death following the Orient.

I ended up going to all of the home games, as well as about half of the aways during the season. The good news was that the coach company used by the supporter's club had been changed again, so that the breakdowns and arriving late for games were thankfully now a thing of the past.

By contrast to the fortunes of my football team in the mid-eighties, at work things were going wonderfully well for me. I had of course made the decision not to go to Uni back in 1978 because I did not want to be Orient-sick living in Birmingham. I had been told by many at the time that I was making a mistake and that I would struggle to get on, career wise, without letters after my name. Well here we were now in 1985, some seven years later and though I was without a degree, I was a foreign exchange dealer in the City of London, earning a really good salary. I was getting nice little bonuses and of course I'd still been able to watch my side throughout the period, so I felt that I had made the right call back in 1978. It may not go down well with many of you reading this, but under Thatcher in the eighties many of us, certainly those working in the City of London were doing very nicely indeed.

Whilst through my foreign currency dealing I was doing fine, as a trader I was not one of the very 'top dogs' in the game making millions for my bank, unlike certain bankers who were making absolute fortunes for their institutions. These boys were well known to everyone in the square mile and salary wise they were really raking it in. They could virtually demand to get paid whatever they wanted, such was their value to their employers, with the huge sums of money they were making for them.

From the early eighties however, although I was not picking up any massive recognition in the game as one of the very top FX dealers, in the close knit community of the traders and brokers I was getting a reputation thanks to one thing. Word got round the City, that there was this geezer at the Australia and New Zealand Bank called 'strongo' (which was what everybody called me) that knew virtually everything about football. Consequently if a dispute arose between traders or brokers over a footy query, the ANZ dealing room was rung, as it was known that the bloke there would probably know the answer. Without being big headed I generally did and resolved many an argument. With the way the City bankers were with their cash there was often a lot of money riding on what I told them, with big bets taking place between them. Nowadays, of course I would not be needed – the answer would just be googled – but in those days I was invaluable. I've got to own up now some thirty odd years later in that I did have a copy of the Rothmans under my desk in case I struggled for an answer to a question that they wanted, but if I say so myself, only rarely was it needed.

Living life as an 'O' as I'm sure many of you can vouch, can make you feel at times that you are leading a bit of a lonely existence. As I said early on I was the only Orient supporter in my year at Larkswood Primary School and this continued when I went up to Chingford Junior High in the seventies. This was a theme that carried on when I entered employment. The ANZ bank was, and indeed still is a wonderful company to work for. (They have been paying me a lovely pension since I was fifty.) In the eighties there were about a thousand of us working for them at Gracechurch Street in the City. Out of that number however, just three of us were O's. Myself and a wonderful married couple, George and Lotte Gatward who were just as nuts about our wonderful club as I was. George sadly passed away at the end of 2014, but for me he was Mr Orient. He had lived in one of the big tower blocks overlooking Leyton Stadium for many a year and when they were finally knocked down, he took residence in one of the houses that took their place. He saw his first game at Brisbane Road in 1942 and didn't miss too many that we played there over the next seventy-two years.

If you went round to George and Lottes before kick-off, and the wind was blowing in the right direction at around 2.30pm, you could open their front door and hear the teams being read out over the Tannoy. Yes it was certainly fair to say that they lived pretty close to our east London piece of paradise. For me it was heaven when I found the Gatwards worked at the bank. At long last I had found a couple who I could share the pain of being an 'O' in work from Monday to Friday, as well as on matchdays. Lotte remains an Orient legend; she is still there at all the homes as well as many of the aways and is still as passionate as ever. Though the three of us spent years working together at the ANZ and found it very rewarding, it has to be said of course that the bank was not as important as another institution that the three of us all knew. The Orient counted for more than the bank for us, of course.

CHAPTER 21

1985–86 – A LIFE CHANGING SEASON

The close season in 1985 was not an ordinary close season. Sure I was still looking forward to seeing the O's play once more come August. Ok so we had got relegated meaning that we would have to endure Fourth Division footy for the first time, but that was partly compensated by the new grounds that we would be able to go to in the last tier of the football league. However, due to events that had happened during the summer, for maybe the first time ever I was not 100% focused on football come the start of the season. I had found myself a young lady.

I still kept in touch with Mike, Tinks and Kevin, those three veterans of many an away trip in the late seventies and early eighties. They all still went to a few home games, though they had all subsequently paired up with females, and were getting serious with them. They decided in their wisdom that it was about time that I saw life beyond Brisbane Road and paired me up with Sonia, who was a good friend of all of their other halves.

We got on really well from our first night out together in May. Looking back now I can't honestly remember what I spoke to her about on that first 'blind date'. I must have told her about my job and talked about my family. I reckon I probably chipped in somewhere about my uncle being a knight and having appeared on *Desert Island Discs*. I do remember that she told me that she was a West Ham fan and had been to the odd game, so I must have said that I too liked football and supported east London's other club, Orient. I don't think though, that I can have mentioned that I had ten scrapbooks full of newspaper cuttings about my side, together with lots of programmes and car stickers, because she agreed to go out with me again at the end of the evening.

From the start we got on famously. As a partnership, even after just a few nights out, I was already starting to draw comparisons with Kitchen and Mayo in 1978. In hindsight it was probably crucial that I met her in May to give our relationship a few non-football months to develop. There wasn't even any World Cup or European Championship to distract me that summer.

I decided at the start of the season that I would start to take Sonia to matches at Brisbane Road, if she wished to go, but that I would play it cool when it came to the away trips. My first outing of the season in 85–86 was to be Hartlepool on 31 August. I figured that a four-hundred and fifty mile round trip to Feethams would be pushing it so early in our relationship, so I enjoyed a 2–1 away victory alone.

In fact Orient's early form in the new division was pretty good, with three wins in our opening five league matches. (Not up to Hendon's first five league encounters in 2015–16 of course, but not bad all the same) The satisfaction this start gave though was nothing compared with the joy that I felt at our match at Brisbane Road on 23 September. It was the first leg of the Second Round of the League Cup and we only went and beat Tottenham Hotspur, 2–0. What a magnificent night it was. Ok so we went on to lose the second leg 4–0 so going out of the cup, but boy was it a sweet victory in the initial game. It was the first time in my eighteen years of supporting them, that the O's had beaten the Spurs. Oh how it would have been nice to have turned back the clock to my youth and

gone into Larkswood Junior School the next day. To have given back some of the stick that I had endured endlessly from my class mates, back in the sixties.

Kevin Godfrey got both Orient goals on the night to steal all the headlines in his finest hour in an O's shirt. Though Sonia did not accompany me that night, I recall going to see her excitedly straight after the match. I informed her that it was the first time that Tottenham had ever lost to a Fourth Division side, and that it was the first time that we had ever defeated them at Brisbane Road. It was a measure of just how well I was getting to know her at the time, that I felt

comfortable giving her all the statto-like facts about the game. If it had been a few months earlier, with our relationship still in its early stages, I don't think that that would have been the case.

By mid-October life was looking really good. Three consecutive wins had elevated us to the dizzy heights of fourth, our highest league placing for years. Ok so we were now in the basement division, but all the same it was still nice not to see the lads struggling every week. Frankie Clark was still in charge, and he even had us scoring goals aplenty, a phenomenon of course, which was most un-Orient like. And there was also the added bonus of going to lots of new grounds in the new division, which was nice.

And then there was Sonia. She was great. Even after only a few months of 'walking her home', I was contemplating marriage. She had come to a few homes, and I decided that the next big step in our relationship would be her first away game. VS Rugby in the First Round of the FA Cup seemed ideal. It was not too far to go, so that she would not have too much time to get bored travelling on the supporter's coach. It was to be played at the beginning of November, which was just before the really cold weather would kick in. Also, it was a game that even I expected us to win easily, which meant that she would not have to endure the pain of watching me getting really worked up witnessing an Orient away defeat.

The afternoon, though – as so often seems to be the case with our club, of course – did not go entirely to plan. With just fifteen minutes to go we were 2–1 down to the non-leaguers. I was getting well ratty with our team. What's more it had started to rain, so that Sonia was starting to get a bit fed up. The form of Orient was putting a strain on our relationship. Things were getting a bit tense, but then a saviour arrived in the shape of Sean Brooks. He possibly saved the partnership of Sonia and myself by scoring a late penalty to rescue a draw. I was saved from seeing us lose to non-league opposition for the first time in my Orient career. Had we lost I think it would have been a very stressed journey back on the coach, but we had just about managed to survive. I had also managed to get a new lapel badge for my collection, so it wasn't such a bad day.

VS Rugby was to be the first of a series of away trips that Sonia and myself were to share that season. We had some wonderfully romantic days out at the likes of Scunthorpe, Chester and Rochdale. She appeared to quite enjoy the experiences, though I wonder how she would have felt had we kept the same coach company on the away trips as we had had in 83–84, when we had broken down every five minutes.

My life was certainly changing. It was on the way back from Rugby that Sonia suggested that we might go away for a first holiday together in December by obtaining a last minute cancellation. I said yes straight away. I had started to realize that there was a world beyond Brisbane Road after all. I would always love my club needless to say, but I was twenty-six, most of my mates had settled down and I did not want to end up like those guys I used to see at the programme fairs – into middle age, still living at home with mum and dad and wearing Columbo raincoats. And I would make sure that the holiday did not coincide with any of the new league grounds that the Fourth Division was bringing. I did not think that anyone could seriously start calling me a 'glory hunter' for simply missing a few games. As far as I was concerned I was still a pretty decent fan.

We booked up to go to Tenerife. The two weeks together would, I thought, be as big a test for our relationship as VS Rugby away had been. Although we had only been going out for about six months, I decided that if we got on really well on holiday I would pop 'the big question' to her soon afterwards. (The 'big question' actually being would she marry me, not did she want to join me in starting another sequence of watching consecutive O's games.)

It was for sure going to be strange in that for the first time ever the lads would be playing and I would not even be in the country, but I guessed that our players would just about manage to cope with that. And I knew that the lads in the club shop would save all the missed programmes for me, so that was one worry that I would not have.

We sneaked in another new ground together, Chester on 23 November and left for two weeks in the sun the following Wednesday. The fortnight was wonderful; we got on really well and had just one tiff during our vacation. It was on the first Saturday. Sonia was getting in some serious sunbathing, but I just could not settle. The O's were playing at home to Swindon. I found it a weird feeling. Our boys were playing at Leyton Stadium, yet I was not even within a few hundred miles of Brisbane Road. It was a similar feeling to that which I had had some fifteen months earlier when Orient had entertained Gillingham during Di's wedding and I was not there.

There were no mobile phones or Internet then of course to keep me informed as to how the boys were getting on. Though I tried to hide my inner emotions, Sonia could see that I was restless, and muttered those words that all non-football believers often hide behind: 'It's only a game.' At six o'clock we made our way back from the beach, passing a public phone box. I knew that my dad, bless him, would be waiting for me to ring him up to get the result, so I phoned him. It had ended up 1–0 to the Orient. I punched the air and kissed Son. Three more points on our road back to the Third Division. I looked upon 1–0 as being the ideal result. We had won, but I had obviously not missed a classic.

Sonia was not happy, however: 'You're on your first holiday with me, we're having a great time, yet the happiest I've seen you since we arrived is now because of that football team.' Things remained a little strained for a few hours, but we ironed out our differences in the evening over a couple of sangrias. I conceded that, yes she was more important than a Fourth Division football team, and that yes it was only a game and that yes there was more to life than watching football. (Like collecting the programmes I was thinking at the time, but I did not let on.)

The remainder of the holiday went really smoothly. During the second week I found a bar that said that it had all the English football results on a Saturday night. By pure coincidence, of course Sonia and myself just happened to be passing it the following Saturday evening. Having won the VS Rugby replay 4–1, we were playing more non-league opposition in the Cup that day in Slough. I found out at the bar that the game at Brisbane Road had ended 2–2. The chap serving drinks told me that we had been 2–0 down and were lucky to escape with a draw. How the hell he knew that I did not know, but I took his word for it.

I had now missed home games on consecutive Saturdays, a feat which at one point in my life would have been treasonable. With the replay the next Wednesday, the day we were travelling home, I was even missing out on a new ground. Yes, the days of the 100% Orient obsessive were behind me, now that there was the 'Sonia factor.' I had decided already that I was going to marry her. I still had the other passion in my life, however, namely Orient Football Club. At the time, I could foresee that the rest of my life was going to be a careful balancing act between my club and my future wife and family. As I've been happily married to Sonia now for thirty years, and continue to be a Leyton Orient season ticket holder (albeit currently only number 2,034), I guess I've made a pretty good fist of that balancing act. For the record we won the Slough replay 3–2 and subsequently got drawn away to Oldham in the Third Round.

Things for me then at the tail end of 1985 were on a real high. The O's were in the middle of an eight match unbeaten run. Frankie had them playing some decent stuff, as indeed we had been doing all season. We had a big target man up front in Paul Shinners. He was the type of player the papers then and now like to call: 'a good old-fashioned English centre-forward.' In the *Soccer Stars in Action* album in 1970, Shinners would have been described as 'a bustling spearhead.' For an Orient striker he was knocking them in at an alarming rate. In his first season with us he scored sixteen goals in thirty-two games in the league. And to enhance this Kitch-like ratio, he even supported a silly moustache as the great man had done a few years earlier.

Christmas that year was wonderful. I had achieved the double of having acquired a young lady, and also seeing my team into the Third Round of the FA Cup. As the supporter of any lower league club will tell you, the Christmas turkey always tastes that little bit sweeter, when you know that your team will be mixing it with the big boys in the FA Cup in that first week in January.

There were two big questions on everybody's lips at the turn of the year. Firstly would the O's be able to sustain the promotion push in 1986, and secondly when and where would I propose to Sonia? Yes what better way, I thought than combining the romance of me and Son with the romance of FA Cup Third Round day, and popping the question to her during half-time at our game at Oldham. The FA Cup had, for sure, given me many a happy moment over the years, so why not let it give me another? We were not looking at a mega-giant killing, if we had won at Boundary Park, but they were still two divisions above us so it would be a fine achievement to win up there all the same. I booked two tickets for the supporter's coach, and we set off together on a four hundred mile round trip, on a day that I thought would change the rest of my life.

Things do not always turn out the way one plans them however, and the trip did not materialize as expected. Upon passing the Watford Gap on the M1 it started to snow. The forecast had not been good, but we had phoned the ground before setting off and they had told us that the game would definitely be on. The weather though was clearly deteriorating the further north we got. We pulled into a service station near Birmingham and someone got out to call the ground again. I dearly wanted the match to go ahead as I had built myself up to asking Sonia to become my wife during half-time. It would be a major disappointment if I was unable to do so. There was also the fact that I knew that I would be unable to get the time off work the following Tuesday to go to the re-arranged game.

Alas though, we could tell by the look on the guys face as he returned to the coach, that the game had been called off. It was announced that we would not be proceeding up to Oldham, but that the coach would detour to Highfield Road to take in Coventry City versus Watford, which we knew would definitely go ahead due to the fact that the 'Sky Blues' had undersoil heating.

Now I had a dilemma. I was keyed up to asking Sonia to become Mrs Strong that day, but if I did it now it would have to be done without watching the O's. I had nothing against Coventry (even though the only time I could remember us playing them, they had thrashed us 4–1 in the Cup in 1973) or Watford. (although our record against them was pretty poor.) It did just not seem quite right however, that I should carry out one of the biggest acts of my life in front of two teams whom I barely cared about. It would all have seemed a bit unreal.

After much soul searching, while the diversion was taking place, I decided that the proposal would have to wait until we saw our next Orient match together. I ended the afternoon with a Coventry City lapel badge, and I was able to tick off another new ground, so that the day had not entirely been a disaster. Watford won the game 3–1, incidentally.

I was round Sonia's the following Tuesday, when news came through that our boys had won the re-arranged game 2–1. It was a magnificent result and it meant an away trip to Sheffield Wednesday in the next round. The revised date of my official proposal to her I decided was to be 14 January – Bournemouth at home in the First Round of the Freight Rover Trophy.

I'm often asked – even today, usually by non-football believers – why I did not choose a quieter, more romantic place than a football stadium to make my proposal of marriage. I just point to the attendance that evening, all 947 of us, to explain that it was hardly a cauldron of noise that night at Brisbane Road. And as for romance, you could not really ask for a more romantic place than Leyton Stadium E10, in my opinion. My season ticket on the North Terrace did not apply to Freight Rover games, so I decided that we would watch the game together sitting in the west-side. It was a strange kind of first forty-five minutes for Paul Shinners, with our illustrious 'bustling centre-forward' managing to score at both ends of the pitch, as we went in at the interval at 1–1.

Looking back now, I feel a little guilty that I did not splash out and at least buy tickets for the best seats in the East Stand that night. (At least those seats had backs to them, unlike the ones in the west-side.) This though was just the Freight Rover Trophy – the competition Frankie had said was silly – and it was after all just the First Round. 'Sonia, will you marry me?' was therefore conveyed to my young lady, accompanied by the traditional half-time cup of Bovril, in the cheap blue seats of the west-side. The answer was in the affirmative, and we were on our way to becoming as solid and reliable a partnership as Tommy Taylor and Terry Mancini were at the back for us, in our promotion winning team of 69–70.

News of my action must somehow have filtered through to the Orient dressing room during the interval, as goals from Ian Juryeff and Paul Shinners in the second half, secured a 3–1 win for us. To the majority of the 947 present that evening, witnessing our victory, it would have been quickly erased from the memory. For three people, however it was an unforgettable night. Sonia, myself and Paul Shinners. I was tempted to write off to the club at the time to try to obtain the match ball used for the game to keep as a souvenir of the proposal that I made to Sonia that evening. I figured though that it would have been given to Paul Shinners, as our striker had scored three that night. (Even if one was an 'o-g'.)

We went back to both sets of parents to convey the two bits of good tidings, that we had seen an Orient win, and that there was going to be a forthcoming wedding. Both pieces of good news were well received, and plans started to be made for our big day, which was to be in August.

To round off an exciting week I took in another new ground on the Friday night at Tranmere. Looking back at the hundreds of away games that I've been to over the years, It's kind of strange how little things often stick in the memory about certain trips, rather than the actual game itself. At Prenton Park that night I always remember the fact that the toilets in the away end had no lights in them. This made it a real struggle for the forty or so of us who had made the trip up north that evening. (Sonia was left at home for this one.) I thought it remarkable at the time that the only club in the country who regularly played their home games on a Friday night (this was pre-Sky, of course) should be the only one, as far as I knew, that did not have any lights in the loos. The incredible thing about it though, was that we played them on a Friday night again three years later and when I went again, there was still no illumination in the toilets.

Though we won the Tranmere game 3–0 back in 1986, in typical Orient fashion we started to wilt in the league and won only three of our next thirteen. Sonia and myself were part of an eight-coach convoy that went up to Hillsborough for Fourth Round day, but summing up how we were doing at the time we contrived to lose 5–0. Though at the end of the campaign, things picked up and we managed to win five out of our last seven, the damage had already been done mid-season, and we finished the campaign in fifth position. Possibly summing up the everlasting luck we inevitably always seem to have supporting Orient/Leyton Orient, it was the year before the play-offs were introduced, which we would have been in, had it been twelve months later, so we missed out on going up by one place.

Part of what was once the world's biggest collection of Orient car-stickers.

Sonia accompanied me on the last two away trips to Swindon and Rochdale. It was a measure of how far our relationship had developed in just a season, in that the previous August I had been too frightened to ask her to go to Hartlepool, yet now some eight months later we were enjoying a day together in Rochdale.

Indeed my last occasion watching the O's as a single man turned into some day as we hammered the Dale 4–1. Steve Castle in particular seemed especially keen on giving me a good send off as a 'bachelor boy'. He scored all four, had a perfectly good fifth goal disallowed and for good measure, managed to get himself booked.

1985–86 was then, like 77–78 had been, a season to shape the rest of my life. The Orient, as they always would be, were still very important to me, but for the first time, I fully discovered that there was some kind of life beyond the heaven that was Brisbane Road. A measure of just how much the goal posts had moved for me was the fact that at the end of the season I took the monumental decision that I would stop collecting Orient car-stickers. The irony of that was that at around the same time I had decided to buy my first car, an old Ford Escort, which I could take Sonia out in.

CHAPTER 22

1986–87 – HAMMERS HAMMERED, 1–1.

It was a close season half spent getting ready for our big day in August, and half spent watching the World Cup in Mexico. It was generally accepted that England had done a good job in reaching the quarter-finals there. That Leicester 'reject' Gary Lineker had given us a summers footy to remember, though there had been no sign of Mark McNeill in an England shirt. After twenty-seven years I prepared to move out of 125 Old Church Road, Chingford, me and Sonia having bought a small house just up the road in Maida Way, E4.

I had certainly enjoyed an agreeable life living at home with my parents and three sisters since 1959. Ok, so I was never allowed to stay at school lunchtimes for school diners, and because of my dad's reluctance to use Esso petrol, my 1970 World Cup coin collection was frustratingly still five coins short, but I was certainly never unhappy at home. There had been the makings of a fall out with my mum in the seventies, when my bedroom started to get full up with football stuff (even post *Scorcher*) but she had relented in the end and allowed my room to be overrun with anything related to the Orient.

It goes without saying that I still keep in close touch with my parents. My dad still does the *Telegraph* crossword every day, and rest assured if England make it to another World Cup Final, he'll be out there tendering the garden, even if there's a hurricane blowing at the time. The wedding went very well, and as expected there were many O's references in best man Mike's speech. He obviously mentioned the Oldham/Coventry trip as well as the Bournemouth Freight Rover match. I felt a little upset for Paul Shinners, however as Mike omitted to mention his three goal haul whilst discussing the game. He also conveniently forgot to mention the Liverpool Subbuteo football team fiasco from 1970, which he was responsible for.

Over one hundred were invited to the reception and evening 'do', including a very good turnout of Orient fans. There were four or five of the supporter's coach regulars, together with Kevin and Tinks who were both ushers. We had the whole day videoed and indeed the old cassette is still up there on the shelf to this very day, next to Orient versus Chelsea in 1972, and of course my appearance on BBC *South East News* with Michael Wale in 1985.

We went to Lanzarote for our honeymoon, which went wonderfully well, and came back refreshed for the new season. On the pitch we won our first five home matches, and though our away form was letting us down a little (surprise, surprise) we weren't doing too badly. Frankie had basically kept the same team as he had had for the previous campaign, though a few of the players – Alan Comfort in particular – were starting to perform really well.

Married life was going marvellously, though initially we both had a lot of adapting to do. For me after twenty-seven years in a single bed, I was now sharing one with Sonia. For her, after twenty-seven years of having her own wardrobe, she was now sharing it with fifteen hundred Orient programmes. Of course concessions were made. Lots of old O's memorabilia, including old scarves, pennants, programme duplicates as well as reserve team-sheets were red carded up to the loft.

The days of going to every away game were gone of course, though I still went to a fair few of them, and all of the homes. Sonia had by this time realized that I would be a changed man if Orient were playing and I was not there to see them. It's still the same today. I tend to find that I am more nervous thinking and worrying about the team, if I am not there witnessing events, than I would be if I were actually at the game.

On a Saturday afternoon, if the O's are playing and I am not there, you can basically write me off between 3.00pm and 4.55pm. Tactics of finding out how we are doing have, of course changed dramatically over the years. In the late sixties, and indeed for a fair amount of the seventies there was often no knowledge of our plight until the legendary *Grandstand* tele-printer from 4.40pm onwards informed us of the final score. How different that was to how it is now. You've got every score updated within seconds on *Soccer Saturday*, or *Final Score* on the telly, and then there's twitter in which some people seem able to tell you about a goal before the ball has even hit the back of the net. And there's even Orient Player on the web site, which even gives you a complete live commentary, if you're willing to fork out for it.

In the days of the late eighties though, it was just a question of sticking on the local radio, and crossing your fingers. LBC, in those days would have reporters covering every London team in the League. Whilst they would concentrate on one top local match, which believe it or not never seemed to involve the O's, they would go to the other games whenever a goal had occurred. I used to sit there listening to the radio, hoping that the reporter would **not** go to the Orient game. You knew, of course that news of a goal at one of our away games was more often than not, not good news. If the sports show did not cross to our game all afternoon, we would at least have got a 0–0. Alas, this rarely happened at the time.

Very occasionally the immortal words 'now over to…for goal news in the game involving Orient', would mean it was us who scored. I would at these times go potty. The most barmy celebrations during the 86–87 season occurred on 6 December. The O's were away to Bournemouth in the Second Round of the FA Cup. They were a division above us and were expected to win. We ended up as 1–0 victors however, and news of Lee Harvey's winning goal that day was greeted with a leap in the air. As I returned to earth though, I fell sideways and knocked over Sonia's favourite lamp. Ironically the reason for my non-attendance that afternoon had been because of a lack of funds, yet replacing one of her favourite household items ended up costing me twice as much as a trip to the south coast would have done anyway.

Whilst my days of total obsession with the O's were a phenomenon of the past, certain habits still remained in my guise as a football fanatic. One of these was – and indeed still is – the fact that no matter what the score was, or what the conditions were, I always stayed until the end of the game. It had all dated back to an encounter with Oxford United in 1974, when I'd missed a late Derrick Downing equalizer by leaving before full-time. I vowed at the time that never again would I commit the crime of leaving before the end of any match, and it's something that I've stuck to ever since.

On 15 December 1986 I was one of the seven hundred and forty-nine present at Leyton Stadium to witness our boys playing Brentford in a group game of the immortal Freight Rover Trophy. Thanks to the proposal at the legendary Bournemouth game in the competition the season before, the cup held a special place in my heart. Yet in 86–87 it was a slightly different story. In the group stage, we had lost our first game 3–0 at Swindon. Entering injury time in our second match, we were 5–0 down to the team from West London. It's fair to say that we would not be progressing any further in the competition. The rain was beating down. I was standing on the north terrace, soaked to the skin, yet I still had to stay till the conclusion of the match.

With practically all of those around me having long since gone home, Peter Mountfield scored what must be a candidate for the most meaningless goal in Leyton Orient's 135-year history. About three of us cheered, the ref blew for time to signal a 5–1 loss, and I made my way home. A totally pointless goal for the O's had been scored, but I felt somewhat proud that I was one of about a hundred of our fans who had been there to see it. I may not have been at the very top of the Premier League when it came to being an Orient supporter any more, but I felt that I was still up there at least fighting for a Champions League spot.

After another useful start to the campaign, things started to turn somewhat flat for the lads around October. We won only one league game in November and December, so that by the turn of the year we were twenty-first. The low point came on 3 January. We got beaten 3–1 at home to Halifax. I remember arriving home afterwards distraught. It had been only six years before that we had been fifth in the Second Division and we were having dreams of going into the First Division. Now here we were losing at home to Halifax and in danger of going out of the league all together.

After the Second Round FA Cup victory at Bournemouth, the wonderful blazers at the Football Association had given us West Ham at home in the Third Round draw. It really should have been something to get very excited about, yet with our team in their lowest ever position in the league, many of us feared a complete massacre on the day. However as events transpired, not for the first or last time when watching the Orient, the FA Cup defied all logic. Completely out of the blue, our boys were simply brilliant against the Hammers. Players such as John Cornwell and Colin Foster, who had been woeful in the weeks leading up to the encounter, had blinding games. We gave them a goal start after twenty minutes, Paul Hilton scoring against the run of play, but our boys never let their heads go down and remarkably did most of the attacking for the rest of the match. West Ham 'keeper, Phil Parkes however was having a blinder and it looked as if it was going to be one of those afternoons when we were destined not to score.

As the game entered injury time, I had resigned myself to an honourable 1–0 defeat, thankful that the universally predicted hiding had not materialized. Then there was an Orient throw in right in front of where Sonia and myself were sitting in the East Stand. Alan Comfort collected it turned and crossed. The ball hit Hilton on the arm. We all went up appealing. Penalty! The ref pointed to the spot. The ball was given to twenty-one year old Steve Castle, the four-goal hero of Rochdale. He had never before taken a pen for us. Yet despite having the massed ranks of Claret and Blue in front of him on the South Terrace, he stepped up and hit the perfect spot-kick. He gave a little clenched fist salute to the Hammers hordes behind the goal and ran back. There was barely time to restart

The Castle pen. A glorious moment.

as the final whistle was blown. I gave Son an almighty hug and can remember tears running down me. My wife too was pleased. She always professed to being a West Ham fan, but she supported her husband more than her team now, and was happy for me.

The most lasting memory of the afternoon for me was the sight of manager Frank Clark running around afterwards kissing every Orient player. Our Frankie, the somewhat dour Geordie, never seemed to show any kind of emotion. Although it was not a game that we won, the West Ham 1987 cup encounter is right up there with the all-time great games. Partly because it was against our nearest rivals, partly because it was against a side seventy-nine places above us in the league, and partly because we had been so crap in the weeks preceding it. It was all just so unexpected. I went back to Chingford with Sonia, and we celebrated together at home that evening. Our first child, Barbara was born exactly nine months later.

Our boys put up another stirring performance in the replay on 31 January, although we lost it 4–1. They scored two late goals and it was generally agreed that the final scoreline flattered them. The big consolation for our club of course, was the bonus of all the money that had been made out of the two games. In fact the two matches against the higher opposition really seemed to rejuvenate the O's and after the replay we won five and drew two of our next seven. Paul Shinners came back into the side, having missed a lot of the season through injury. Colin Foster, our promising but inconsistent centre-half was swapped with Mark Smalley at Nottingham Forest. Shaun Brooks and John Cornwell started to find some form in midfield, while Alan Comfort on the left-wing was starting to look a really classy player. After the disaster that was mid-season we had lots of ground to make up, but we were certainly going in the right direction.

My video cassette recorder had been moved to my new abode, but Orient wise it had been pretty idle recently. Our games were not being covered at all on the box. However the West Ham game heralded the start of a new era at Brisbane Road. From that game onwards all home matches started to be recorded and could be bought on video cassette for £25 each. Of course I bought the Hammers game, but I refrained from spending all of my hard earned cash on more of the things as I would have done a few years earlier. Had they been around at the start of the eighties, when my footy addiction was at its peak, my bedroom would have been filled with 5–1 home defeats and relegation winning Orient performances. But thankfully I was a bit different now. I started to buy just the odd one or two.

In fact the recordings themselves in the beginning were very primitive. The person controlling the camera was often a couple of seconds behind the play. It was indeed highly fortunate that our equalizer against the Hammers was a penalty, just about allowing the cameraman to catch up with play and capture the spot-kick. In the early ones there was no commentary, but a large microphone was placed at the side of the camera. You could enjoy some lovely swearing emulating from the west-side just under the gantry. The chap who did all the recordings in the early days was a bloke called Charlie Dunsford, who was employed by the club. It's probably best we do not dwell on what became of Mr Dunsford, in later years. His videos did improve however, a commentary was eventually added and a 'highlights of the season' one started to be produced, costing just a tenner. They did become a must-have item in the Strong household.

An Orient institution was started just a month after our wedding, one that just like our marriage is still going strong today some thirty years on – The Orientear, aka The Leyton Orientear. From the start I thought that our new fanzine, started by Dave Knight and a few lads who were fed up with events going on at the time at Brisbane Road, was brilliant. A drop from Division Two to Division Four had meant that there was little coverage for us in the national papers. There was always the local press, the cuttings in their newspapers were still cut out by me every Thursday, but coverage in them at the time was always a little too biased for me in favour of the O's. Now though, through the *Orientear*, there was something written by the fans for the fans. For the first time you could read about the real issues. The bad burger in the west-side, or the fence in front of the North Terrace. Every one of the two thousand Orient programmes I possessed seemed to be written by people with the sense of humour of a Roy

THE ALTERNATIVE ORIENT
SUPPORTERS MAGAZINE

Hodgson, yet the fanzine was totally different. Everyone at Leyton Stadium knew that Tommy Cunningham was not the greatest centre-half who had ever played football, but now for the first time you could pay 30p and see it in print.

Nowadays there's twitter, facebook, etc to keep us amused, but the *Leyton Orientear* the second oldest fanzine in the country is still going strong. Mat Roper's *Pandamonium* is an admirable publication having been produced for some years too, but nothing for me beats the *'ear*. I am biased of course having written my column in it for most of those thirty years. Needless to say I started collecting all the buggers and have got the entire *Orientear/Leyton Orientear* collection at home, now numbering two hundred and fifty.

1986-87 continued to be a real up and down season for the O's. It was ending on a real high though. Six wins out of eight leading into our final game meant that we still had an outside chance of the play-offs if we won it. What a final game though. We were to play Burnley away, who were bottom of the league. They had to beat us to have any chance of staying in the division. The national papers had been full of our opponents all week. How could a famous old club like Burnley go out of the league, was the talk of all of the press.

Following on from the West Ham cup match, Sonia was now four months pregnant, and experiencing a few difficulties, so that I was unable to go up to Turf Moor that afternoon. The game though was the biggest in the country that day. On BBC radio, *Sport on Two* actually carried commentary of it, the first time they had ever done so for a Fourth Division fixture. It seemed like the whole planet was against the Orient that day, with everyone rooting for the Lancs club. No one mentioned anywhere, that it was just as important a game for us too.

Fifteen and a half thousand packed into their ground and the kick-off was delayed. We duly lost 2–1 and Burnley stayed up, condemning Lincoln City to the Conference. Yet again we had missed out on promotion. Speaking to many O's who attended the game that afternoon, if we had prevented Burnley from staying in the league, it could well have been Middlesbrough 1978 re-visited for our fans. They would have faced serious problems from a set of supporters who would not have been overly happy. It also came out a few years after that Frank Clark had been told by the local constabulary that they would have problems guaranteeing our players safety at full-time had we won. O the joys of supporting Orient in the eighties.

Come the end of the season Sonia was starting to look as large as Neville Southall did at the time. With our baby on the way, she stopped going to games with me. It was decided that our small house in Maida Way, Chingford would not be big enough to house the three of us when the new arrival came, so we started looking for a new abode in Loughton. More space would be needed for baby clothes and toys, not to mention the new collection of Orient fanzines, which had been started that season.

CHAPTER 23

1987–88 – BYE-BYE NEWPORT

As the new season started, I was very excited on two fronts. Firstly, in just a couple of months I was going to become a daddy. Sonia had got over her bad morning sickness and was in fine health. Secondly, as they had been relegated from the Third Division, I was looking forward to seeing us finally erase the jinx that was Newport County by beating them for the first time since 1956. They were a club in turmoil, going rapidly downhill, surely we could beat them in the Fourth, couldn't we?

I was really bullish about the O's chances for the new season in August. Long overdue, after a campaign led by the lads at *The Orientear*, the club had reverted back to its proper name of Leyton Orient from plain Orient, which it had been since 1967. This seemed to give everyone at the club a lift. Surely after just missing out the previous two seasons, we would make it back to the Third this time round? With the state that Sonia was in, all of the away games were out of bounds early on in the season, though I was still keen to go to all of the homes. Just one defeat in the opening eight matches meant that we were actually threatening to go top, and the way we were playing it looked as if we might even stay there this time round.

Towards the end of September the full implications of the timing of the West Ham match, and our subsequent celebrations began to come to light. We had two home games in the space of four days and my wife was nine months pregnant. Sonia and the impending arrival had to come above anything else, of course, but our boys were hitting true promotion form and I desperately wanted to be there at every home game to see it. A couple of wins could very well see us hitting that top spot. I left to go and watch the game with Peterborough on the Saturday, with Sonia resting. The phone number of Brisbane Road was left by the telephone and Sonia was given orders to ring the club if she felt any twinges, so that I could rush straight home to her.

Nowadays, thanks to the arrival of the mobile phone, the days when a message would be announced over the Tannoy asking expectant dads to rush home to the missus, who was about to produce, have sadly disappeared. When it used to happen, a big cheer would inevitably go up from everyone at the ground, so adding to the afternoon's entertainment. Alas it does not happen anymore. I guess that's progress. I would have loved to have had my name read out to all, that Saturday afternoon during the Peterborough match, but it was not to be, as Sonia remained twinge-less for the ninety minutes of the game.

I was able therefore to watch all of another fine display by the O's, as we defeated the Posh, 2–0. Arriving home Son congratulated me on our victory, and she told me that she did not think anything was about to happen on the baby front. Sunday and Monday saw no change in her condition, but twinges did start to occur on the Tuesday morning. As I drove her to Harlow Hospital that day, I resigned myself to the fact that I was going to miss our home game that evening. Ironically the team we were playing were none other than my beloved Newport County. The auld enemy.

I remember sitting by her bedside at around kick-off time that evening waiting for the action to start on the baby front. Not unnaturally my mind started to wander to Brisbane Road. What was happening there? We had the chance to go top if we won; yet we were playing Newport who we had not beaten for over thirty years, so we were surely bound to be losing. Yet County knew that I still despised them. They would have seen that I was not there and out of spite they might deliberately have lost, so that I would have missed it. I was a bundle of nerves on two fronts. Around ten o'clock everything was quiet with Sonia, so I slipped out of her room to listen to the *Sports Desk* on Radio Two. The news was good. Very good. A 4–1 victory had actually taken us to the top of the league that evening.

I punched the air twice while walking back down the corridor, going back to Sonia's room. This totally confused a couple of young nurses who I went past, who could not understand why someone was celebrating wildly in the maternity ward, when their baby had yet to be born.

I focused my mind back to Sonia and within a few hours I had become a father. My little girl, Barbara had been born, and Leyton Orient had gone top of the league. Just how good was that. At the time I felt I knew exactly how Frank McClintock must have felt when he lifted the FA Cup back in 1971 to complete Arsenal's double that day. We announced the birth in the local paper, and I wrote to the club asking them to mention it in the club programme for the next home match. Orient entertained Rochdale on 20 October on a wet Tuesday night, and news of Barbara's arrival was there in black and white, on page seven of the match-day magazine. Upon reading it before the game, I figured that this had to give our players a lift before the game, the fact that one of their keenest supporters had recently become a father for the first time. It actually turned out to be an extraordinary ninety minutes of football. After a quarter of an hour, it was still 0–0. We had had plenty of chances, but I can remember turning to the bloke standing next to me on the North Terrace that evening, and giving one of the all-time classic Orient quotes:

'It's going to be one of those evenings when we are destined not to score.' Oh really. Seventy-five minutes later we were 8–0 up. For the last fifteen minutes we again failed to hit the back of the net, yet we had crammed eight goals into the games middle hour. News of the birth, I felt, had obviously spurred our lads into performing great things that night. I had now seen us play Rochdale four times. We had won every time, scoring twenty goals and conceding just one. At the time, I loved them almost as much as I despised Newport County.

We continued our good form in the league, especially at home. The away results meant that we were unable to hold onto top spot, but a 3–1 victory over Tranmere on 12 December took us up to second. I was confident as Christmas approached that promotion could be achieved. Yet again though, it was not to be. Once more our fortunes flagged as the New Year came. We had a fine win at Peterborough on Boxing Day, but the game saw a crucial injury to Paul Shinners. The big man had been having a fine season. He had scored twelve in just twenty-one games, including two in the Rochdale massacre. He had also got the last minute winner in a glorious 4–3 victory at home to Darlington, when we had been behind with just ten minutes to play.

With Shinners out of the team, he was replaced by Kevin Nugent, someone who was to develop into a prominent figure at Brisbane Road over the next four decades, but who was only young at the time. Our form sagged alarmingly in the league as we won just three of our next fourteen games, after the Peterborough victory. The only consolation during this period was that my Orient television-video collection was boosted by one, thanks to an FA Cup appearance on *Match of the Day*. Wins over Exeter, Swansea and Stockport had taken us into the Fourth Round to play First Division Nottingham Forest at Brisbane Road. There was a fair amount of interest in the game, not least of all because Brian Clough had already nominated our Frankie as his eventual successor at Forest. It was indeed a prediction that actually turned out to be correct. The Beeb duly picked our match as one for *Match of the Day*.

After my stunning television performance before the Southampton game back in 1985, I awaited a call from Michael Wale, wanting another pre-match interview, but somewhat surprisingly it never came. Forest defeated us 2–1, though we actually played very well on the afternoon, and initially took the lead. I noted at the time that it had been our first goal on *Match of the Day* for seven years.

The second half of the season was to say the least disappointing. My one lasting memory of those few months after Christmas that year however, will be of Michael Marks. Every club can boost them – the big money flops. Ok so we only paid twenty-five grand for Marks, but in Leyton Orient terms, £25,000 was (and indeed still is) somewhat of a big money signing. And he was rubbish.

Frankie bought him in February from Millwall to give us one last push for promotion. He arrived with a lot of promise. Marks had played in all but six of his team's Second Division games in the previous season. He had scored ten goals including a hat-trick. A fine partnership had been developed at the Den between him and a promising young striker called Teddy Sherringham. However during the close season the Lions had signed Tony Cascarino from Gillingham to play up front, and Marks was the man to make way. As a result he dropped two divisions to join us. On paper it looked a really decent signing, especially with Shinners injured.

He made his debut on 27 February at home to Wrexham. We won 2–1 but Marks was hopeless. Size wise he looked a bit like Sonia had done prior to the Newport game. Clearly a couple of stones overweight, he looked totally unfit and Frank pulled him off after an hour of the game.

Yet because of injuries he miraculously kept his place in the team for our mid-week trip to Newport County. I had not been going to away games, yet this was one that I could not miss. By now my most despised team were eleven points adrift at the bottom of the league, and clearly going out of it. After my non-appearance at the home game with them, I just had to be there at Somerton Park. There was a very good chance that it would be the last time we would play them, and after years of trying I just wanted to see us beat them. Those unfinished programmes from the sixties still haunted me. Then there were all those painful defeats to them in the early eighties. Going into the game they had conceded sixty-six goals in thirty-two games and were an opposing centre-forward's dream opponent. We simply could not fail to beat them.

Yet being Leyton Orient, we only drew 0–0. Once again I was gutted. Marks did not have a shot all game and was once more hopeless. Not surprisingly he did not make the team for the following Saturday's game. An injury to Kevin Nugent brought him back for our game at Rochdale however at the end of April.

Being Rochdale we knew we would win, of course, but the big question was, would our man manage a goal, or at the very least a shot on target? I did not venture to Spotland, but our customary win was achieved, this time 3–1. For all O's followers at the game, though the highlight must have come in the second minute – Michael Marks' one shot in a first team shirt for the Orient. The ball hit a Rochdale defender, and there were apparently half-hearted appeals for a penalty, but it was not given. Alas, it was to be the nearest he ever came to scoring for us, as he never started another game. Like all rubbish Leyton Orient strikers, he eventually moved on to a non-league club never to be heard of again. In Marks' case he went to Fisher Athletic.

Having now spent fifty years supporting a not very good football team, I've seen more than the odd duff forward wearing the famous Leyton Orient shirt. We certainly can attract them down at Brisbane Road. Your definitive O's centre-forward over the years has been quite tall, usually overweight, with no first touch at all. He is always hopeless in one-on-ones with opposing keepers, and generally has the speed of a three-legged tortoise. He has been known to be quite good in the air, in fact quite deadly providing he's no more than six inches away from the goal. And of course (unless his name's Jay Simpson) he's never allowed to score twenty league goals in any one season. McCormick, West, Snowcroft, Plasmati. There are indeed a wonderful list of legends that we've had over the years, to be sure.

Older fans of your big clubs, your Spurs, your Liverpools, your Arsenals, I'm sure spend much time debating amongst themselves about who have been the best for them – Chivers or Greaves, Hunt or Owen, Ian Wright or Malcolm MacDonald. I suppose it sums up in a funny kind of way how different it is when you support the Orient. I've had numerous conversations and friendly arguments with fellow O's over the years over the forwards that we've had, yet more often than not the discussion will be about who the worst of them has been. It's generally been agreed that unless you were lucky enough to have seen Tommy Johnston, then Peter Kitchen has been the top man as far as strikers go, but as for the worst of the bunch, now that's where the real arguments can start. You are basically so spoilt for choice with the Orient.

Personally my vote for the all-time turkey of Leyton Orient forwards that I've ever seen still has to go to Michael Marks. Looking at the bare facts he made three appearances for us, scoring no goals and having just one woeful shot. Probably the easiest twenty-five grand Millwall ever made.

Back in 1988, a little spurt towards the end of the campaign meant that thanks largely to our fine start, we were still just about in with a chance of reaching the play-offs if we won our final game. It would have been lovely to have played against one of the division's lesser lights, but unfortunately we faced Wolves. The team from the Midlands had already won the championship and were far and away the best side in our league. It came as little surprise, therefore that they beat us 2–0 to consign us to yet another season of Fourth Division football at Brisbane Road.

When it comes to picking out seasons that have ended in major disappointment, as a Leyton Orient fan you are spoilt for choice. You don't have to turn the clock back too far at all to come up with the last three for starters: 2013–14, 2014–15 and 2015–16. For us veterans though this 1987–88 vintage is right up there with the best of them. We had spent much of the season up till Christmas in an automatic promotion place. Yet in the end we could not even make it to a play-off place. Barbara had been born with the lads top of the league in September, yet she would be celebrating her first birthday with us still in the same division, as we were when she was one day old.

It could have been worse, of course. We could have supported Newport County. They finished bottom and were duly dispatched to the Conference. I have to say though that as far as I was concerned it was a case of good riddance. In all I saw us play them nine times before they went out of the league. We drew four and lost the rest, including once in a penalty shoot-out. I hated them. They actually only lasted half a season in the Conference the following year, before going bust. Resurrected as a new club, they fought back to re-enter the league, and low and behold we've started playing them again. Indeed after all this time, in the 2015–16 season, not only did I see us finally beat them, but I actually saw us do it twice, as we managed to do the double over them. I travelled down to Wales for our away match with them in September 2015 and talking to the locals down there, nobody could still tell me why they kicked off their games at 3.15pm back in the sixties. After all this time, it remains one of life's great mysteries.

As well as Barbara's birth the big news on the home front was that we moved to a bigger abode in Loughton, four miles away from Chingford, to a house where we still reside to this very day. Despite the bigger residence, a lot of Orient memorabilia was red-carded up to the loft, due to a lack of space. This included my collection of lapel badges from other clubs. They are still up there now collecting dust, though they have had their uses over the years. I remember the

Sunday after Arsenal had famously lost to Wrexham in the FA Cup, going up to the loft and digging out a wonderful big badge from the welsh club that I had bought up there some years before. I wore it proudly on my suit going into work on Monday morning, attracting some top banter from the Gooners and Spurs fans at the bank.

A lot of the wally-ness that I had had as an Orient obsessive at the start of the decade had thankfully gone (like watching grass grow during parties at Brisbane Road, etc), but I was still inclined to do some pretty daft things in my capacity as an O's fan. For Barbara's first Christmas I forked out £25 for Dunsford's video of the Leyton Orient versus Newport County game, the match played a few hours before Sonia delivered her. I figured that in years to come, it would be nice for her to be able to view the match that was being played whilst mummy and daddy were at the hospital waiting for her to be born. She's now twenty-nine and unsurprisingly she hasn't watched it yet.

Despite me now being a family man, I was still present at all of the homes that season, with the exception of the Newport game. If the lads were playing away on a Saturday afternoon, then I would of course be glued to the radio between three and five, waiting for news of the boys. I had become pretty proficient at changing nappies, but Sonia knew not to trust me to do it between these hours. I would have been my normal nervous self with the O's playing, and it would have been a real danger for the safety of my young daughter.

One consequence of our move was that I started to travel to work via the Central Line on the Underground every weekday. Upon boarding the tube at Loughton, I always took a seat on the left of the train. It was a habit I had for years, the reason being that I was able to see the floodlights at the heaven that was Brisbane Road, as the train passed Leyton. I may have had those Monday morning blues, the weather may have been dire, but as long as I could see those floodlight pylons when on the train, then world was still a good place.

I celebrated ten years at the Australia and New Zealand Bank in March 1988. My foreign exchange dealing was going fine, and around April, I was given the opportunity to go and work for the bank at their head office in Melbourne. I declined, of course. I had turned down going to Aston University some ten years earlier because I could not make it back to Brisbane Road every two weeks to watch the Orient. If I was unable to return from Birmingham every fortnight, what chance would I have of making it back from Melbourne to watch O's games?

CHAPTER 24

1988–89 – YET ANOTHER PROMOTION SEASON

As we started the season, the feeling around Brisbane Road, was that surely this time the O's would get it right. It transpired later that a disillusioned Frank had offered his resignation after the Wolves defeat in May, but the board had turned it down. He was to be given one last chance in 88–89.

When the season started however, the first few games were dreadful. Of the first five league games we drew two and lost three. As a result we found ourselves just one place off the bottom. A rather fortunate 1–0 home win against Darlington improved matters slightly, but any thoughts of promotion seemed a million miles away at the time. The next game saw a 3–0 defeat at Torquay, so that the pressure was really on the manager as we entertained York City on a Tuesday night in October.

'Clark Out' banners that had been hoisted on the North Terrace were ordered down by the police, causing much argument between supporters and the boys in blue. The club really had hit an all-time low. The corner was turned just a little that night with a convincing 4–0 win. The second was scored by Alan Comfort, which was to be the first of nineteen for our winger that season. The O's always had a fine tradition of producing good wide men. Comfort followed in the steps of Laurie Cunningham and John Chiedozie, both of whom went on to successfully join First Division clubs. Moving onto the present, in the past few years it's probably fair to say that the best player at the club has been wide man Dean Cox. I've always had a theory that the size of our pitch – we've got one of the widest in the league – has got a lot to do with it. I've always felt that it has given wingers more time and space.

Of all the splendid wingmen we've had over the years, I actually rate Comfort as the best. Like Cunningham and Chiedozie he was quick, could easily beat defenders, and was capable of supplying a decent cross at the end of it. For me though, the big advantage that he had over the other two was his finishing. Having skipped past a couple of defenders, he could crack home a wicked shot, hence his high tally of goals for us in the 88–89 season. It might be argued that while Cunningham and Chiedozie shone for the O's in the Second Division, Comfort did it two leagues lower, but I'm sure if he had been given a proper chance, he would have been just as effective at a higher level.

LEYTON ORIENT SUPPORTERS CLUB
01 539 6156
O's AWAY TRAVEL

LEYTON ORIENT   SEAT NO: __16__

COACH NO: __1__

Stoke City

DATE: __Oct 11__   DEPARTURE TIME: __2 pm__

coaches leave from Leyton Orient F.C. Brisbane Road, E10

NAME: _____   Fare Paid £ __10__

MEMBERSHIP NO: _____

PLEASE NOTE: No alcohol is to be taken aboard any of our coaches.

With the form he showed in our promotion season, we were never going to hang on to him, and he was sold to Middlesbrough at the end of it. Alas, he played only a few times for the North Eastern club with the lovely supporters, before getting a career ending injury. Apparently he was just beginning to establish himself as a favourite at Ayresome Park, his popularity helped greatly by scoring a cracking goal against local rivals Sunderland. When he was forced to give the game up he became a vicar, eventually becoming the Orient's chaplain. He can still be spotted today watching the odd match at Brizzy. After the York match, we gained a 0–0 at Scarborough on the Saturday, to set us up for a trip to Stoke City the following Tuesday evening, in the Littlewoods Cup. We had lost the home leg 2–1 and were not given too much hope in the return leg, against a side two divisions above us. I made the trip up on the supporter's coach and it turned into a wonderful evening.

An early Kevin Hales penalty had put us all square over the two legs, though we were still down on the away goals rule. Just five minutes before the end though, Simon Stainrod made it 1–1 on the night, and 3–2 to Stoke on aggregate. It looked all over for us. Step up Alan Comfort, however. A magnificent mazy dribble, followed by a fierce shot past the 'keeper with only a minute left on the clock, took the tie into extra-time.

The few hundred of us who had made the trip up to the Midlands were standing in the away enclosure at the side, and we went bonkers as Comfort's effort went in. The best though was yet to come. 1988–89, which transpired to be our first promotion season for nineteen years, saw many magic moments. Yet just as memorable as anything in the league that year was the penalty shoot-out, which followed the goalless extra time at Stoke that night.

The shoot-out took place in front of the Stoke kop end, where their most vociferous fans were gathered. This I felt at the time was not going to help our boys. It was also a well-known football fact at the time that we had never, in nine years of trying, won any penalty shoot-out. Initially we went behind, but Paul Ward and Ian Juryeff bagged their pens for us to pull it back to 2–2 on spot-kicks. 'Biffo' Ward's effort was particularly memorable for the little wave he gave to the Stoke boys behind the goal upon scoring. Simon Stainrod then stepped up and smashed his attempt against the bar, which meant that it was all down to Kevin Hales. If our man converted we went through. He calmly placed his effort wide of the 'keeper, so sending our small gathering of away fans delirious.

It rounded off a blinding evening, one still fondly remembered some twenty-eight years later. Once again it highlights what it is to be a supporter of Leyton Orient Football Club. As I've said on so many occasions, fans of many teams look back to glorious days out at Wembley, Championship wins and Cup victories for their memorable moments when following their teams. At the Orient we like to reminisce about winning penalty shoot-outs at the end of Second Round Littlewoods Cup ties.

After the ecstasy of Tuesday night, the week could surely not get any better, yet remarkably it did. The following Saturday we were at home to Colchester United in what appeared on the face of it to be a routine Fourth Division fixture. Yet amazingly, just five days short of the first anniversary of the Rochdale 8–0 massacre, we once again contrived to win by the same margin against the Essex club. It was certainly beginning to look as if the O's had finally turned the corner. Barbara's speech was coming on nicely at home, yet after the dramatic week, I decided I would stop trying to teach her to say 'Clark Out'. Things, so it seemed, were beginning to move in the right direction for the club. We were still struggling away from home, but at least we seemed to have sorted out the home form, so we were half way towards getting it right.

Then though, came a dramatic setback. The FA Cup had paired us with non-league Enfield in the First Round. A new television agreement at the beginning of the season had seen ITV get total coverage of all live League matches, with the Beeb having no League soccer at all. It seems strange these days when talking about television agreements and there being nothing said about pay per view channels, but that's the way it was in those days. The Beeb had lost *Match of the Day*, except on FA Cup days, when they were allowed to show recorded games. They had never before covered the FA Cup from the First Round, but deprived of any footy for most weeks they decided to do it in 1988. In their wisdom they chose Enfield versus Leyton Orient as the top game of the First Round and showed it on their programme in the evening.

MOTD had been an institution for twenty-five years, but it had been temporarily halted at the start of the 88–89 season. I stood along the side at Enfield's Southberry Road ground, directly opposite the cameras. As a result I made my first television appearance since the legendary Wale interview in 1985. The Orient being on the television meant that the whole nation would now have the chance to see the team who just a few weeks earlier had scored eight against Colchester. They could thrill at a side that had recently taken part in the most thrilling Littlewoods Cup Second Round, Second Leg tie ever. That afternoon however, the O's were crap. A late, long range 'Biffo' Ward effort gave us a fortuitous 1–1 draw. It was a match however to give more ammunition to the 'Clark Out' army who were still in force on the Brisbane Road terraces.

Possibly the most surprising aspect of the afternoon, given that it was such a dire match, was the fact that the Beeb again picked our replay as their main game on *Sportsnight* the following Wednesday. There had been great debate about the new television deal at the beginning of the season. It was said that with just live League coverage on ITV, the smaller clubs would be frozen out and they would not appear on the small screen at all. Yet here we were in November and the first teams to be featured twice on the box during the 88–89 season were to be Leyton Orient and Enfield.

The whole country waited with baited breath for the replay. Our boys started much better, Ian Juryeff scoring twice in the opening six minutes, but we were pegged back and ended up drawing 2–2. A third game was needed. The BBC decided in their wisdom to save the taxpayer's money and the third match at Brisbane Road was not broadcast. Ironically over the three games we played against Enfield, our best performance was in the last game, yet ended up losing it 1–0. We had gone out of the FA Cup to a non-league club for the first time in over forty years. I was gutted. We kept saying that things just could not get any worse supporting the O's, and yet they always did. It had been just ten years since we had been one game away from Wembley in the competition, now we were going out in the opening round to non-leaguers.

My little girl had been born just a year earlier with the Orient top of the league, yet where would she be by the time she was ready to watch her first game? Was I being a responsible father if I was to bring up my daughter to support a team who were simply no good? I did not want her to be teased at school. It was a difficult period in the Strong household, though Sonia was being very supportive. I can remember having a long discussion with her on the subject: 'Frank Clark – should he stay or should he go?' The man had taken us to our lowest ever league position at the start of the season, and we were losing to sides that would not have lived with us a few years before. Yet our Frankie had just moved close to us in Loughton. Sonia had spoken to him in the local Post Office, and said what a lovely man he appeared to be. She had seen his wife and two daughters and she told me that they were a really nice family. It would not be fair, she argued, to take their dad's job away from him and put him out of work. As far as she was concerned he should stay. Here was one person the 'Clark Out' brigade would not be recruiting.

Now I think that my wife would be the first to concede that her knowledge of football is about as good as Karren Brady's is these days. Yet in this instance she turned out to be absolutely correct. By the end of the season, after a dramatic turnaround Clark had become something of an Orient hero.

Initially the situation got no better. At the turn of the year we were still in the bottom half, and had still not won away. Yet the first game of 1989 saw us gain our customary win against Rochdale, this time 3–0, which moved us into the top ten. Around this time Paul Shinners moved on to join Barnet. It may not mean a great deal, given the not-so-hot competition over the years, but when it comes to Leyton Orient centre-forwards 'Rambo' Shinners was certainly one of the better ones. His goal scoring record for us was not bad at all and he, of course, left that abiding memory of the three goals in the famous Freight Rover Trophy proposition match against Bournemouth in 1986. Unfortunately Shinners has had some bad headlines over the past few years, but we'll gloss over that here.

Looking back now, it's fair to say that Leyton Orient's season back in 88–89 effectively started at the end of January. On the twentieth of that month the local *Guardia*n ran the headline that was to put a new complexion on the rest of the campaign: 'Arsenal striker to play for Orient.' Kevin Campbell was to join us on loan, initially for a month but with a view to stretching it to three. The eighteen-year-old had scored a massive fifty-nine goals in the Football Combination the previous season. He was once again the leading scorer in the reserve league in

88–89, when he joined us. Also attracting attention at the time was another forward who came to the O's on loan, this time from Gillingham. A chap named Mark Cooper. Both players, in their own differing ways were to become Leyton Orient Legends.

Campbell was not your typical Orient centre-forward. He was big, quick, powerful, he could finish, and most un-Orient like, he had a first touch. He scored in his first game for us, a 2–1 defeat at Crewe, but he really made his mark on his home debut against Rotherham. After going in 1–0 down at the break, he scored twice in five minutes at the start of the second period to turn the game on its head. We went on to win 3–1 and were on our way to finding a new hero.

I got my first look at Cooper that afternoon. He came on as a sub after eighty-eight minutes. He too was big. That though, it appeared at the time, was where the similarities with Campbell ended. He did not look quick, and he had just one shot, which ended up on the South Terrace. In fact he did look, like your typical Orient centre-forward. Although only twenty-one at the time, Cooper had already enjoyed what you might call an interesting career. He had shown a lot of promise in his early days at Cambridge, so much so that Spurs had paid a lot of money for him. Yet for some unknown reason the north Londoners had not played him, and he was sold on to Gillingham for £110,000. Things had not gone well for him in Kent however, and they wanted to sell him for just twenty-five grand. On his full debut for us, a 3–1 victory at Darlington, Coops had found his way on to the score sheet. Yet he also managed to concede ten of the sixteen free-kicks we gave away that afternoon, to give us some idea of the kind of player he was.

He obviously did enough to impress Clark however, who paid just over £20,000 for him without even waiting for the end of his loan period. Thanks largely to Campbell things on the pitch started to improve dramatically. As spring approached we were ever improving as a team. It was not until the home game with Burnley on 4 March, however that people at the club really started to believe in promotion. We won 3–0 to take us up to ninth and within range of the play-offs. Alan Comfort had a blinder, scoring two wonderful goals and setting up King Kevin Campbell for the third. It was to mark the beginning of a run where we were to win nine out of the next eleven.

While Cooper was struggling to make the starting eleven, Campbell was playing out of his skin. It was obvious to everyone that he was far too good for the Fourth Division and would have to go back to the Gunners when the three months were up. He certainly gave our whole club a lift however, in the time that he was here.

His penultimate game was a 5–0 thrashing of Grimsby and the Arsenal loanee was once more magnificent. He scored one, made two and forced the Mariners to substitute the young centre-half, Lever, who was supposed to be marking him. Campbell signed off for us following a 2–0 home win against Halifax on 4 April. When he joined us we were 14th in the table, and as he left we had risen to sixth. He had scored nine times in fourteen appearances. As we all knew he would, he went on to bigger things at Arsenal, Nottingham Forest and Everton but I'm sure he must look back and remember the time he spent in east London as the time that made him a half-decent player. (In much the same way as we made Harry Kane an England striker when he played for the O's, of course.)

Upon his exit, the *Ilford Recorder* ran the headline: 'Campbell hands in that O's number ten shirt, but to whom?' The answer was Mark Cooper. Would Cooper be able to make an impact in his first game back against Wrexham? Yes he made an impact alright. He threw a punch at Joey Jones after an hour and got himself sent off. It was our first red card of the season in the League. Now he would miss three games in the crucial run in. Until his sending off, we had had the third best disciplinary record in the country.

He had one last game to play before the suspension kicked in, a home encounter with Torquay. We won 3–1, Coops did not score but left two abiding memories from his performance that afternoon. First he clattered his 6ft 1in, 13 stone frame into Torquay's young 'keeper Ken Veysey, putting the Gull's custodian out for the rest of the season. Then he famously rounded stand-in keeper Phil Lloyd after a bad back pass, only to hit the ball wide of an open net. Most agreed at the time that it was the worst miss they had ever seen at Brisbane Road, narrowly edging out Ian Juryeff's effort against Bournemouth in our relegation game some four years earlier. Mind you, the same day saw the horrendous Hillsborough disaster, which of course, put our disappointment at the miss into some kind of perspective.

Clark had been furious with Cooper's dismissal at Wrexham. There was a Barclays Bank £25,000 Blue Riband Award that season, where sending offs and cautions were offset against goals scored by every team. Before the Wrexham game we had been top in our division, but the red card had changed that. Not surprisingly on top of the three-match ban the FA gave our man, our Frankie also fined Cooper.

We had been stumbling a little since Campbell had left, but we were still up there near the top, and it came as a great relief to everybody when a 1–0 win at Lincoln on 6 May secured a play-off place. We had come close to getting one the previous two years but had just missed out, so it was wonderful news to get one this time round. It meant that we could relax in our last game of the season at home to Scunthorpe. That was not the case for our opponents however, who required a win against us to secure automatic promotion. Cooper was back in the team. Since his arrival in February he had scored just one goal for us at Darlington. He had made Michael Marks look like Lionel Messi. I remember moments after *Tijuana Taxi* was played, the boos rang out as his name was announced from the team sheet. He was not a popular man with anyone at the club at the start of the afternoon.

What followed however, was one of the most bizarre ninety minutes I can recall seeing at Brizzy. At the end of it quite remarkably Cooper was running off with the match ball, having just scored one of the best hat-tricks anyone had ever seen by an 'O'. There had been some wonderful goals scored by Alan Comfort that season, yet Cooperman's twenty-five yarder after twenty minutes to get the ball rolling that day was as good as any that our winger had managed. The big man then converted a centre from eight yards out some nine minutes later, to leave us six thousand punters stunned. Yet he saved the best till last. With just minutes remaining and the O's 3–1 up, Scunny 'keeper Paul Musselwhite rushed from his goal to punch clear a Keith Day free-kick. With the custodian well out of position the ball fell at the feet of Coops, who was well outside the penalty area. To the utter amazement of the crowd he lobbed it quite brilliantly back into the empty net. We were all speechless. I can never remember a crowd so gobsmacked as we all were at the end of the 4–1 victory, thanks to Cooper.

As a result of their loss, Scunthorpe missed out on going up automatically, having famously been wrongly told by Keith Simpson on our PA that they had been promoted. But all O's had witnessed something that was much more important to us. Here, in Cooper was a player whom everyone had resigned themselves into thinking was a complete donkey and yet we'd just seen him put in a performance that was world class. It was just crazy. His three goals had wiped the slate clean with Frankie, and they ensured that we ended up winning the Barclays award after all, and with it £25,000 which were to go towards ground improvements.

So we were nicely set up for the play-offs, to be joined in them by Scunthorpe, Wrexham and Scarborough. Our first game was to be at home to Scarborough in the semi-finals. A crowd of over nine thousand gathered at Brizzy for a twelve o'clock Sunday kick-off. I got there really early to secure my customary position on the North Terrace. (By now the country's laws had been changed, so that there was no free gate anymore.) There was plenty of talk around me, much of it concerning Cooper. After the Scunny game, was he a Kitch of a forward or had those ninety minutes merely been a fluke? Well he answered us within six minutes of the kick-off, rising high to head home a Kevin Hales cross magnificently. Our man, along with the rest of the team continued to torment Scarborough all afternoon, yet a vital second just would not come. Then with just seven minutes left on the clock Lee Harvey was wrestled down on the edge of the box by Craig Short.

As the resulting free-kick was directed into the area, Cooperman stooped low to head home for ours, and his, second. How we all loved him now. A 2–0 win had given us plenty of hope for the second leg. Up at Scarborough in the return, it was our defence that this time took centre stage. Being a couple up from the first game meant that you knew that we had a bit of breathing space to begin with. I ventured up to Yorkshire for the Wednesday evening game and was feeling comfortable as it remained 0–0 well into the second half.

In the seventieth minute however, Martin Russell scored for the home team. Even now some twenty-seven years later, I still consider those last twenty minutes of that Scarborough match to be the longest I've ever known watching the O's. Our opponents were kicking towards the goal behind which we were standing, the few hundred O's fans just willing the ball not to go into the net right in front of us. Sitton and Day however were both enjoying their finest hour in an Orient shirt, so that despite some desperate defending at times we just about managed to hang on, to go through to the play-off final by winning 2–1 on aggregate.

It was great stuff. At the games conclusion I felt shattered. Indeed as we all boarded the supporter's coach we were all exhausted. But we were through. Wrexham had somewhat surprisingly defeated Scunthorpe to set us up for the two-legged final against the Welsh side, with the prize of Third Division football at the end of it, for the winners. You just had to love the play-offs. The team who had finished sixth were playing the side that had come seventh for the right to be promoted. If all of this had happened a year later, we would now be looking at the end of this book. The following year all the play-off Finals were moved to Wembley. I would indeed have reached the end of that twenty-three year road to the twin towers. Typical Leyton Orient. Just as we had finished fifth in 85–86 so just missing out on the new play-off system that was introduced a year later, now we were once again a year too early, this time for a trip to Wembley. The result of that is that this book is not over yet, and you lot have got to plough through an extra ten chapters of my writing before the ultimate destination is finally reached.

The first leg of the final, back in 1989 was to be away on a Wednesday night. Unfortunately I was unable to get time off work at the bank to make the trip up to North Wales. There was no coverage of the game on the television or radio, and of course these were pre-Internet days. Back then the only way to meticulously follow the game at home was via the commentary on the Orient Club-call telephone line – 0891-12-11-50. Sounds good, but just one small problem – 39p a minute. I calculated at the time that to listen to the entire commentary on the phone, even allowing for just two minutes of stoppage time would have cost me £35.88. That's about twice as much as the evening would have set me back if I had been able to have gone to Wales to actually watch the match.

I faced a dilemma. After our recent move our mortgage had trebled. There was now a toddler to feed and clothe in the Strong household. That £35.88 could have bought a couple of pairs of shoes for Barbara. Yet this was our biggest game for years. After nineteen fruitless years, we were finally knocking on the door of promotion.

After much soul searching I decided on my tactics for the evening. I would ring every fifteen minutes for an update, and then catch the last ten minutes in full, on the phone. The total cost I calculated at being around six pounds, which was the equivalent of a large pack of Pampers disposable nappies, at the time. I thought this a fair compromise.

First call of the night after fifteen minutes: 0–0. Second call: 0–0. Half-time and it was still goalless, though Cooperman had apparently hit the crossbar. It really was turning into a highly nervous evening. If I had been at the game I would not have been more on edge. My hand was shaking simply dialling those ten numbers every quarter of an hour. Fourth call: 0–0. Fifth call: 0–0. We were holding on. At 9.20pm, with just ten minutes remaining I rang again to listen to the remainder of the match. There were no goals however, and at the end we had secured a no score draw. The £6 I felt had been fully justified, as we were nicely set up for the final act of the season at Brizzy in the second leg.

Our extraordinary season was about to reach its climax in June. On the same day as our game, England were due to play Poland at Wembley in a crucial

World Cup qualifier. We were therefore forced to change the kick-off time of our encounter to a twelve o'clock start. I got to Brisbane Road desperately early on the day, thus securing my normal North Terrace spot. I didn't have much time for Wrexham having missed my only game of the 79–80 season up there, if you remember. By mid-day punters were still streaming into our theatre of east London dreams, so that kick-off was put back twenty minutes. Thirteen thousand were present that afternoon. It was never going to be a classic as there was too much at stake, but no one cared as long as we won. The players were all knackered anyway, after a long ten-month season.

Chances were few and far between and as half-time approached it was still goal-less. Then a minute before the break, Alan Comfort's cross found Lee Harvey on the edge of the area. He chested it down and rammed it past keeper Salamon to make it 1–0. It was a stunning shot, a wonderful goal scored right in front of us, sending everyone delirious. We had a happy half-time, but just ninety seconds after the restart Wrexham were level. John Bowden scored a soft goal, which meant that although it was now 1–1 on aggregate, the Welsh side had the advantage, an away goal.

Our boys kept plugging away but time was passing quickly and worry was beginning to set in on the North Terrace, and elsewhere around the stadium. Then with just eight minutes remaining Harvey collected the ball on the right and crossed low. Mark Cooper had done nothing all afternoon. He had been tracked everywhere by Joey Jones, but now for the first time he lost his marker to shoot past the keeper and put us 2–1 up.

It was a glorious moment, though celebrations of course were tempered. We were Leyton Orient after all, and there were still eight minutes to go. God those eight minutes were long. There was one moment when from point blank range a Wrexham forward headed

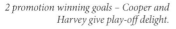
2 promotion winning goals – Cooper and Harvey give play-off delight.

179

against our 'keeper Paul Heald's face, the ball flying into the air. It seemed like the ref added three hours of injury time, but finally the man in black blew for time and we all went crazy. We had waited nineteen years for this moment of promotion, and boy was it glorious.

We all flocked onto the grass; many gathering in front of what then was still the main stand, the East Stand. The players came into the Director's Box and each one of them took it in turn to hold the microphone and make an idiot of themselves. Even Frankie was seen to manage a brief smile for the first time since the West Ham game some two and a half years earlier. The only player who missed the celebrations was Alan Comfort, who had been whisked away by helicopter then jet, to get married in Bangor, Northern Ireland.

I had gone to the game with Mike and Tinks and after we finally left Brisbane Road, we found a nice pub in Walthamstow where we carried on drinking till late into the evening. It was not until the next day that I discovered that England had won 3–0. Needless to say, I cared little for my country that day.

Looking back now, that 1988–89 season was for sure a pretty bizarre season. At the beginning of it, the only chant heard at Brisbane Road was 'Clark Out'. After our first defeat to a non-league side for decades, Frankie was probably the most hated manager in the history of the club. (This, of course, was pre Brush, Liverani and Hendon.) Likewise after his dreadful miss against Torquay and other poor performances, Mark Cooper was arguably the most derided forward ever to put on a Leyton Orient shirt. (This, of course, was pre Snowcroft and Plasmati.) Yet by June both were being treated as heroes at Brisbane Road.

To be honest, I think a lot of punters at the time, myself included, still considered Mark Cooper a pretty average player. We thought that he would get found out in the higher division. However, the fact remained that at the most crucial time for the club in years, he had delivered six goals in five games to help to take us up. This was an achievement that nobody would ever be able to take away from him, and we would always remember him for it. King Kevin Campbell may have done the business for us earlier in the campaign, but Cooperman was lethal at the business end of it. Lol Ross, together with the lads at the *Leyton Orientear* produced a magnificent record, 'Super Cooperman' as a tribute to him. Along with *Tijuana Taxi*, of course, it will be one of my eight selections on Desert Island Discs, when I finally follow Uncle Sir Roy onto the show.

Although we had only finished sixth in the league, the team for that season was certainly one of the better Orient sides we'd seen for some time at Brizzy, and probably deserved to go up at the end of it. Paul Heald, who had taken over from 'Bomber' Wells in December, was a fine young 'keeper. 'Ooh' Terry Howard and Kevin Dickenson were a useful couple of full-backs, Howard chipping in with five goals. Keith Day and John Sitton were reliable centre-halves, who had their finest hour in the Alamo at Scarborough. The two Steves, Castle and Baker ran midfield, and Frankie often boldly chose to play four up front, with two wide men in Harvey and Comfort. We were rewarded with eighty-six goals that season in the league, more than anyone else in the division. It all just seemed a tiny bit unreal watching a Leyton Orient side who actually knew where the back of the net was. To actually watch an exciting home team at Brisbane Road was almost unheard of since I'd been going.

It was a great season for my scrapbook collection as with all the publicity we got at the end of it six more books were added. There were also a few silly stories in the tabloids to keep us entertained, like the headline in the *Daily Mirror* on Christmas Eve: 'Lloyd Webber bids for Orient', referring to cellists Julian. It came to nothing, of course. Yes, looking back now some twenty seven years on, 1988–89 is right up there with the best when we're talking about memorable Leyton Orient seasons.

CHAPTER 25

1989-90 – BEESLEY FOR ENGLAND

Nineteen eighty-nine–ninety started with the O's in the Third Division for the first time in four years. In fact the season turned out to be a bit of an anti-climax after all the excitement that had been generated in 88–89. We ended up in fourteenth place, but the really disappointing aspect was that the bright, entertaining football that we had previously been playing seemed to disappear. We played a lot of the promotion campaign with a couple of wingers, but now Alan Comfort had gone to Middlesbrough and Lee Harvey was often played in the middle of the park, alongside Mark Cooper. As a result, after scoring so many the season before, we only managed fifty-two goals a year later. As an attacking force normality had returned to Leyton Orient. We were back to being the Leyton Orient we had all got to know and love for the seventies and most of the eighties. Our top scorer in our first year back in the Third was Coops with just twelve.

One of the few highlights of the season was a Second Leg of a Second Round Littlewoods Cup tie against First Division giants Everton. We had lost the first game at home 2–0, so we all travelled up to Goodison Park on a Tuesday evening expecting a good hiding. Having held our own for most of the first half however,

LEYTON ORIENT SUPPORTERS CLUB
01 539 6156
O's AWAY TRAVEL

LEYTON ORIENT   SEAT NO: _____0016____

v   COACH NO: ___/___

Everton

DATE:_____Oct 3_____   DEPARTURE TIME: ___12.30pm___
coaches leave from Leyton Orient F.C. Brisbane Road, E10

NAME: _____   Fare Paid £ __/2___

MEMBERSHIP NO: _____

PLEASE NOTE: No alcohol is to be taken aboard any of our coaches.

twenty-one-year-old Danny Carter, who had replaced Alan Comfort in the side, won a ball wide on the left. He cut inside and fired past Neville Southall from twenty-five yards out. It was a truly wonderful strike. Southall indeed conceded afterwards that it was one of the best scored against him for years. A couple of hundred of us gathered behind the goal at the opposite end of the pitch celebrated wildly, whilst even Everton supporters in the ground applauded, which I thought at the time was jolly decent of them. We held out until half-time, so that going in just 2–1 down on aggregate at the interval, incredibly we still amazingly nurtured dreams of going through to the next round.

I remember just after the restart Cooperman had a good chance to level the aggregate score, but he headed over from a few yards out, right in front of where we were standing. The tie unfortunately though, was effectively settled, within seven minutes of the second period, when Whiteside and Sheedy scored after 72 and 79 minutes. There was still time for Geoff Pike to score with the last kick of the game, but in the end we went down 4–2 over the two games. It had however been an admirable showing from our lads over the two games, particularly in the away game.

Everton however, was a rare highlight in 89–90, most matches just seemed to come and go, leaving little in the memory. The only other thing that really sticks out from the campaign for me was Carl Hoddle. When we heard that we were getting Glen's younger brother at the Orient, there were the inevitable cries from certain supporters that he may turn out to be as good as his sibling. The truth was however that he had started out with Glen at Spurs, but they had shown Carl the door, as he was simply no good. He had spent four years touring the part-time circuit and had ended up at non-league giants Bishops Stortford. Our Frank though, for some strange reason paid the Hertfordshire club a massive ten grand for his services. They must have laughed all the way to the bank, in much the same way as Millwall had done when we bought Michael Marks from them. Hoddle junior looked like his brother. He played in midfield like his brother. That though, it has to be said was where the comparisons ended. While Glen could pinpoint a pass up to fifty yards, Carl's range was fifty centimetres. Glen could take on players and beat them, while Carl would get knocked off the ball and end up on his backside. The elder Hod could pack a wonderful shot, while the younger was a constant threat to the trees of the Coronation gardens and the houses behind the North Terrace.

It has to be said however that Carl did have one decent game in an Orient shirt, scoring for us in a 4–1 win against Reading. For that reason he cannot be considered a candidate for an all-time worst ever Orient XI, because that's one more good game than a few have had for us over the years. Indeed inevitably after the match the newspapers were drawing comparisons between the two brothers.

Said Richard Lewis in *the Waltham Forest Guardian*; 'We had the mastery of Hoddle. It is a name that conjures up such majestic moments in English soccer and what a bargain Frank Clark has picked in the brilliance of Carl Hoddle, brother of the illustrious Glen.'

Oh really. The next home game against Chester we lost 3–0 and Carl had a stinker. He gave away a penalty and was pulled off after less than an hour. When selected he continued to look out of his depth in the Third Division, and was eventually packed off to Barnet. It's the kind of phenomenon that would make a good Channel Four documentary. How can one man be so good in his profession, yet his brother be so pathetic in the same trade? Sadly, the Carl Hoddle story does not have a happy ending, the poor man dying at just forty of a brain aneurysm in 2002.

There really was nothing of note that happened all season at all at Brisbane Road. The biggest laugh of the year was provided by the *Daily Express* with a report linking Mark Cooper with a move to Liverpool. The equivalent these days would be saying that Manchester United were showing an interest in Ollie Palmer. In fact in the prize for the wit of the year, the *Express* were only just beaten by our Frankie and the Wigan manager. We bought Paul Beesley from the Lancashire club for a club record £150,000 and though eyebrows were raised at the time at the price paid by us, it turned out to be a very good signing, the player being sold on to Sheffield United for double that just eight months later. The laugh was though, that there was a clause in the transfer contract when we bought him, stating that we would pay Wigan a lot more money, if Beesley ever played for England, whilst he was with Leyton Orient. The thought of any O's player representing the national team at any time was about as believable then, and still is now, as Ian Hendon ever becoming England manager, but once again I suppose it did give us all a good chuckle at the time.

Despite Beesley some of Clark's transfer dealings, as highlighted by Hoddle, continued to baffle. At one time he gave a trial to a chap called Paul Reynolds, who was a convicted armed robber. He was at the time serving a nine-year jail sentence for raids on betting shops. He spent a period of time training with our club by special arrangement with the authorities at HM Prison Springhill. At the end of the period, however it was decided that he would not be offered a contact at Brisbane Road. Then in March, Clark bought former Norwich striker Justin Fashanu to the club. He though was well past his sell-by date though, and lasted just four games.

Our Frankie still had lots of credit though with most fans, after the memorable campaign the year before. Sonia remained his biggest fan. She no longer came to games with me because of the toddler we now had, but she said that Clark continued to be very polite to her, on the occasions that she saw him in Loughton High Road.

CHAPTER 26

1990–91 – ANOTHER BORING SEASON, ANOTHER GIRL IN THE FAMILY

The World Cup in Italy had filled some time before Brisbane Road beckoned again, with some wonderful moments for the English. Pleat's last gasp goal against Belgium, and Gary Lineker scoring twice against Cameroon, together with his semi-final goal against the Germans were magic to be sure. At home Barbara was now three, and we decided it was about time we got her a baby brother or sister whom she could play with.

I remembered that the timing of Barbara's birth had not been ideal in 1987. It still hurt that we had beaten Newport 4–1 and that at the time I was sitting in a maternity ward waiting for Sonia to give us our first child. Wives delivering babies during the football season should not be allowed, I decided. The best time for the new arrival I thought would be the middle of May, just as the season had ended. A birth out of 'football hours', so to speak, would mean having to forgo an announcement in the Orient programme, which had been so nice when Barbara had arrived, but that was a sacrifice that would have to be made so that I did not miss a home game.

So after some careful family planning we were given the due date of the new Strong as 20 May 1991, two days after the Cup Final. I thought it perfect timing. Ok, problems might be encountered if we made it to the play-offs, but the way the team had played in 89–90, together with the look of the squad that we had assembled for the new campaign, meant that it was a dilemma that I did not think we would have to face come May.

Back at the heaven that was Brisbane Road, Frankie had brought in Peter Eustace as chief coach, which basically meant that our man from Loughton had unofficially moved upstairs. He had started to handle the clubs financial and administrative affaires, leaving the playing side of things to the new Yorkshireman at the club. To my utter amazement the lads started to produce some fine performances, and unbelievably by Christmas the O's were third in the league. As with Barbara's pre-birth, my wife's pregnancy had heralded an upturn in the fortunes of the club. Although our away form was typically Leyton Orient at the time, with only two wins out of the first nine, we were virtually unbeatable at home, winning nine out of the opening ten. We beat Second Division Charlton in what was now called the Rumbelow's Cup, Second Round, before taking Crystal Palace to a replay in the Third.

There was an historic day for the club, and a sign of things to come in the future, as we made our live debut on Satellite television in a boring goalless draw away to Colchester in the FA Cup. It was shown on 'BSB', which was the least popular of the pay-per-view companies at the time. Only about thirty people in the country had one of the BSB square aerials, but I managed to find one of them and so added to my Orient video cassette collection with the match.

On the pitch one of the highlights of the season was a game against Tranmere Rovers in February. We won 4–0 with Chris Bart-Williams making his first team debut at the age of just seventeen, and scoring after just eleven minutes. The afternoon's most memorable moment, however was provided by Cooperman. The great man had been side-lined all season with a knee problem and he came on as substitute just before the end of the game. Within minutes he had scored on his comeback, a simple header from about four inches. What followed was wonderful. A seemingly possessed Cooper running round Brisbane Road, waving arms in all directions in a celebration of his return to the real world of first team football. We had been 3–0 up by half-time, so it was actually a pretty meaningless goal, but try telling that to Cooper at the time. Coops certainly divided opinion on the Brizzy Road terraces in the early nineties, in much the same way as Ollie Palmer does today, but I loved the guy.

Following the Tranmere match, I had a letter published in the *Ilford Recorder* stating that Bart-Williams had become the first double-barrel named player to score for the O's since A.R. Haig-Brown in 1906. I also said that Geoff Pike's strike against Tranmere had been his first league goal for two years. Although now a changed family man, I continued to be a bit of a sad bloke. The anorak in me would not go away.

After the Tranmere victory we went up to sixth. There was talk on the terraces of a play-off place from the optimists, or even an automatic promotion from the lunatics. Some of us just waited for the standard Leyton Orient collapse. It came alright, and how. After we got an away draw at Rotherham on 5 February, the O's suffered seven straight defeats in a row in the league. In spectacular style we crashed down to sixteenth place. As I suspected all along worrying about missing the birth of my child to see us play a play-off match was not going to be a problem. Luckily we had collected enough early season points for relegation not to be a cause for concern at the end of it. We won our last home game 4–0 against Reading, but by then the season had already fizzled out badly and we were left with a final position of thirteenth.

With all Orient's football having finished, we were left with three clear months to concentrate on the new birth, which we were told could happen at any time. As it was, Sonia was rushed to hospital on Cup-final eve, 17 May. Driving her up to Harlow Hospital that Friday night, I resigned myself to missing my first FA Cup Final since I had started watching the great game back in 1967. It was not, of course as big a blow as it had been some three and a half years earlier, when I was forced to miss an O's home game because of Barbara's birth, but it was a blow all the same. At the time, I still loved Cup Final day. Staying at home all day watching football related stuff on the television in those days was still a big deal for a lot of people. Yet this year there was to be no *Cup Final Grandstand* for me for the first time in twenty-four years. On that journey up to Harlow any normal expectant father would have had thoughts only of their wife and her forthcoming great event. I though was thinking also of other things. Visions of Cup *Final Mastermind, It's a Cup Final Knockout,* and even *Cup Final Wrestling,* were appearing as I drove to the maternity ward.

Our planned timing of the birth then while not as bad as Barbara's, could have been slightly better. Cup Final day 1991 was spent at Sonia's bedside as she gave birth in the morning to another girl, Rebecca who soon got to be known by everybody as Becky. Three and a half hours later Tottenham Hotspur v. Nottingham Forest kicked off at Wembley. At around 5.30pm a boy passed the bedroom window outside the maternity ward chanting: 'there's only one Des Walker'. I guessed that Forest had defeated Spurs in the big game, with Walker scoring the winner. What a memorable day 18 May would be remembered as, I thought. Not only because I had become a father again, but because Des Walker had scored. Everyone knew at the time that though he was for sure an ace defender, Des Walker simply never scored a goal.

Imagine how stunned I was when I finally got home that evening and found out the truth. Des had scored alright, but had put through his own net to give the cup to Spurs, who won 2–1. Although I had bought Barbara a copy of Leyton Orient versus Newport in 1978 to commemorate the day she had been born, this time around I refrained from getting a copy of Spurs versus Forest on video for Becky. All in all, although there was the drama of a new addition to the Strong household at the end of it, 90–91 was another pretty mundane season O's wise. And we were still no nearer to getting to Wembley.

CHAPTER 27

1991–92 – HURRAH! ANOTHER CUP CLASSIC AT LAST!

One crucial decision was taken during the close season. After many years of standing behind the goal at Leyton Stadium, I decided that I would treat myself to a season ticket in the East Stand. Entering my thirty-third year, it was time I felt to give the old legs a rest. I bought a seat next to George who I have spoken about before, the Leyton Orient legend who sadly passed away in 2014. Previously I had been going to matches mostly alone, although Mike, Tinks and Kevin would go to the odd one or two. This was something that had never bothered me at all. I had always looked upon watching the O's as a personal thing between myself and the club.

It had never bothered me either to stand at all the games, either. Having a seat in the East Stand though, did have many advantages. There was certainly a better view now, and what's more my programmes started to arrive home in mint condition. The ritual became that I would go to the programme shop before the home matches, buy the match-day magazine together with any aways I might have missed and put them in the carrier bag. From season 1991–92 however, this bag could now be placed under the seat. Worries that it could be trodden on by some idiot on the terraces were now a thing of the past. Plus, of course, it could rain like hell, but for the duration of the game anyway, the dam things would not get wet. The regular nerds at the programme fairs of the early eighties with their Columbo coats, would have been proud of the new found quality of my collection, I thought at the time.

All I needed now was some decent football to watch in front of me. The start however was not good. Under Peter Eustace, who was now officially first-team manager, we failed to win any of our first four league matches and found ourselves in the bottom four. Amazingly though somewhat out of the blue, there was a dramatic sudden improvement and five wins out of our next seven took us up to seventh. The highlight of this period was seeing Andy Jones, a forward signed from Bournemouth, score one of the best goals ever seen at Brizzy Road, against Chester City. Collecting the ball just inside his own half, he powered his way past two defenders before drilling an unstoppable shot from twenty yards out, past the 'keeper. It was a real stunner scored by a player who I felt could have gone on to become a lethal striker for the O's, but he alas suffered from a suspect knee and was so forced to give up the game really early.

Another player to make his mark at this time was Ricky Otto. He was a wide man, who looked as if he could follow in the footsteps of Cunningham, Chiedozie and Comfort into the books of the wing-greats of Brisbane Road. Otto was an interesting character. He came into the professional game at a late age, partly because he had spent much of his early life in prison. I first saw him in a pre-season friendly at Leyton against Real Valladolid, a Spanish First Division side, who had included Columbian World Cup star Valderama in their line-up. Watching the West Indian warm up before kick-off, I genuinely thought from a distance that with ponytail flowing behind him, he was a female mascot that evening. It actually came as a bit of a shock when the game began and I saw him bouncing up and down the left-wing. His league debut at Brentford saw a 3–4 reverse, but the performance of Ricky that day is still recognized by many Brizzy veterans as being one of the best first outings of any O. All three of our goals that day were made by Otto runs and crosses. His two goals against Darlington in a subsequent game, turned a 0–1 reverse into a 2–1 win, though it soon became clear that he was a very erratic player. When he was up for it he could be brilliant, brushing aside right-backs and putting in a fine cross. He also possessed a powerful shot to compare with any that Comfort might have produced. However, when he did not want to know he could be dire. On occasions you could see after about ten minutes that he needed to be substituted.

More history was made for the club in the Second Round of the FA Cup. We had defeated Welling in the First Round, thus setting us up for an encounter with West Bromwich Albion at home. The game was chosen to be our live debut on the major satellite channel, Sky. Nowadays with practically every football match ever played available to watch on YouTube, it seems a strange thing to say, but back then I was thrilled at the time that I'd have another O's match to add to my video-cassette collection. That fifty stone, five hundred pound video cassette recorder that I'd acquired back at the start of the eighties had long since gone, but a more modern version had taken its place. And I was getting more and more Orient stuff now, which I could play on the thing. O how I loved the machine.

Sky did a wonderful job on their first outing to our east London paradise. They wonderfully chose Sir Peter Kitchen as their match-day summarizer. I found out afterwards that they got a few phone calls from viewers wanting to know why the man analyzing the football match had a halo on his head. Our hero even managed of course, to correctly predict a narrow victory for the O's, as we won the game 2–1. I didn't have a Sky 'dish' at the time, but had of course designated three folk who did have one to record it for me to be absolutely sure that I got a copy on tape.

We had a good Christmas in 1991. It was the first one when there were four of us in the Strong family after Becky's arrival earlier in the year, and the O's defeated Bolton 2–1 on Boxing Day. As any footy buff will tell you, Christmases are always a whole lot better when your team wins on Boxing Day. In the Trotter's encounter we had been a goal down at half-time, but had come back to win thanks to two second half goals from Mark Cooper. Yes Cooperman was still around. Usually in and out of the team thanks to injuries, he still split opinion, yet he was still a player who had the ability to score in any game. And of course none of us had forgotten his 1989 experience for us.

Two days after the Bolton game, we defeated Brentford 4–2 at Brisbane Road in a never-to-be-forgotten match. It was our first victory over them in six attempts in the League. To many an O, this was considered one of the best results for years as they thought of Brentford as being our number one enemies, though personally I would have preferred to have seen us beat Newport. The game saw what many present at Brisbane Road that day agreed, was one of the most inept refereeing displays since football began. David Ellery was the man in black. He had had trouble controlling the game all afternoon, and by the end of it he had totally lost the plot. It culminated in our player, Kenny Achampong being hit and felled in the middle of the pitch. A mass brawl erupted involving most of the players. After it had all calmed down a little, Ellery went to consult his linesman who had been miles away from the action and clearly didn't have a clue what had happened. Our referee knew that he had to be seen to be taking some action so he laughingly sent-off just about the only innocent party in the whole affair, Kenny Achampong. Whilst it was all going off, our Kenny was lying flat out in the middle of the pitch. Everyone agreed it was a joke decision. At the end of the game you would never have seen a home crowd so incensed after a victory. There were mass protests at our club about the sending-off afterwards, and by strange co-incidence David Ellery did not referee a match at Brisbane Road for years afterwards.

On the brighter side, the turn of the year came and Leyton Orient were lying in seventh place. Despite the fact that Chris Bart-Williams had been sold to Sheffield Wednesday for a tidy little sum, it had been a good first half to the season. And we had been given a Third Round FA Cup trip to top Division Oldham to look forward to. This brought back memories of that infamous non-trip to Boundary Park some six years earlier, when I had not popped the 'marry me' question to Sonia. This time I travelled up north alone, Sonia stayed at home, as she always did now, to look after Barbara and Becky.

The game itself saw a typical backs-to-the-wall performance from any lower division team away to a First Division side. Remarkably, however we took the lead in the first half thanks to a Keith Day goal, though Oldham equalized and in the end we were more than happy to hang on for a 1–1 draw. As we left the ground and headed back to the supporter's coach, the electronic scoreboard that they had at Boundary Park flashed up the latest score in an FA Cup game being played at the time: 'Wrexham 1 Arsenal 1'. I remember thinking to myself at the time, I hope Arsenal score a late winner. The reason being that I wanted our result to be the best performance on the day by a smaller team against a First Division side, so giving us a lot of publicity. I still remembered back in 1972 when we had defeated Leicester away in the Cup and the result had been overshadowed by Hereford's victory over Newcastle that day.

Though I usually wanted the underdogs to win against the giants, I was somewhat disappointed this time, when finding out Arsenal had actually lost, when I got back onto the coach. In fact over the years there has been a general theme of seeing O's good performances in the FA Cup being overshadowed by other results on the day. In 2006 as a fourth tier club, we won 2–1 away at Premier League side Fulham, yet on the same afternoon non-league Burton Albion held Manchester United to a goalless draw, and so captured all the glory. It's been yet another of the joys of being a Leyton Orient supporter over the years, that our timings are often not very good.

The Oldham replay turned out to be a great game. The 4–2 victory was another Oriental FA Cup classic. Ever the ace-statto, however my first thought at the end of the match was just how much the one hundred and twenty minutes football that we had just witnessed had followed the pattern of the 1966 World Cup Final. Oldham – like West Germany – had scored first, we had equalized through Lee Harvey and then taken the lead thanks to a Kevin Nugent goal. With just ten minutes left however, the visitors levelled to take us into extra-time. This time the scorer had been Palmer though and not Weber.

As at Wembley some twenty-six years earlier, the game turned on a controversial fifth goal. Andy Jones was clearly body-checked for an obvious penalty, but Steve Castle's effort was blocked by Hallworth. Yet referee Lodge, after consulting with the Russian linesman ordered the kick to be retaken and this time Castle scored. Then just like back in 1966, with Oldham pushing forward, our boys broke away and Nugent added a fourth, though this time round there were no spectators on the pitch who thought that the game was over, as the ball hit the back of the net.

It was indeed, a wonderful night at Leyton Stadium. We were long overdue a memorable FA Cup evening, and here it was. I actually refrained from a few celebratory pints afterwards however, rushing home to view the highlights that were on the Beeb's *Sportsnight* programme that evening. Tony Gubba made his debut as a commentator at Brisbane Road and thanks to the result, he like Barry Davies was now welcome back at any time.

There were no other cup shocks on the night and as a result we managed to get a lot of publicity after the game. My press cuttings collection had a massive boost the next day. The nationals love it when the O's do well, as we are a dream for the headline writers. The day after the Oldham match, the *Daily Mirror*

had, 'Wizard of O's', together with 'Better Leyton Never', while *The Sun* chipped in with the inevitable 'Orient Express'. The scrapbook collection was now up to thirty and growing.

At the Orient, Eustace really did seem to have got his act together with the team. Including cup games we went ten without defeat after Christmas. Portsmouth beat us in the next round of the cup, but sitting seventh in the league there was all to play for in the remainder of the season.

There was a remarkable match at West Bromwich Albion on 3 March. I ventured up there

Great cup win, shame about the kit

on the supporter's coach for the evening game in the Midlands. Entering the game the Albion sat third, while we were four places behind. Defender Keith Day had been excused duty, as his wife was about to give birth, while Ricky Otto was given leave to attend a family funeral. Eustace started with a very defensive line up, playing Kevin Hales as a sweeper. With the team we had out, the general consensus amongst us before the action started, was that 0–0 would be the best we could hope for that evening. Yet incredibly after just eighteen minutes we were 3–0 up. We held them to the same scoreline until half-time, when a couple of people asked me when we had been so far ahead of anyone away from home in the league at the interval. It had, I recalled been at Notts County during our near promotion season back in 73–74. By the end of the match our formation was a somewhat unorthodox 7-2-1, with strikers Robert Taylor and Kevin Nugent playing as twin right-backs, but we held out to win 3–1.

Results continued to go well. A 4–0 thrashing of Hartlepool on 5 April saw us go fifth and in a play-off place. We even had a game in hand on all but one of the clubs above us. With just six games remaining, talk was of finishing at worst in a play-off place, and at best of automatic promotion. Ok so we had fallen apart at the end of the previous two seasons, but it surely would not happen again, despite the fact that Kevin Nugent had been sold to Plymouth.

By the law of averages we were due a good finish to a season, despite the fact that we were Leyton Orient, collapse-kings extraordinaire. O dear. We proceeded to lose all of our last six matches and ended up finishing tenth. In 1991–92 we thus achieved the nineties hat-trick of dramatic failures at the death.

Just why it kept happening to us was one of football's great unsolved mysteries. We just put it down to the fact that we were Leyton Orient. It was such a shame it had to happen in 91–92 because take away those last six encounters and it had been a fine season for us. We had done well in the league, had had a good FA Cup run, and had held Sheffield Wednesday to a draw in the Rumbelows Cup which was an excellent result.

One thing that 91–92 will always be remembered for however, in my opinion, was the hideousness of our kit that year. In my opinion the worst we have ever had. The white shorts and red socks were fine, but the shirts were different class. They were basically red, but across the chest and on the sleeves it appeared that some nerd had tried to paint a zebra crossing. On top of that the name of the club sponsors at the time, 'Bamen' was written in red over the top. And just to make the shirts more colourful the numbers on the back were yellow. It reminded me at the time of the kind of design that four-year-old Barbara was bringing home every day on her paintings from playgroup.

I felt a little normality returned to my life at the end of the season when I was once more able to watch the FA Cup Final live, after missing out the year before. Liverpool defeated Sunderland 2–0 in a dull match, but it was nice that I could once more watch all that footy stuff on the box all day, which I had not been able to do in 1991. At the time the thought of the FA Cup Final not kicking off at three o'clock and not being the most important domestic match of the season would have been unthinkable. How times, alas change.

CHAPTER 28

1992–93 – 1972 REVISITED

There was a happy event in the Strong household over the summer as we had an extension built. This was great news for the ever expanding programme and video cassette collection, as well as giving more room for the kids. I once more got a season ticket in the East Stand next to George. I remember at the start of the season walking down Brisbane road to the game when 'Gatters', as everybody knew him, suddenly veered off sharply to the left towards a chap coming the other way. He shook his hand and started talking to him. Eventually he rejoined me and explained that the man was Eddie Brown, a famous old Orient player from the late-fifties who he had not seen for thirty years. George had recognized him instantly, as he would have done any player from that fifties era.

At the time I thought this all a bit strange. George struggled to remember the results of O's games from a few weeks previously and the names of players playing for us at the time, yet take him back three decades and he knew everything about the club. Yet turning the clock forward now to 2016, I have to say that I find myself in virtually the same situation as George did then. If I was walking down Brisbane Road now and Kevin Godfrey, John Jackson or Barry Silkman were coming towards me, I'm sure I'd spot them straight away. The present day squad though, now I'd find it a lot more difficult to pick those players out. And it's the same with results too. Most from the eighties are ingrained in the brain, seemingly forever. I can just about recall that Boxing Day game against Portsmouth in 2015 (3–2), or the 2–0 Crawley win at home in February this year, but I'm finding that it's getting more difficult with the recent results. The joys of being an ageing supporter, I suppose.

The 92–93 season started and the O's, along with most of the other clubs in the league found that they had got promoted. Because of re-organization and the introduction of the Premier League, we found ourselves back in Division Two. It was though still football's third tier in proper money. We celebrated the 'new' division however, by starting like a house on fire. Unbelievably, considering how 91–92 had finished, a 1–0 victory at home to Bournemouth on 17 October took us to the top of the league. We had won seven out of our first twelve games. The defence was conceding few and Andy Jones along with Robert Taylor were doing the business at the other end.

Despite the sound performances however, one little incident stands out from the beginning of the season at Brisbane Road, and it had nothing at all to do with events at the time, on the pitch. It occurred during a routine match against Blackpool in August, which resulted in a 1–0 win. During the game the referee stopped the match to complain about a colour clash between the top worn by of one of the spectators in the west-side, and the linesman's flag. Police and stewards got involved and after some delay the fan, Graeme Baumber, was sent higher up the stand. It was a bizarre happening; surely a first in football history and it duly made the news in the evening, and was in the papers the next day.

Our magnificent stadium has indeed been party to other weird incidents over the years. We generally average one a decade. The first that I can recall went back to 1974 during a goalless draw with Hull City. One of the worst games in the history of football was enlivened during the second half when a spectator ran onto the pitch, picked up the ball and drop volleyed it into the net. It was a strike that most Leyton Orient forwards over the years have only dreamed about. (His one shot on target was indeed one more than Michael Marks managed in his nine months at the club.) The intruder soon scarpered back into the crowd and whether or not he was caught, I could not tell you. In those pre-CCTV days the boys in blue were caught totally napping on the day, and he may well have escaped.

Not so fortunate was the pitch-protester from 1983, during Kitch's comeback match against Preston North End. With the score at 1–1, during another lousy game, a man with crutches climbed over the lowish wall in front of the East Stand enclosure and went onto the sacred turf. He ventured up to the centre circle, where he threw his crutches down in the direction of the centre spot. With the crowd – all 1,666 of us – cheering, a couple of young policemen eventually arrived onto the pitch not knowing how best to deal with the situation. After handing him back his supports, he half walked, was half carried back to the police-room at the corner of the North Terrace. I thought at the time that the man was brilliant. It was a monumental gesture summing up totally the mood of the Brisbane Road punter at the time. We had slipped into the bottom four of the Third, having been relegated just the season before. His action, right in front of the management team and the Director's Box was in effect his way of saying 'what the hell is going on at our club?' Thanks to Kitch we went on to win the game, but our friend had made his point and we all echoed his sentiments at the time.

Bizarre event of the current decade? That goes back to just the end of last year at the Portsmouth encounter on Boxing Day. End of the game – job done by the boys with a 3–2 victory, another pitch invasion, this time by our esteemed owner Francesco Becchetti. This was no ordinary pitch invasion however. Our man proceeded to kick our Assistant Manager Andy Hessentaller from behind, just in front of the dugout. Our management team had apparently been given stick by Mr Becchetti for the duration of the match and at it's conclusion Hessentaller had evidently gestured and shouted back at the owner. The club tried to play the event down afterwards, Hess stating that it was all friendly banter, but the FA didn't see it that way and gave Francesco a six game stadium ban.

Getting back to the 92–93 season, we had a wonderful game against Dagenham and Redbridge in the First Round of the FA Cup, winning 5–4 after being 2–0 and 3–1 down. That secured a live Second Round tie on Sky. A Saturday night match at Reading though resulted in a poor 3–0 defeat. Despite the cup setback the league form remained excellent though, particularly at home. Full-back Terry Howard of all people chipped in with a hat-trick on 28 November as we defeated Mansfield 5–1 at home. For all the fine achievements in the league before the turn of the year however one game stands out for me more than any other. A match in the First Round of the Auto-Windscreens Trophy – the new name for the cup for lower league teams – against Gillingham. The evening began like any other mid-week home game in those days. I boarded the Central Line at Loughton to go the six stops to Leyton at around a quarter to seven. This usually gave me plenty of time to get to Brizzy, buy a programme and enter the ground in time for kick-off.

That night however, between Snaresbrook and Leytonstone the train stopped. After ten minutes it was still there. About as static as Peter Bonetti had been for West Germany's three goals in the 1970 World Cup quarter-final. An announcement was then made to us that there was a points failure ahead and that we would not be making any further progress for some time. In the end it was quarter to eight before we reached the theatre of dreams station, which was kick-off time. I ran to the ground thankful that I was only going to miss about five minutes of the match.

When I got to Brisbane Road however, I discovered that as it was so late, there was only one turnstile still open. (Season tickets did not cover those cup games.) The turnstile that you had to use to enter the ground was purely for the South Enclosure. Yes, after an absence of twenty years I was going back to stand on that sacred terrace where I had seen us defeat Chelsea 3–2. The place where I had stood for the most magical ninety minutes football the world had ever seen. The place though where I had vowed never again to frequent, as a tribute to that wonderful day, 26 February 1972.

As I watched the game, it all seemed a bit unreal. I felt that I should not have been there. This was the 'Chelsea Match Terrace', and always would be. It was an insult to the memory of that great encounter that I was standing there, watching of all things an Auto-Windscreens Trophy First Round match. I felt that I had let Barry Davies down, too. It was an affront to his finest moment commentating for the Beeb.

We went on to win the game 4–1 that night against the Gills. I'm sure though, that at one point watching from the enclosure, I saw Bonetti and Webb collide to give Mickey Bullock an open goal from which to score from. At times I could see not seventy-seven Gillingham supporters standing behind the Coronation Gardens end, but thousands wearing blue and white Chelsea scarves, ready to invade the pitch near the end of the game, looking for an abandonment. I kept looking round expecting to see my dad, upset at being crushed and not being able to do the *Telegraph* crossword.

As I travelled back to Loughton after the game had ended, I must have been the only Orient fan not overjoyed at seeing an easy victory. When I got home I turned on the television. I half expected to see the game on *Match of the Day*, along with Davies doing that famous commentary. I felt bitter towards London Transport that evening. Yet again I vowed that I would not watch another O's game from that part of the ground. Thankfully twenty-four years on I've so far been able to stick to the promise this time round.

The boys continued to play well after Christmas, Exeter were hit for five in January, this time Robert Taylor got a hat-trick. At the end of the match Orient were second in the table and looking really good. Then, remarkably Brighton were defeated 3–1 at the Goldstone Ground on 6 February, and this time it was Ricky Otto who scored three. In the space of twelve league matches three different O's players had scored hat-tricks. Was this really Leyton Orient we were watching? We all awaited for the traditional post-Christmas collapse to reassure us that it was. Well it came, of course and in 1993 it started on 6 March.

The season, and indeed looking back now, it could be said that the decade of the nineties, peaked on 27 February 1993. A home game against Stoke pitted the third placed team, the O's, against the league leaders from the potteries.

Bye, bye 'Big Match'. Our last appearance on the show

Stoke were unbeaten for a record twenty-five matches. 10,798 were attracted to Brisbane Road, which was our biggest crowd in the league for years. Even *The Big Match* cameras were there along with Brian Moore, to show the highlights the following day. Stoke were the better team on the day, it has to be said, yet that man Mark Cooper stooped low to score with his head after forty minutes and we held on to record a rather fortunate 1–0 victory.

Talk on the terraces, and in the clubhouse after the game was yet again about the O's going up. Many were once more talking about stealing one of the two automatic promotion places that were up for grabs. Certainly it would have needed a highly dramatic reverse in form for the club not to make at the very least the play-offs. But then again we were Leyton Orient. We always blew it come this time of the year. And sure enough we did once more blow it. Of the next twenty-one points on offer we claimed two. We dipped below the play-off line, never to return. There was a mini recovery at the end of the season but the damage had already been done and we finished seventh. It was the most disappointing finish to a campaign since…well the season before.

Oh the continued joys of being a Leyton Orient supporter. And despite the victory over Gillingham in the First Round, we did not make the Final of the Auto-Windscreens Trophy, so another year went by without a Wembley appearance.

CHAPTER 29

1993–94 – BYE-BYE EUSTACE

The close season saw Frank Clark finally depart Brisbane Road after eleven years at the club to take over from Brian Clough at Nottingham Forest. Eustace had been first team manager for two years, but Clark had still been highly influential at the club in his role as Managing Director. Even more so as chairman Tony Wood was spending more and more time overseas. Like many an Orient manager, Frankie divided opinion at the O's. His record in the transfer market had been patchy. There had been the good in Comfort and Beesley, but there had been the bad in Marks and the like. However it has to be said that for much of the time when he was in charge, certainly at the beginning of his reign, he gave us a very entertaining team to watch. This was most un-Orient like, of course. He also presented us with that one memorable season back in 1988–89, giving us our first promotion in nineteen years, and we also had the odd good cup result along the way. And the most important thing of all, of course was that he was always polite to Sonia when he met her in Loughton High Road. If he was ok with the wife, then he was alright with me.

There were big changes among the playing staff in the summer. Eight were given free-transfers, while Ricky Otto and promising young centre-half Adrian Whitbread were sold to Southend and Swindon, respectively. It was, of course the age-old story at Leyton Orient that we had to sell to survive. As had always been the case at our piece of heaven in east London, we just did not get enough punters through the turnstiles to keep the club running on gate receipts alone.

There were the usual letters written to the local papers stating that the club lacked ambition, but most of us realized that the O's were, as they always have been, a selling club. There was no way of course, that we would ever be taken over by a rich Italian willing to put money into us (!). Indeed, as we were to find out a year later, even a continual stream of player's leaving Brisbane Road in the early nineties would not be enough to guarantee the club's survival.

The main addition to the playing staff in the close season was Colin West. He was a big, tall striker with no first touch and certain not to get you twenty goals a season, so that he was a centre-forward made for the Orient. He had played for seemingly every Football League club in England and Wales, and had even chipped in with a spell at Glasgow Rangers, where he had obtained a Scottish League winners medal.

Season 93–94 always looked like it was going to be a pretty boring campaign, and so it proved. As we never really looked good enough to mount a promotion challenge, it was just a case of trying to accumulate enough points, so that when the annual post-Christmas collapse came, we had enough in the locker to be safe. As it was this time we peaked on 5 March. A 2–1 home victory against Plymouth took us up to ninth. Unlike the previous few years however, this time nobody even mentioned the promotion word. We had seen enough of the O's in the nineties not to be that naïve.

Everyone was just preparing themselves for the annual free-fall down the table. And we were not to be disappointed. On this occasion it took the form of just one win in our last thirteen as we cartwheeled down to finish eighteenth. Just why it happened yet again, once more remained a mystery. Yes, we had a few injuries, but then so did every club. In 93–94 the playing staff had been boosted by the addition of Ian Bogie and Glen Cockerill who were both decent players. It had been a brave attempt to give us a final push up to the second tier, yet we ended up just about avoiding relegation.

Indeed it was later to transpire that the club had signed Bogie and Cockerill, when they really could not afford to do so. It was strongly rumoured that when Bogie was later sold on to Port Vale for £50,000, £35,000 of that was paid back to the player as a signing on fee that he was promised but never received when he joined us. As was so often the case at Brisbane Road at the time however, there was a cloud of secrecy over the real financial position at the club. It was clear, though that all was not well at Leyton Orient money wise, the real extent of which we were to find out at the end of 1994.

There were very few games to get excited about during the 93–94 season, yet one result had quite a significance to it, although no one realized it at the time. On 30 October we won 1–0 at Hull City. Amazingly it was to be the O's last away victory in the league for twenty-three months. Our second half of the season collapses became legendary in the nineties. Towards the middle of the decade however, the two words 'legendary' and 'infamous' also came to be associated with Leyton Orient's away form. It quite simply became hopeless.

As we started to slide down the table in March, it became clear that unless there was a dramatic turnaround, Eustace's days at the club were numbered. At the time I went along with the masses (in so far as there were any masses at the time at Brisbane Road) and joined in the 'Eustace Out' cries. As he did not live in Loughton, he could not even call on Sonia to lend him her support in his hour of need, and he thus ended up getting the sack in April.

In these pre Brush, Liverani and Hendon days there was a general consensus among a lot of O's fans at the time, that the Yorkshireman had been the worst manager we'd ever had at the club. Yet whilst in charge we had actually spent plenty of time in the play-off places in the third tier, and had on a couple of occasions actually been top of the league. We finished seventh in what was then called the Second Division or third tier in 92–93, just missing out on the end of season lottery, yet at the time it was considered a failure. He went back up north after he left us, eventually opening up a pub in Yorkshire.

The O's got around five hundred applicants for the vacant managers job, which was not bad at all, considering that we did not even advertise the post. The board ignored all of these however. In a characteristic Leyton Orient move they appointed assistant manager Chris Turner and youth team coach John Sitton as the new joint bosses. Now you did not need to be a brain surgeon to realize that it was a move made purely for financial reasons. Eustace's contract had to be paid off and the cheapest option at the time was to upgrade Turner and Sitton, rather than employ a successor from outside. We had seen the same thing done at our wonderful club when Bloomfield was made up to player/manager in the late sixties, and also when Clark was promoted to being made the boss in 1983.

Many of us feared the worst when the appointments were made. Lovely as they all are, Leyton Orient supporters, like I suppose all football fans, can be a funny bunch. I remember having an argument with one in the supporter's club back in 1994 after Sitton and Turner had just got upgraded. He tried to tell me that our situation was similar to that of Liverpool at the time. They had employed Kenny Dalglish from within, with no previous managerial experience, and he had won them the double in his first year. Apart from the fact that we once shared the same Subbuteo kit however, I could see no real similarities between the O's and Liverpool at the time. In fact drawing comparisons between the two clubs in red, was akin to comparing Jay Simpson with Gianvani Plasmati when it came to comparing goal-scoring ability. As it was though, I don't think anyone can have envisaged just how bad Sitton and Turner's spell in charge was going to be.

Back on the domestic scene all, as was usually the case, all was going well at home. Barbara was now six and Becky two. Just one small hiccup arose with

Barbara at school however, a problem that I had anticipated that she would encounter, someday. She came home one afternoon and said to me, 'daddy we were talking about football at school today, and Robert who sits on my table asked me who I supported. I said Leyton Orient and he laughed. He said that they were rubbish and that I should support a good team like his daddy, who he said supported Manchester United. But Leyton Orient aren't rubbish are they, daddy?' It was a moment I'm sure many a small-team supporting parent must have encountered over the years. A situation that you know you are going to have to face eventually, but you just try to put it to the back of your mind until it actually happens. I was however prepared for it, and had my answer ready: -

'Just ask Robert how many times his daddy goes to watch Manchester United and tell him that your daddy sees Orient play every week, because he is a true supporter.' I did not tell Barbara to let Robert know that her dad had seen his team play on over one hundred different grounds, and once went nearly five years without missing a game home or away, or that he had over two thousand Orient football programmes and a Leyton Orient car sticker collection in his loft. If he had known these things, I figured Robert might have been withdrawn from St John Fisher School, his parents not wishing him to mix with such a weird family.

As the forgettable season on the pitch petered out for the O's, I reached a landmark in my football fan career on the last day of the season. I'd worked out, with the help of my little black book started in 1974, that I'd been to 91 out of the 92 league grounds. Most of those in deed, had been with the O's – it had helped of course, that the team went sliding down the league in the eighties which gave me the opportunity to go to lots of new grounds.

It was just left for me to do the City Ground, home of Nottingham Forest, to complete the 92. I went up there for their game against Sunderland in May, with Joe a good work friend of mine from the ANZ dealing room in the City. He was, and

---

through this terrible ~~length~~ to get you very much."

COMPLETING THE SET

Leyton Orient supporter Martin Strong will "complete the set" when he watches our game against Sunderland this afternoon.

He has visited 91 of the 92 grounds, seeing Orient on 82 of them, but has chosen the City Ground as his final port of call.

His friend Joe Morgan told us: "Martin was present when Frank Clark achieved promotion with Orient in 1989 and he's hoping to be around when Frank celebrates the 'double'."

TRAVELLING COMPANION WANTED

A supporter in the West Country is looking for a companion to travel to our home games.

Executive Stand season ticket holder Keith Pettit, who lives in

indeed still is a big Newcastle fan, and he was lured to the game in the hope of seeing Sunderland lose. It was a philosophy that I could relate to. I'd have travelled a few hundred miles if it meant seeing Newport get beat. Unfortunately for Joe, however the Mackems after being a couple down at one stage, pulled back two late goals, thus earning a 2–2 draw.

I got a little mention in the Forest programme that afternoon, and at the end of the day I had done the lot, every league ground in the country. It had been twenty-seven years since I had been to the first, Leyton Stadium on 1 April 1967. After some thought I decided against joining the '92 Club' for those that have done the full set. I remembered my days going to those programme fairs in the early eighties, seeing all those sad blokes still living at home with mum and dad. They all had '92 Club' lapel badges on and I did not really fancy being associated with those strange people. Having finally reached the 'Mount Everest' of football following, I contemplated starting on grounds in the Scottish League. After due consideration though, I thought better of it, however. I decided that I'd just wait for them to resurrect the Anglo-Scottish Cup before I started going to places north of the border.

CHAPTER 30

1994–95 – HEARN THE HERO

To be honest, the early years of the nineties were frankly a bit boring, both on and off the pitch at Leyton Orient. Well all of that certainly changed in spectacular fashion with the 94–95 season. One word you could never in a million years describe that campaign as was 'boring'. There is though many a word that could be used to describe the season, most of them along the lines of 'dramatic' although for a lot of it 'disastrous' or 'awful', would be more appropriate.

Before the 1994–95 season started, many veteran Orient campaigners like me feared that it would be a poor one for us, but realistically nobody can have envisaged the carnage that was to follow during the next nine months. In August the footy started with most considering that to avoid relegation would have been a success, yet come the end of the year avoiding relegation actually became the least of all our worries. By December it became obvious to all that there merely still being a Leyton Orient FC to support would be an achievement come the summer of 1995.

The bookies had placed us as 50–1 rank outsiders for the Second Division title when the season began, and their pessimism was clearly not misplaced. Sitton and Turner were going to give it all they had, but they were clearly going to be out of their depth with so little managerial experience between them.

We basically started off with the same team that had struggled so badly at the tail-end of 93–94, though alas Mark Cooper was given a free transfer, and he had been snapped up by Barnet. I had always been a big Cooperman fan. It was real comic book stuff the way that he had picked himself up from such a disastrous start at the club, including that legendary Torquay miss and the sending off at Wrexham, to play such a major part at the end of our promotion winning campaign in 88–89.

He had been plagued with injuries in the years afterwards, yet had still managed to score over fifty goals for us in all matches. In Leyton Orient terms, when it's usually a cause for celebration when a striker makes it into double figures for the season, this was a wonderful achievement.

Also, unlike many a player to wear the Orient shirt over the years, he actually seemed to have an affinity for the club. I met his dad outside the ground just before he left us, and he told me just how happy Cooper was at the club. I don't actually think that the new management team at the time, really wanted him to go, but it was just a question that he could not play alongside Colin West. The two of them were basically too similar. The rumour was that West still had a year of his contract to run, whilst with Cooper's having expired, the later had to leave.

We were paired with Barnet and thus Cooperman, in the First Round of what was now called the Coca-Cola Cup (the League Cup in proper terms) just after he had left. We got hammered 4–0 and surprise, surprise Cooper got two for them for the Bees. Despite this though, although he may not be in the Kitchen, Jackson or, coming up to the present, Cox class, for me he still remains a bit of a Leyton Orient hero, in my eyes.

In the early part of the nineties, we had got used to the O's falling apart every year after about thirty-odd games. In 94–95 however, it's fair to say that the collapse started after just one game. On the opening day of the season we were paired at home to promotion favourites Birmingham City and almost unbelievably beat them 2–1. Seeing as to how the next nine months were to pan out, this was an extraordinary result. The Blues lost just one more time before Christmas in the league, while we were to win just five more all season. They finished top, we ended up bottom a mere 63 points behind them. Our midfielder Ian Bogie said in the *Daily Express* after the opening encounter that we were a good outside bet for promotion. In truth there was more chance of me burning my Orient programme collection at the time than that happening.

Yet despite all of the difficulties we started to have on the field, it was the revelations off the pitch that broke, that were to really shake up everyone at the club. It all started with a report splashed across the back page of the *London Evening Standard* on 4 October, reporting that £55,000 had to be borrowed from the PFA to the club to pay our player's wages. It was said that until this money was repaid to them, we were unable to buy any new players, or even take any on loan.

The truth at the time was that for a little while Leyton Orient had been dependent on chairman Tony Wood's money. It was said that he had put well over a million pounds of his own cash into the O's, just to keep the club afloat. The big problem however, was that he had made his fortune through the coffee plantations of Rwanda. In 1994 the small African country became wrapped up in a vicious civil war, so that Wood – who had been nicknamed 'Compo' by fans, because of his likeness to the *Last of the Summer Wine* character – lost a fortune.

Whilst the war in Rwanda could not have been foreseen, the club had also gambled on bringing expensive players into the club, with a view to it gaining us promotion. Glen Cockerill, for example, had been acquired from Premier League side Southampton, where he had been club captain. One would assume that he would not have taken much of a pay cut to join the O's, so that he must therefore have been on a very good salary at Brisbane Road.

With the Orient struggling at the foot of the table, and with major financial worries, the boys of the press contrived to cheer us all up with one of the funniest stories ever, concerning the O's. A report in the *Daily Mail* on 21 October stated that Rod Stewart was interested in buying Leyton Orient Football Club. Hilarious. Some wag at the paper had seen that we were in dire straights financially, knew that Rod was a keen football man, and with the O's being the nearest League club to his British abode in Essex, had put two and two together and got five.

Elton John and Watford at the time was the obvious parallel, yet any chance of the Tartan Terror following suit and buying us was laughable. He had never been anywhere near Brisbane Road and the only danger of it ever happening would have been if his beloved Scotland had chosen to play a World Cup qualifier there. He actually lived in a mega-mansion in Epping Forest, just a few miles away from where I lived. He had been seen in a few of the local pubs, although nobody had actually spotted him at the bar buying anyone a drink. With an apparent reluctance to buy anybody even a beer, it would hardly seem feasible that he would be willing to put his hand in his pocket and take over an ailing football club, who he had never even see play. If I'd have thought that there was any truth in the story then I would have taken a trip up to his mansion. I would have gone up to the big

Rod may head for the Orient

ROD STEWART may emulate Elton John by becoming chairman of a football club.

The soccer-mad singer · is said to be interested in taking over Second Division strugglers Leyton Orient. Elton John was chairman of First Division Watford.

Stewart, above, who has a home in Epping Forest, Essex, has been invited to Orient's Brisbane Road ground, in East London, for talks with chairman Tony Wood.

Rod at Brisbane Road? I don't want to talk about it.

iron gates and tied a few old Leyton Orient scarves around them. Indeed I might have even treated myself to one of his CDs. at the time. Knowing though that a Stewart takeover would never in a million years happen, I did not bother. Nothing believe it or not ever came of the story, whilst we were *Sailing* towards the fourth division.

Amongst all the gloom, we actually managed to win an away game in November at mighty Tiverton in the First Round of the FA Cup. I ventured down to the west country, but even this trip was not without its problems. A wall that was holding back the Orient supporters collapsed as we scored our equalizing goal. Fortunately, nobody was injured and I got yet another fifteen minutes of fame with a picture of the incident on the back of *The Times* on Monday morning. There I was right in the corner on the far left. I wondered if anyone in the country looking at the paper had recognized me from the Wale interview on the Beeb, back in 1985.

Unsurprisingly though, we crashed out of the FA Cup in the next round, losing 2–0 at home to Bristol Rovers, and by Christmas we were third from bottom of the division. With the situation in Rwanda becoming increasingly desperate, Tony Wood made what was to become a legendary statement on 'Clubcall', the clubs premium rate telephone news line. Stating that he was prepared to sell the club for a fiver he said; 'I will hand over the keys to anyone who gives me five pounds. That's the stage I've reached now. I've put a lot of

Wall down at Tiverton

money into this club in the last eight years, but with the situation in Rwanda I can't do any more. I've lost everything. I am faltering in the deep sea and I'm just hoping something will turn up. Unless something happens the club will just keep going down and down.'

News of Wood's passionate speech broke in the national newspapers one morning. I though had already heard his message by dialling the Clubcall number, 0891-12-11-50 at work the evening before. At the end of the call I was stunned. I was so stunned in fact that I forgot to 'click-out' at the end of the call, as you had to do in those days with our ANZ work phones. As a result the call lasted until I got back into work the following day at eight o'clock in the morning. At 47p a minute which was the Clubcall rate, and with the call lasting all of sixteen hours, I could not actually understand why the club still had a financial crisis the next day.

There had been money worries at the Orient before of course, but somehow you always thought that the club would pull through. In the spring of 1933 the O's were threatened with closure unless a £2,000 debt was not instantly met. It was said that donations to help save us included £50 from the Prince of Wales, though as I had not yet started my Orient press cuttings collection, I am unable to confirm or deny whether this in fact was correct.

Just months before I had attended my first game, there had been the infamous 'pass the bucket' meeting at the ground in November 1966, when donations from the fans had again kept the O's afloat. Indeed throughout my time as a Brisbane Road punter, stories had regularly surfaced about the club going out of business, yet somehow you always believed that they would get out of it. This new crisis however, appeared different.

Maidstone and Aldershot at the time, had recently been forced out of existence, and now it looked a real possibility that we could follow them. In many a previous crisis there had always been a player whom we could sell to keep us going. A Bart-Williams or a Chiedozie. This time though, there appeared to be nobody in the squad who you could call upon to be a saviour. And on top of that there had also always been the impression in the past that come the crunch, the directors always had enough reserves in the bank to bail us out. The crisis in Rwanda however, meant that this was clearly not the case with Wood. The other directors would do their best, but they were clearly no multi-millionaires or Rod Stewarts.

Travelling home from work, having just heard our chairman on Clubcall, it really hit home just how bleak things were at our beloved club. I really did feel devastated. I tried to comprehend what my life would be without my beloved Leyton Orient. Sure I had never had an easy life supporting them. Starting off with other kids taking the mickey out of my lowly team in the sixties, failed promotion pushes and disastrous FA Cup semis in the seventies, relegations in the eighties, post-Christmas collapses in the nineties, it had always been a hard existence for me as an O's fan. But at the end of the day though, you always took it for granted that no matter how bad the results were on the pitch, the club would always at least be there. Now though it looked as if this might not be the case for much longer.

Just how was I going to cope? It would mean the end of life as I knew it. What was I going to moan to Sonia about on a Saturday night? Would my ANZ work colleagues stop talking to me on a Monday morning if they could not give me stick about my football team? What was I going to do on a Thursday night, when I traditionally cut out all the weeks Orient press cuttings and put them in my scrapbook?

There would be the humiliation of Barbara going to school and having to say to Robert that daddy didn't support anyone anymore, because daddy's team was not there anymore. I could picture myself spending all day Sunday looking at the league tables in the papers, trying desperately to find 'Leyton Orient' somewhere. But they would not be there. There had already been lots of defeats to mull over at that point during the 94–95 season, but all of these losses now just seemed to be a minor point, compared to what the bigger picture held for the club.

I cursed my luck that whilst other club chairmen had made their fortunes in profitable businesses at home and abroad, we were unlucky enough to have one who made his wealth in Rwanda. Wood had said that he had seen at first hand the plight of the war-torn country. He had witnessed the massacres and the killings. He had lost friends and people who had worked for him for over twenty years. He said that the civil war in the country had put the plight of Leyton Orient into its true perspective, and that football could never be more important than life and death. He was, of course 100% correct, and I must admit that when I read what he had said I felt just a little ashamed that I felt the way I did about what was after all just a football team. All the same though, losing Leyton Orient Football Club was going to be a hard pill to swallow if the worst came to the worst.

News broke just before Christmas that Phil Wallace, a local businessman was going to help bankroll the club for a few weeks with a view to buying out Wood's shareholding. This really should have cheered me up, but it didn't. It was clear to most that the club had monster debts that the possible new saviour would not be able to handle. He was managing director of local 'L and M Food Group', who were hardly J. Sainsbury Ltd. Wallace at the time was chairman of Boreham Wood FC, who were hardly in the same league as the O's. I must admit that I never had any confidence in the man rescuing us.

Nineteen ninety-four was not a good Christmas. The whole year had been a disaster for Leyton Orient FC. Summing up what a mess the twelve months had been was the farce of the last scheduled game of the year at Brisbane Road against Bristol Rovers. The referee decided to call the match off just twenty minutes before kick-off time, with a couple of thousand already inside the ground. The man in black, Keith Cooper declared at the desperately late stage that the pitch was unplayable. The few hundred Rovers fans who had made the journey up from the west country were forced to queue up for a refund, meaning that many of them would have arrived back in Bristol no earlier than if the game had actually gone ahead. It was all a complete shambles, summing up the year.

Anyone who had been following us to all the games away from home in the league in 1994 would have ended with a record of seeing us that read:

Played 24   Won 0   Drawn 4   Lost 20.

Incredible stuff. And there were still more bizarre twists to our season to come as we entered 1995. There was the Paul Hague transfer saga. The man had been bought from Gillingham as a big, dominating (yet if truth be told, dreadful) centre-half. He was the last player Sitton and Turner had been allowed to sign before the transfer embargo that had been slapped on us. No one really knew quite how much he had cost, though anything up to £60,000 had been mentioned. What was certain however, was that the fee was linked to the number of appearances he made for the O's. As we had no money though, we could not afford to pick him as we could not give the Gills anymore cash. We had therefore signed a player whom we could not play. Only at the Orient.

There was also much amusement at the clubs expense when Terry Howard, who had been at the club for many years and had made three hundred and twenty-eight league appearances for us, was sacked at half-time during a home defeat to Blackpool. We were rapidly turning into a laughing stock. To top it all, with a great sense of timing, a local journalist Jo Treharne, had asked at the beginning of the season if she could be given access around Leyton Stadium, with a view to making a fly-on-the wall documentary about the club. She was around Brisbane Road all season and produced what was, to say the least, an interesting programme, which was eventually shown on Channel Four in October 1995.

In February after looking at the club's books for eight weeks, it came as no great surprise when Phil Wallace pulled out of a possible salvation act. He said: 'My decision was purely financial. As I delved into the club, the situation got worse. It is just too big a hill to be climbed.'

It was at this point that the club really did hit rock bottom. There had been eleven games without a win as we cruised towards relegation, but even that seemed an irrelevance when compared to the difficulties behind the scenes. There were rumours that the coach company who took the team to away games had not been paid, and were thus refusing to take the team to any more matches. There was also a story that the milkman was another who was owed money and was refusing to leave any more milk at the ground.

Leyton Orient we were told were £500,000 in debt and losing £10,000 a week. According to the press two or three parties had shown an interest in buying us, but surely after delving into the books, as Wallace had done, it was hard to see anyone taking over what was a complete mess. I was on a real low in February. You became almost too nervous to look at the papers in the morning, or *The Standard* in the evening for fear of finding any more bad news concerning the club, possibly even news signalling the end for us all together.

At the start of February it looked as if the O's needed a miracle just to stay alive. Then on the sixth of the month, totally out of nowhere, it appeared that the miracle had, quite amazingly arrived after all. I first saw it looking over somebody's shoulder on the tube, whilst travelling into work. There it was, a headline in *The Sun;* 'I'll save Orient.' Straining to see the article on the crowded train, I could just about pick out what followed, 'Fan Hearn is on cue to rescue crisis club.' My God, how good did that sound? In typical Martin Strong fashion, as I had done many a time over the years after hearing good news, I punched the air. No doubt it was a baffling sight to the others in the carriage, but who cared. When I got to Bank Station I parted with 20p to read the article in full. It was the first time any member of the Strong family had bought *The Sun* since they gave away those 3-D footballers in the early seventies. There had been some dodgy things written in the paper over the years, yet when I read the story, it actually all seemed plausible.

Well known sport's promoter Barry Hearn said in the article that he was looking into a rescue package for the club. 'I have always enjoyed a challenge

Hearn the hero.

and I can't think of a bigger one.' Too right Barry, I remember thinking at the time. If he had wanted something a little less demanding, he could have climbed Everest with both legs tied together.

I can remember standing there at Bank Station in the middle of the rush hour reading the piece over and over again. I at once felt like a new man. Unlike the Wallace affair, Hearn appeared to be genuine. We knew he had the money, if not to do a Jack Walker/ Roman Abramovich, at least to save the club. We knew that he was the kind of man who would relish the publicity

of being a chairman of a Football League club. He had made a success out of snooker and boxing, so our little east end team would present him with little problem I thought.

At the same time that all the problems off the park were going on, there was another bizarre twist to a truly bizarre season on the pitch. With the team near certainties for relegation, and the club close to bankruptcy, the O's had miraculously sneaked to within one game of a Wembley appearance.

We had lost the first game in the Auto-Windscreens Shield to Gillingham, but had then defeated Fulham at home. The next round in this, as ever the most illogical football competition in the world, paired us with...Fulham! We duly beat the Cottagers yet again, and were then paired with Bristol Rovers at home. The match was goalless after ninety minutes so that for the first time ever the O's were involved in a 'sudden death' game. This had been newly introduced at the time, where the scorers of the first goal in extra-time would go through. In this match though, there really was no need for them to bother at all with the extra added thirty minutes. Rovers had rested all of their goalscorers for the game, and we didn't have any goalscorers anyway, so that the match was always likely to end up going to penalties. And in keeping with the true craziness of the season, we actually managed to win the shoot-out. The Gods then presented us with another home tie against Shrewsbury, and we managed to sneak a 2–1 win which ensured a two-legged Southern Area Final against Birmingham City, with the winners going through to the Final at Wembley.

It was in deed, the furthest we had ever got in the annual mickey-mouse competition, which Frank Clark had famously hated. By now the Blues were top of the league, yet our boys did remarkably well in the first leg to hold them to a narrow 1–0 defeat at St. Andrews, particularly as Birmingham had scored after just four minutes. This set up nicely a Wembley showdown at Brisbane Road.

The night of the second leg transpired into one of the weirdest I have ever encountered at our east London theatre of dreams. The game was made all ticket and over ten thousand, many of them down from the Midlands, had gathered inside Leyton Stadium to witness the duel.

Yet somehow for me the result was a minor factor compared with the real business of the evening. It had just been announced that Barry Hearn had cleared the most pressing debts of the O's, and had acquired a twenty-eight day option to complete the purchase of the club. It was a formality that he would buy out the directors. In short he had saved Leyton Orient Football Club.

Through his snooker players and boxers, Hearn had often been in the headlines. Many sports people had an opinion about the extrovert, though personally I'd never really thought one way or the other about him. Now though

that had all changed. He instantly became a Kitch-like hero with me. Ok, so he had not actually saved my life, but in saving my football club, he had come pretty damn close to doing so. I loved the man.

The home game with Birmingham was to be his first match. Around twenty minutes before kick-off time he made his entrance into the Director's Box. We rose as one in the East Stand and gave him the welcome he fully deserved. As a great Brisbane Road

One step from Wembley.

moment, I felt at the time that it was not far behind Fairbrother's goal in 1972, and the final whistle at the Play-off Final in 1989. There was just a wonderful feeling of relief that swept around the ground. We could once more watch our team without wondering if it might be the last time that we would be able to do so. It was all so wonderful. Ok so we were Leyton Orient, and there was a good chance that we would see them lose that night, but what the hell, at least we could now be guaranteed of seeing them play in the future.

The applause for Hearn lasted about four or five minutes, he stood up and milked it, of course, yet for me it could have gone on a lot longer. As I finally took my seat to watch the match, the bizarre thing was that the result suddenly seemed of little consequence. Since my first match against Swindon back in 1967, I had had a dream about watching the O's at Wembley and here we were, the closest we had ever got to achieving it, yet in some ways it all seemed a bit of an irrelevance. The main thing was that Leyton Orient were still alive. That mattered so much more than anything that was going on in front of me.

As the game started, the O's had a great chance to level the aggregate scores after just a couple of minutes, but Colin West missed a good opportunity from an Ian Bogie corner. This was as good as it got, however. The tie was effectively settled in the thirty-eighth minute, when Steve Claridge netted for the Blues, though from where I was he looked a mile offside. Two quick goals after the break gave the visitors a 4–0 aggregate lead, and despite a couple of late goals we ended up losing 3–2 on the night. The Wembley dream was gone for yet another year. Under normal circumstances I would have been gutted that the road to the twin towers was not finally at an end. But these were not normal circumstances. Ok, so I would not be watching the O's at Wembley, but I was just elated that I was able to watch the team play anywhere. When I arrived back in Loughton, I remember thinking at the time that the only time I had ever got home so happy having just witnessed a Leyton Orient defeat was in 1989 when we lost 1–0 at Scarborough, but went through to the Play-off Final 2–1 on aggregate.

Not everything changed upon Hearn's arrival at the club, such as the fact that we were still losing virtually every week, but the atmosphere around the place was different. It's true that not everyone at the club shared my view that Hearn was a wonderful human being. Many saw him number one as a businessman and wondered what his ulterior motive was in taking us over. Lots said that he would be gone after a year or so. He actually ended up staying for nineteen more than eventful years.

One thing the man did bring to the club was a smile. For some time at Leyton Stadium everyone had been going around with long faces, speaking of nothing but doom and gloom. From the outset though, it was obvious that Hearn may have known little about the game of football, but one thing that you could never accuse him of, was going around preaching doom and gloom.

He always was, and of course still is, a pretty positive character and at the time, it was so refreshing to have someone at the top of our club who was like that.

On 30 March he held a high profile press conference. 'You may think that I'm crazy but we're going to have some fun in this place. We're a little fish now, but we'll grow and it's going to be a rollercoaster ride. I'm having trouble sleeping at the moment. I can't stop thinking about the club and the players.' He then went onto the pitch and took a couple of penalties against our 'keeper Paul Heald. It was all good pretentious stuff. I loved it. Hearn announced that for the next season, a season ticket in the west-side would be £10 for children. I considered at the time that this was just about the best announcement that any chairman of Leyton Orient Football Club had ever made. Indeed over twenty years on, it's fair to say that even now the club are still reaping the benefits of that ground-breaking statement. To this day, it still remains for me the best decision any O's chairman has ever made at the club.

Many kids took up the offer of the cheap season tickets, lured by their dads who could not afford to take the youngsters to the bigger clubs. As a result a lot of those children actually acquired the 'Orient bug', in much the same way I suppose as I had done back in 1967. A lot of them I know still go today. Now, of course the kids have all grown up so that the club are raking in a lot more than a tenner for their season tickets every year.

One of these was my nephew, Robert Stone. His dad Graham, who's married to my elder sister Carol, started taking him to Brisbane Road when he was ten in 1995. Twenty-one years on and Robert hardly ever misses any Leyton Orient game, home or away. In fact the only games he does miss are when they clash with an England away game, as he follows the national team wherever they play. I'm not saying that he's keen but last year he went to the England away friendly in Spain on the Friday night, and flew back to England the next day before getting a plane up to Newcastle so that he could travel down to Hartlepool to see the O's play there on the Sunday morning. It's fair to say that had it not been for his introduction to football, via Hearn's tenner tickets, he would not have got hooked on Leyton Orient.

Whilst I was delighted to see Barry Hearn come to the club, joint managers Sitton and Turner were not. To nobody's great surprise, he sacked the pair of them almost straight away. They departed with a record of just seven wins out of forty-eight in the league. You had to feel more than a little sympathy for the pair. They had been made managers purely for financial reasons, but it was clear at an early stage that with no managerial experience, they could not cope. Despite what folk said about the duo however, they gave it all they had and had worked for hours on end to try to get it right. And knowing the Orient, one imagines that when they were made up to be joint bosses, their salaries hardly went up at all, despite their added responsibilities. Ordinarily, Sitton and Turner would have been quickly forgotten about as a managership pair. There was however still that fly-on-the-wall documentary to be shown. It was to be in October 1996 when the programme was finally aired that the two of them and particularly Sitton, were to infamously return to the headlines, thanks to Jo Treharne.

Hearn replaced the duo by appointing the Tottenham youth team coach Pat Holland as the new manager. With all the traumas off the pitch dominating throughout the season, it was probably just as well that events on the park were somewhat overshadowed. Throughout the campaign we were awful in the league. The defence was not too bad; Heald was a sound enough 'keeper having returned to the team after a long-term back injury. Bellamy and Purse were passable as defenders in the third tier, but in midfield and upfront it's fair to say that we were dire

After the initial freak game against Birmingham, we only scored another twenty-eight times in the league. It really was like turning the clock back to the pre-Kitch days of the seventies when we always struggled to average a goal a game. Colin West battled bravely up front when he was not injured, but he had little support and was often a lonely figure in the final third of the park. We managed to go eight league games without a goal between November and January.

After the match on the opening day there was only really one more game in the league to shout about. A home encounter with Peterborough, who were defeated 4–1. It was a strange result, coming as it did in the middle of an awful spell, and it was made even more peculiar by the fact that makeshift centre-forward Mark Warren scored a fine hat-trick that day. Warren stayed with the club for some years and turned into a pretty useful defender, but he was never a striker. His record when he left us read seven goals in one hundred and forty-seven appearances; highlighting what a freak afternoon he had had in scoring three against the Posh in 1985.

At least in 94–95 there could be no second-half-to-the-season collapse to worry about because as we were one but bottom in January, it would not really have been possible for us to collapse any more. Even so a season in the nineties would not have been a proper season for the O's without some kind of slump, so that we still contrived to lose all of our last nine and so finished bottom.

And then of course there was the legendary away form. Out of a possible sixty-nine points on offer away from Brisbane Road throughout the season, we managed to pick up two. Nine goals were scored in twenty-three games on our travels. I went to a few of them and my God they were painful. One of the best moments of the season came before the Plymouth home match in October when as previously mentioned I acquired a video cassette of the magnificent Orient versus Chelsea cup classic from 1972. It highlights what a crap campaign 1994–95 was, when I look back and remember this as much as anything I saw on the pitch that season.

Ninety-four–ninety-five was the most dramatic for events off the park I had ever seen at the time. It took until 2014–15 for anything to match it for continual drama at Brisbane Road. The recent season was one that in many ways actually mirrored the one back in 1994–95. Two seasons ago we once again saw a new owner come to the club, and at the end of it we had to suffer a relegation. In May 1995 though, I remember just being thankful at the time that I still had a Leyton Orient to watch, no matter what division we playing in.

CHAPTER 31

1995–96 – A DROP BELOW THE DOTTED LINE

So at the start of 1995–96, we were back in the bottom tier after a six year absence. In those days, if I remember correctly it was officially called 'League Three'. On the home front I decided that it was about time I took Barbara to watch a match at the theatre of east London dreams. She was now seven, which was the age at which my dad started taking me and I thought that she was ready for her initiation. Bazza had introduced those £10 season tickets for kids in the west-side, so I bought her one. After four seasons sitting in seat R49 in the East Stand, I moved to the opposite side of the ground to sit with her. It meant not sitting next to George, but I still saw him a lot around the place.

The new seat was not as comfortable – the west-side ones did not have any backs to them – but the move had saved me a few bob, and the programme could still be kept in mint condition under the seat there.

I took Barbara to the first game of the season at home to Torquay on a lovely August day. I remembered how excited I had been some twenty-eight years before, when my dad took me to Brisbane Road for the first time, and I loved it. I hoped that my eldest daughter would feel the same way. Unfortunately though, unlike me, Barbara had never shown any interest in the great game at all. I could understand that she may not have wished to go to 244 consecutive Orient games as I had once done, but I did hope that she would want to see the O's at least on the odd occasion, and enjoy it.

I knew though, that I might be facing a losing battle when we arrived at the ground and I asked her if she wanted a programme. She said no. I had planned it that we would arrive just before kick-off so that she would not get bored waiting for the game to start. We took our seats at 2.55pm, just as an announcement was made that kick-off time had been delayed by fifteen minutes because of crowd congestion. It had not been a good start. Barry had given away a few thousand free tickets to entice the punters and over eight thousand were present. Eventually the match started just as my kid was beginning to get a little bit restless. I really hoped that we would see a cracker for Barbara's sake. At half-time it was goalless. My mind inevitably went back to 1967 when my first game had finished 0–0.

As the second period began, I just prayed that we would score and Barbara would get off to a winning start in her Orient-supporting career. My prayers were answered after seventy-five minutes when an Alex Inglethorpe through ball sent Shaun Brooks clear, and our midfielder slide the ball past the 'keeper to put us 1–0 up. Barbara cheered and I felt a great sense of relief. We held on for the victory. My daughter had gone one better than I had done for my initial match, although, it was obvious that she did not have the same enthusiasm that I had had. When we got home she told her mummy that she had enjoyed it, but I could see that she said this just to please her daddy, and that going to football was, regrettably, not going to be for her. She had not even wanted to start a programme collection.

I took her a couple more times, but it was clear that I was fighting a losing battle in my attempt to make her a keen fan. For some reason she was more interested in going to swimming lessons on a Saturday afternoon with mummy, rather than watch an ailing fourth division football team with daddy. I must admit at first I was a little disappointed, but remembering all the difficulties that I had encountered in my youth from being an O's supporter – ie problems with programme swaps and graffiti, not to mention other kids taking the mickey out of my not-very-good football team – I mellowed into thinking that maybe her attitude it was not such a bad thing after all. And at least as she had showed no interest at all in the wonderful game, I knew that she would not start supporting Spurs, Arsenal, West Ham or Newport – now that would have been catastrophic.

On the pitch after all the trials and tribulations of the previous season, it did seem as if some sense of normality was returning to our club. Mr Hearn was doing a lot of talking, but it was nice to hear an Orient chairman not continuously having to go on about financial problems. Some of his statements were wonderful: ' At the end of the season we'll have the biggest party the East End has ever seen when we are promoted to Division Two. It will be an extravaganza of opulence the like of which the world has never seen.' Brilliant stuff, Bazza.

Leyton Orient under Hearn was certainly a totally different place to be around as it had been before. The club shop, which had previously been like a garden shed in the corner of the ground was totally revamped and moved to beneath the main East Stand. With the new influx of the '£10 kids' you could barely get near it before home games. The great thing for the club about the new youngsters, of course was that they were bringing their dads along to the games. Fathers, who could not afford to pay 3 x £25 to take their two kids to watch

Spurs or West Ham in the Premier League, were now taking them to Brisbane Road instead.

As well as bringing in money through the turnstiles, the dads were being dragged into the shop as well. Hearn was really doing his best to breathe new life into the club, though inevitably there were party poopers around. He was accused of being sexist when he dropped the price of season tickets for women. Yet the reality was that in 1994–95 we had had twelve female season ticket holders. Something had to be done. Thanks to the new policy, we went from having a total of seven hundred and forty season ticket holders the season before, to having over three thousand in 95–96. Alas the old programme shop in Brisbane Road, which had been so magnificently manned by Dave Staplehurst over the years, was given the chop, but that was something saddos like myself were forced to accept in the name of progress.

New manager Pat Holland made a few signings for the start of the new campaign. Alex Inglethorpe from Watford, Danny Chapman from Millwall, together with Roger Stanislaus and Tony Kelly from Bury arrived at the club. Financially with Hearn in control, the club was in a much better position now, thank God, and the finances were helped dramatically as 'keeper Paul Heald was sold to Wimbledon for £125,000. We also got another lucky summer bonus, as our former midfielder Chris Bart-Williams was transferred from Sheffield Wednesday to join Frank Clark at Nottingham Forest. There was a sell on clause in the contract when we had initially sold him to Wednesday, so that we netted a £228,000 windfall when the player moved clubs. Yes, after all the headaches of the previous season, it finally seemed as if the O's were back on the right track.

At the time O's fans were generally happy with Holland's appointment as manager. He had done well in charge of the youth team at Tottenham, and there was certainly more confidence in him as there had been in Sitton and Turner. (Not that that was too much of an achievement.) Indeed we started the season very brightly, a 3–1 home win against Doncaster on 30 September took us up to third place.

The early season run included one of the all-time classic Leyton Orient matches. Throughout the football world at the time the O's away form had become legendary. It had been 30 October 1993 since a league victory had been achieved away from Brisbane Road. It was clearly going to be one to remember when the dismal run was finally broken.

As it was the red-letter day turned out to be 12 September 1995 at Northampton. Every little detail about that Tuesday night turned out to be perfect. I made it up there to see it all that evening, partly because of the lure of the Cobblers new stadium, Sixfields. Whether it was the attraction of a new ground, or whether O's fans just had a premonition that it was going to be a lucky night I don't know, but our away support that evening was much larger than we would normally have expected to get for such a game, particularly as it was mid-week. The South Stand for away fans behind the goal was full.

The game itself was hardly a football classic, yet it turned out to be one of the most enjoyable for years. Northampton took the lead with a deflected goal off of our defender Alan McCarthy, but our boys levelled through an Ian Hendon free-kick. As the game entered its final stages, we all hoped that a winner would come under our noses with the O's kicking towards us, though after forty-three unsuccessful away league trips, 'hope' was the operative word.

It was heading for 1–1 as the match entered injury-time. We looked set for a valuable away point, which we would have all taken at the start of the evening. Then a low Shaun Brooks cross from the right saw Alex Inglethorpe stick out a leg to deflect the ball past the 'keeper and into the net. The massed hordes behind the goal went crazy. As ever the period between the winner being scored and the final whistle seemed like an eternity, yet we amazingly held on and as the referee's whistle blew for time, all hell let loose in the away end.

In the twenty years I'd been watching the O's play away from Brisbane Road, I'd never seen anything like the atmosphere that night at Sixfields. Folk were going round kissing fellow fans, shaking one another's hands and congratulating each other. Punters who you had seen around for years, yet never spoken to before, suddenly became your best buddies, as everybody shared the wonderful experience of seeing an away win with their fellow comrades.

Many of us then jumped the wall to join the team on the pitch. Many supporters did a lap of honour. It was quite a sight as the home fans had quickly dispersed and we were running around the ground to three empty stands, but we did not care. The attitude of the Northampton stewards was one of complete bewilderment. How could the followers of any team get so worked up over what was to them a routine away victory? It really was quite a night though for us. Ever since the Chelsea 3–2 cup classic in 1972, I'd always believed that the best games were the ones when your team had come from behind to win, with the winner coming in the last minute, and this Cobbler classic certainly further enhanced that view.

The general mood around the place had picked up dramatically under Hearn, but there was just one own goal that he had managed to score since he came to Brisbane Road. He had inexplicably replaced *Tijuana Taxi* with *We Will Rock You* by Queen, as the tune to lead the lads out at Brizzy every home game. The whole world knew that Leyton Orient always took to their field of play accompanied by *Tijuana Taxi*. My dad and I had been present for its debut back in 1968 and it had been virtually unchallenged ever since.

For the O's not to be led out by Herb Alpert was like watching Arsenal play at Highbury in those days and not wear red shirts with white sleeves, or like having Manchester United play at Old Trafford with a stadium full of Mancunians. It was just not cricket. There had been one attempt in the mid-eighties to replace '*Taxi*', but it had proved futile and our tune soon came back. When he saved our club back in February, Hearn had said that he knew little about the great game and this gesture seemed to prove his point. He had saved the club, so we would put up with Queen, but it was nevertheless a hard pill to swallow.

For all the headlines that Bazza had brought to Leyton Orient, ironically it was an event that he had little to do with that was to get the club most publicity during the 1995–96 season. The long awaited Jo Treharne documentary was shown on Channel Four on 12 October. Rather unsurprisingly they called it *Leyton Orient – club for a fiver*, after the infamous Tony Wood quote. The programme was supposed to be all about a year at the club, but in reality it turned out to be all about John Sitton. Seventy odd times the 'F' word was used, with the majority of those emulating from Sitton's mouth. To say that our former joint-manager came out of the programme badly would be something of an understatement. To the 1.3 million who watched it, he came across as a foul-mouthed bully, who knew nothing about football or man management.

Sitts said afterwards, 'I feel betrayed by the people who made the film.' Personally I felt just a little bit sorry for the guy. Hour upon hour of film must have been taken by Treharne in her time at the club, yet most of it must have been ditched, allowing for a sensationalist documentary to be made mostly about Sitton. Despite taking FA coaching exams he found it impossible to get another job in the game in the years that followed, and became a taxi driver.

At the bank where I was still working at the time, everybody seemed to want to talk to me about it, the day after the programme was aired. This saddened me somewhat. Folk always used to come up and have a chat about the O's with me after a memorable match, but there hadn't really been any memorable matches for us since the Oldham cup game in 1992. No one I worked with had noticed the significance of the Northampton game. It had taken this programme to make anyone I worked with notice Leyton Orient again, which was sad.

Whilst things under Holland had started to look a little brighter at the start of the season, we all knew that we were the O's and this was the nineties, so there had to be a collapse at some point. Some said though that with the new management things would be different this time around. Indeed it was different. Under Holland the fall down the table began not after Christmas, but on 7 October. Of the last thirty-six league games, we won just seven and finished fourth from bottom.

As the cherry on the cake, we were knocked out of the FA Cup by Torquay, who ended the season bottom of the entire league. The O's managed to get more unwanted publicity at the beginning of January when our full-back Roger Stanislaus became the first player in the country to test positive for cocaine. He had failed a random test after our game against Barnet in November. The level of cocaine found was regarded as being sufficient enough for it to be 'performance enhancing'.

Indeed it must have done wonders for Roger's performance that afternoon as he helped us secure a 0–3 defeat to our local rivals. Poor old Bazza. Here he was doing his best to promote us as London's new 'Community Club' and one of our players gets done for smoking dope. Hearn had little option but to sack him, so writing off the £40,000 that we had paid for him at the start of the season, more than we had done for any other player in August. Could surely only have happened at the Orient.

So at least financially under Hearn we were ok now, which was very reassuring, but on the pitch we were basically still hopeless. It was thought that after the victory at Northampton, the stigma concerning away wins had been broken. Yet we failed to win again on our travels for the rest of the season.

If 94–95 had been a disaster as far as results went, it's fair to say that in many respects 95–96 was an even bigger disappointment, the reason being that we had started so brightly. Yet again it was hard to fathom out just why we cartwheeled down the league so spectacularly, but fall apart we did. We failed to win any of our last ten, and finished the season fourth from bottom.

At the end of the season my mind went back some thirty years to the late sixties. I remembered when I used to go away with my mum, dad and three sisters on holiday every August to places such as Clacton and Broadstairs. In those pre-*Rothmans Football Yea*rbook days, my dad used to buy me the *News of the World* football annual every year, just as we were going on holiday. The idea was that it would make the journey in our Morris Oxford go quicker for me. Reading the book in the car would help pass away the hours spent travelling. It certainly worked, it did indeed make the journey seem a lot shorter as I browsed through the statistics in the book, fascinated by them.

There was always a page in the handbook with the previous seasons English League tables in them. Lines were drawn at the top and bottoms of the various divisions denoting where clubs were promoted and relegated at the end of the season. Play-offs, of course, had yet to be invented. There was one exception to the lines drawn however, denoting where teams had changed divisions, and this was at the bottom of the Fourth Division. Here there was always a dotted line drawn above the club finishing fourth from bottom. As I understood it there was no relegation as such for sides finishing so low, but they had to re-apply for their place in the Football League for the next season.

After a couple of years it became clear to me that the same names regularly appeared below that dotted line. Hartlepool, Workington and Darlington were nearly always there. The Orient, of course, were in the division above so that the dotted line was never an issue for us, thankfully. I remember thinking at the time how awful it must be if you had been born in one of those northern places, and your dad had taken you to support one of those teams. You had little hope of ever winning anything, and all you had to play for every year was trying to end up above that dotted line. I was so thankful that I supported the O's. Ok so we were only in the Third Division, but just a few years before in the early sixties, we had been in the First Division, and we would surely return there some day. Teams such as Hartlepool and Crewe had never been there, and it appeared to me that they never would. At least I had some kind of future to look forward to when it came to watching football, unlike those poor boys who had been taken to watch their local sides.

Yet here we were now in 1996, some thirty years later, and Leyton Orient were, low and behold, ending the season in the bottom four of the bottom division. The rules had changed now, of course and the dotted line no longer existed, but if there had been one then we would have been below it. We would actually have had to have gone to the Football League in June and beg them to keep us in the league. It was really all so depressing. And as for that long awaited trip to see my team play at Wembley, I was still waiting for it to happen. The road to get to the twin towers was indeed turning out to be a very, very long one, and there appeared no end to it at all.

CHAPTER 32

1996–97 – AYORINDE, SHILTON AND STEVE DAVIS

The summer of 1996 really should have been a good one. A nice one weather wise and the country as a whole revelling in the joys of Euro 96, which was being played on our doorstep. I did not enjoy the close season however. The O's had got to me in a big way. I had just completed my thirtieth season at Brisbane Road. The last two had seen the worst ever off the pitch, with the club nearly folding in 94–95, followed by the worst ever on the pitch in 95–96, culminating with the O's finishing in our lowest ever league position at its conclusion.

After the events of 1994, maybe I should have just been thankful that there was a Leyton Orient Football Club to support at all, but I still spent a lot of June and July reflecting on where it had all gone wrong for the club. I had started to follow the O's in the late sixties, with the team in the Third Division. We had won a promotion in 1970 to see in the new decade. The boys had been just one goal away from the First Division in 1974. The FA Cup semi-final was reached four years later. Up until the early eighties we were still amongst the top thirty sides in the country. Yet from then on, apart from one little blip in 88–89, it had been downhill ever since. We were continuously saying at the Orient, 'things just can't get any worse for us', and low and behold they always did.

Surely at some point in my life things would turn around for my beloved club? It can't have been asking too much to be able to see some kind of success, however small, to reward mine and a lot of other supporter's loyalty over the years. As always you looked to the new season for some cause for optimism. What did Barry Hearn, Pat Holland and everybody else at Brisbane Road have up their sleeves for us in 1996–97 we all wondered?

Barry Hearn had said on 1 April 1995, when he had just acquired the O's: 'We will treble our outlay on the youth scheme and develop our own talent. This club will never buy another player. Why should we take someone else's cast-offs?' Sixteen months later, with the start of the 1996–97 season looming, Leyton Orient had just signed Alvin Martin (aged 38) and Les Sealy (38) from West Ham. Dave Martin (33) had joined us from Gillingham as well as Martin Ling (a mere youngster at 30) from Swindon. As the season progressed, Ray Wilkins (40) turned out for the O's, and as the icing on the cake Peter Shilton at 47 put on an Orient shirt to play his one thousandth league game. Oh the pleasures of supporting our glorious club were never ending.

I did have one little shock in the close season. Whilst travelling into work one morning, I took my normal place sitting on the left side of the Central Line train, and shut my eyes for a six stop snooze, having entered the carriage around 7.15am at Loughton. As per normal I opened them as the train approached Leyton, ready to view the four floodlights at our wonderful stadium, before it departed towards Stratford. To my horror however, I was dumbstruck as I only saw two of them.

What was the story? It had always, of course, been a lovely sight to see those four pylons whilst making my way into the city for a tough day of international banking. You knew that though there was a lot wrong with the world, with those reassuring four floodlights still there, it was not all bad. Now though two of those were seemingly gone. It could have heralded good news however. There had been rumours that a new South Stand was going to be built to replace the terrace at the Coronation Gardens end of the ground. Had two of the pylons been taken down in readiness for the new structure?

I had to ring the club at 9.00am to find out straight away exactly what was going on. Yes, it was confirmed that a couple of them had been dismantled, and that the whole of the terrace was to disappear in preparation for a new stand. I don't know who it was that I spoke to, but he actually seemed to know what he was talking about. I asked him when the new work was to begin on the new stand. I remember there being a bit of a silence at the other end, before he said that that had not yet been finalized. He went on to add that for the moment we were to have a three-sided ground.

Whilst then it looked like there could be some fun and games off the pitch, we knew of course that being the O's there would be plenty to talk about on it as well. Despite taking us to our lowest ever league placing the season before, most of us were ready to give Pat Holland another crack in 96–97. Holland appeared to be pinning a great deal on a bloke called Sammy Ayorinde, a Nigerian forward who had joined the year before, and who it was said was very good. He had initially been unable to obtain a work permit, and was so forced to play for the reserves, while all of the formalities were sorted out. Apparently he had told the club that he was going to marry an English girl, which would have corrected the difficulty and made him available for the first team. The strong rumour that did the rounds later however, was that he had omitted to tell anyone at the time that his fiancée was already married, so that a long running divorce held up proceedings considerably and he was thus unable to play for us. It could only happen at Leyton Orient. Whilst all of this was going on Ayorinde was scoring goals a plenty for the reserves, so that there was much anticipation in August when he at last became available.

Said our Bazza; 'In Sammy Ayorinde we've got someone who is going to frighten the life out of opposition defences. He's going to make me a million.' So what became of the club's new Lionel Messi? He made just seven appearances for us, scoring twice and like many a rubbish Leyton Orient striker over the years, was quickly packed off to a non-league team, never to be heard of again. In Ayorinde's case it was Dover. It was obvious to all from his first team debut that he was not up to being a league player.

Hearn, needless to say had been on his usual top form around August; 'the whole jigsaw is now coming together, and we're getting a pretty picture. I call it my paradise in the middle of the east end. We were bullish with enthusiasm last year, now we are bullish with knowledge. We will be a successful club.' It was stirring stuff indeed from the great man, and on top of it all, to the great relief of all of us Orient traditionalists, he had given us back *Tijuana Taxi* to lead the boys out.

So after all the build-up to the new campaign, how did we fare as the season began? Basically once more we were hopeless. By the end of October we were seventeenth, and had scored just eleven times in seventeen matches. 'Holland Out' became the new anthem at Brisbane Road, as the shambles that was Leyton Orient on the pitch in the decade continued.

There was one little incident in a match at Brisbane Road in September that, in a nutshell, epitomized Leyton Orient in the nineties. During a game against Colchester, Colin West contrived to take possibly the worst penalty ever seen at our wonderful piece of heaven in the east end. After the initial award just after half-time, our man confidently ran up to strike a powerful right footer into the top left-hand corner. The referee decided however, that the 'keeper had not been ready and that it had to be retaken. Trying to be clever Westie, obviously thinking the custodian would dive the way he had hit the first effort, chipped the ball into the middle of the goal. The opposition player though merely stood his ground and casually collected the back-pass. It really was laughable, magnificently summing Leyton Orient up at the time.

Though Barbara was not coming with me to matches, I continued to watch games in the west-side as I had got to know a few of the regulars there. The

£10 Child season ticket, alas not used

terrace behind the south goal had been removed, so that as we had anticipated, we were watching our football in a three-sided ground. It was a bit peculiar watching games when there was nobody behind one of the goals. The terracing was eventually replaced with a match-day car park, whilst away supporters had been shifted to the south-wing of the East Stand. We were told that the latest news on the new south stand being built was dependent on the club getting a lottery grant. The application for the grant however, was eventually turned down in 1997. Unbelievably there were strong rumours at the time that our case had not been helped by the request for funds to help it being built, being sent in late by us. It could only happen at our club.

When goals were scored at the Coronation Gardens end, somehow it all seemed a bit unreal. There always appeared to be a few seconds delay before the crowd actually realized that a goal had been scored there. Adverts had been put up at the south end, though personally I would have liked the club to have put up a mural, as they had done around the same time at Highbury, during the redevelopment there of their North Bank.

It would have been my dream for the club to paint two thousand glum faces behind the goal, each donning a blue and white scarf. That way whenever events on the pitch were grim, old stagers like me could pass away the time imagining that we were staring at the mass hordes of Chelsea fans gathered behind the goal on 26 February 1972. We could have cheered ourselves up reminiscing about the greatest hour and a half in the history of the world. Alas it was something the club chose not to do.

The 'Holland out' protagonists duly got their way following a 3–0 defeat at Cardiff on 26 October. The man was given his marching orders and was sacked. He left us with a final record of: played 68, won 18, drawn 16, lost 34. At least in his time in control we had managed four away victories, which was four more than Sitton and Turner had managed during their time in charge. It was generally recognized when he went however, that Holland had been the worst Leyton Orient manager since…well Sitton and Turner.

Three days after his sacking we saw one of the most depressing games ever at Brisbane Road as we went down 1–0 to Scarborough to take us down to twentieth in the league. The lowest crowd of the season didn't even have 'Holland out' to sing to liven things up that afternoon.

Things improved a little the following Saturday with a 1–0 home victory over Torquay. The really big bonus from this game though, was that the winner had been scored by a striker who we had brought in on loan from Peterborough, a chap named Carl Griffiths. The new man got the only goal of the game after a defensive mix-up. It was the first time the O's had scored in four matches. From the start Carl Griffiths did not seem like a Leyton Orient striker. He was not overly slow and he actually appeared to have a first touch. He also looked as if he knew the whereabouts of the opponent's goal. As he looked like the type of player who could get you twenty goals a season, there seemed no way we would sign him permanently. Said Barry Hearn; 'He is a class striker. We've got him for a month so let's enjoy him.'

As Bazza looked for a new manager, trainer and ex-player Tommy Cunningham was put in temporary charge. Various names were banded around for the job, among them our own Alvin Martin. Our aging centre-half had made no secret of his desire to get into management. As it was though, Hearn turned to Tommy Taylor to become the new boss. Taylor had previously been the top man at Cambridge, but he had had two spells as a player at Brisbane Road in the sixties and eighties. He had told Hearn that he would walk down the M11 to get the Orient job, which was just the kind of thing that you said to our Barry, if you wanted to work under him. Alvin Martin was clearly disappointed not to get the gig and indeed it seemed no coincidence that he only played three more matches for the club before he left.

Most of us were happy at Taylor's appointment. Unlike Holland, Sitton and Turner he at least had some past managerial experience, and he had not done a bad job in his time at Cambridge. At the time that most overused phase of the nineties at Brisbane Road surfaced again after Holland left; 'things can't get any worse', but get worse once more they did as we duly contrived to lose at home to non-league Stevenage in the FA Cup.

Carl Griffiths scored three times in six appearances whilst on loan for us. A striker with a goals-per-game ratio of one every two games was clearly not going to fit into a Leyton Orient side, so he was sent back to Peterborough at the end of his loan period. At the end of November 'keeper Les Sealy was deposited back to West Ham with Peter Shilton, just three years short of his fiftieth birthday coming in the opposite direction. As it transpired this was a wonderful move by the club. A real piece of Hearn-like opportunism. Shilts had kept himself fit and was obviously still a more than adequate goalkeeper at our level. More importantly though, he had played nine-hundred and ninety-six league games in his illustrious career. He had been stuck on that number for nineteen months, yet amazingly no team in the lower divisions had spotted the publicity that a one thousandth appearance could bring to a club. But then no team in the lower divisions had had Barry Hearn as a chairman before Leyton Orient. Bazza called the signing of Shilton; 'a marriage made in heaven', and of course he was right.

Matches 997, 998 and 999 saw just one goal conceded by the old boy, setting the scene nicely for a one thousandth league match against Brighton on Sunday 22 December. Even the games leading up to the historic encounter had landed the O's a lot more publicity than they would normally have expected. I was staying up late on a Thursday night to cope with the extra newspaper cuttings.

The real bonus for the club however, was the not entirely unexpected decision by Sky to show Shilton's one thousandth match live, giving Hearn a much needed television fee as well as yet more publicity. Despite the presence of the cameras and a bitterly cold day, eight thousand gathered at Leyton Stadium, to swell the bank balance even more. Naturally the occasion called for a classic from the 'Barry Hearn book of quotes', and we were not disappointed; 'If the world were to end in ten minutes, Geoff Boycott would go to the nets, Steve Davies would attempt one last 147 break and Peter Shilton would go and have some more stretching exercises.' Vintage Hearn.

Sky viewers were able to see a red carpet welcome for the veteran 'keeper, a fanfare introduction, followed by four on-pitch presentations. They were then treated to what had to be one of the worst live matches ever shown on the television, certainly the one featuring the two lowest placed league clubs ever, with Brighton being the bottom club at the time. The Sussex side did not give the great man a save to make all afternoon however, as we won 2–0. It was a nice video for me to add to my collection as we kept up our 100% record in front of the live Sky cameras, following our victory against West Bromwich Albion in 1991.

Shilton played four more games for us before being replaced. He had done his job. December 22nd had been his day, but I looked upon it as being as much a success for our Bazza. Ok, so we had probably paid the 'keeper a huge fee, but we had more than recouped it through the satellite showing and the bigger than average crowd for the historic match. No previous Leyton Orient chairman would have dreamed of doing something similar. I continued to have a lot of time for our Barry. There was also peace of mind in that you knew that with him in charge the two words 'financial crisis' would not be raising their ugly head at Brisbane Road.

Despite the Shilton saga brightening up the season though, the general situation on the pitch, despite the new manager, was still bleak. We had finished the previous season fourth from bottom, yet as Torquay had been so far adrift at the bottom, the prospect of us finishing bottom and going out of the league – just one team went down then – was never going to be an issue. Even then with Stevenage top of the Conference, and their ground deemed not good enough at the time for league football, even the West Country side had been safe in 95–96. This was not the case in 96–97 however.

As Easter approached the unthinkable for us was a real possibility – relegation to the Conference. It was a certainty this time round that the team finishing bottom would go down. Brighton were the bottom club, but even they had picked themselves up a little and were just six points behind us. We had had a ridiculous 4–4 draw with them at their place, which included a pitch invasion at the Goldstone Ground. By not beating them that afternoon, they were still well in touch with us and a few others. It was going to be a close thing to decide who was going down.

As the holiday fixtures came, I felt really distraught. Looking at the remaining games the situation for us appeared really grim. We had just seven games left and only three of them were at home. The next game at Brisbane Road was against top of the table Carlisle. It went without saying that it did not really matter who we were playing away from home, because we nearly always lost away. At the time our last victory on our travels had been way back in September.

I wasn't going to too many of the away games at the time, there was usually plenty of running around to do with the girls – ie swimming and piano lessons – on a Saturday, but I had decided that if our last game at Chester on 3 May was to be our last as a league team then I would have to be there. It would be a bit like going to see a favourite relative who you knew was just about to pass away and you would not see her again.

We were away to Scunthorpe on Easter Saturday. A massive game. Having had Good Friday off work, I had had a lot of time to worry about the match. I had picked up Barbara from swimming lessons and sat down nervously at three o'clock, with the radio tuned to Greater London Radio, who were the best source of up-dates at the time for the O's. I did not have teletext or Sky.

They went over to Glanford Park, home of the Scunny at around 3.15pm and we had conceded and were one down. This of course was not entirely unexpected, but the real choker came around ten to four when the other scores were read out, with the O's still one down. None of the five teams below us were losing and horror of horrors, Brighton were 1–0 up at fifth place Chester. Even now I can remember sitting in my chair at home feeling totally distressed at that moment. In footballing terms, at 4.00pm on that day Saturday 22 April 1997, we were at the lowest point in our long history. Just three points above the bottom club, three points away from a ticket out of the league.

I can still recall now sitting in my chair at home feeling totally distraught. Horrible phases were flashing before me; 'FA Trophy', 'Football Conference', 'FA Cup Fourth Qualifying Round.' Disgusting language. How was I going to bring myself to use such terms when talking about Leyton Orient? And to think that I had ever slagged off the Auto-Windscreens Trophy. At least that had proper clubs in it. Now I was facing the prospect of watching teams like Leek Town and Gateshead every week.

I just hoped and prayed that there was better goal news to come in the next forty-five minutes. All was quiet for around half an hour, but suddenly and quite miraculously, everything changed. We were told on the radio that we were going to Glanford Park where there had been not just one, but two quick goals. Amazingly now it was 2–1 to the O's. When they returned to the studio we learnt that it was now Chester 2 Brighton 1. The next fifteen minutes were very long but the scores remained the same. I celebrated wildly as the full times came up. My prayers had been answered. Leyton Orient that night were nine points above the bottom club Brighton with just six matches remaining. What's more we had even got one of our away games out of the way.

How great it all felt. It was yet another experience to highlight just what it's like to support a club like Leyton Orient. I went to bed that night feeling great about my football team. Not because we had won anything, but because I knew that I would be able to watch them playing League football in 1997–98.

Unbelievably there was more Easter joy to come as we incredibly defeated top of the table Carlisle 2–1 at Brisbane Road on Monday, making us well and truly safe from the drop. There were no more alarms before the end of the campaign and we finished the season in sixteenth place. Not great but it could of course have been a lot worse. We could easily have been looking at non-league football come August.

Tommy Taylor had been in charge for six months, but to be honest I had not been too impressed. Results had not been much better than they had been under Holland. What bugged me was the number of players that we were using. By the time of the final game a record forty had worn an Orient shirt during the season. The home match against Lincoln in March was a fair reflection of how things had gone. When the team was announced before the game there were three players making their debuts that day, who nobody had heard of – Paul Atkins, Chris Timons and Dave Morrison. Within ninety seconds of kick-off one of those, Morrison had given away a penalty. We went on to lose 3–2. The constant changes were doing us no good at all. By contrast the only time we fielded an unchanged eleven from the previous game was against Carlisle on Easter Monday, and it had resulted in a victory over the top of the table team.

Some of Taylor's signings were to say the least puzzling. Around Christmas a certain Bjørn Heidenstrøm arrived on loan from Norwegian giants Odd Grenland. He lasted all of three matches before being sent back across the North Sea. There were rumours that there was more than the odd agent that was doing very well out of the fact that Tommy Taylor was manager of Leyton Orient Football Club.

Amongst all the transfer turmoil however, there was one bit of good business that stood head and shoulders above anything else. When Carl Griffiths returned to Peterborough in December, most of us thought that we had seen the last of him. In March however he returned. By the end of the season he had scored six in thirteen games for us. People started to say that we had signed a 'goal-poacher'. This was a term that nobody had used in association with any Orient forward since Kitch, donkey's years before. It was certainly one rare piece of good news at our three-sided theatre of dreams.

Another signing that we made in March though once again highlighted the bizarreness of the decade at Brisbane Road. Snooker player Steve Davies arrived at the club as a director. It was pure coincidence of course, that the six times world champion had Barry Hearn as his manager. It was obvious that he was not really a football man and he went to very few games during his time served on the board. Indeed he had always said that he was a Charlton supporter. It was certainly a strange appointment, the nineties equivalent of some of the weird appointments that Francesco Becchetti makes these days.

CHAPTER 33

1997–98 – A REINCARNATION OF KITCH?

As a Leyton Orient supporter hard as it is, you always try to be optimistic at the start of a season, looking at positives for the new campaign. It has usually been the case over the years however, that come August your first thoughts are often along the lines of, 'let's just hope it's not as bad as last season.' Bearing in mind how things had gone in 96–97 nobody at Brisbane Road was very confident for the new one in the summer of 1997. Well I say nobody, that was not entirely true. It's fair to say that there was one person at Leyton Stadium who was still bullish at the time, and there are no prizes for guessing who that person was:

'I have been involved in various things as we all know, but this is by far my greatest adventure. It has been fascinating here and I am enjoying myself immensely. It's a bit like a snowball I suppose and we have to get it rolling, and when I do I think we are going to shock a lot of people.' So said Barry Hearn in July 1997. Wonderful stuff from the great man. And in a nice little coup for the club he managed to secure a couple of pre-season friendlies with Arsenal and Spurs at Brisbane Road. Although we lost both matches 1–0, twelve thousand turned up at each game, so that it paid off handsomely for us.

We all just prayed that maybe we could see just one decent season in the nineties. Tommy Taylor had bolstered the defence in the close season with the signings of three useful players, Dean Smith, Stuart Hicks and Simon Clark. With Paul Hyde being a decent 'keeper, it did not seem as if there would be much of a problem at the back.

And at the other end of the park we now had 'Super' Carl Griffiths to knock them in. The Welshman missed the first two games through suspension, but when he came back he looked sharp. Of the first fourteen matches he played for us in 97–98, he scored in nine of them. Add a silly moustache and it really could have been Kitch leading the line for us. Indeed after a twenty-year wait it appeared we might actually have found a new goal-scoring hero.

The big problem however, was finding a partner to play with him. Colin West and Scott McGleish were tried unsuccessfully, and both eventually departed. Jason Harris arrived from Crystal Palace and showed promise, but he was not brilliant. Carl seemed the only one capable of finding the back of the net. Largely due to

The three Strongs: Sir Roy, dad Derek and Martin.

a lack of goals, any optimism that there might have been around the place soon evaporated, as the early season turned into yet another struggle. A 1–0 defeat at Lincoln on 1 November took us down to seventh from bottom. The only bit of good news this time round was that Doncaster Rovers looked hopeless at the bottom of the league, so that relegation to the Conference was never going to be an issue this time around, as it had been the season before. Yet again though, generally it was all still ultra-depressing at our still three-sided ground. After nine games without a win there were even rumblings of 'Taylor Out' at Brisbane Road.

I continued to write my monthly column in the *Leyton Orientear*, which indeed I still do today. However in October 1997 my position as the Strong family's main football writer came under threat. Upon buying the BBC's *Match of the Day* magazine, I noticed that my Uncle Sir Roy, who at the time was the David Beckham of the arts world, had written an article in it. Mind you it was headlined: 'Why I hate football.' Reading the article I just thanked my lucky stars that I had been born to my wonderful dad, and not his brother. I cannot have imagined Uncle Sir Roy having taken me to too many matches at Leyton Stadium in the late sixties and early seventies. Heaven forbid, had he been my father I might even have not been present at Brisbane Road on that glorious day, 26 February 1972.

At least the 'Uncle Sir Roy' episode gave me a little chuckle, which was just as well as there was nothing to laugh about when it came to the O's at the time on the pitch. We really did hit a new low when we got beaten by Hendon in the First Round of the FA Cup. Ah, the FA Cup. That wonderful competition that had at one time been a magical one for the Orient. Something to annually look forward to. Even if things in the league were not going too well, you could always rely

A non-footballing Strong.

237

on the old cup to bring out the best in our boys. Not anymore, though. In the last three seasons we had gone out to the ninety-second team in the league, Torquay, then a decent non-league side in Stevenage, and now a crap non-league team in Hendon. And as far as the league was going, Bazza had promised us back in September that we would be top come November, in fact we were sixteenth.

Leyton Orient in the nineties eh, didn't we just continue to love them. Just for a welcome change though, folk who said at the time; 'things just can't get any worse', were actually proved right for once. The 1–0 Hendon defeat in a replay at Brisbane Road appeared to give everyone a kick up the backside and our fortunes did indeed improve, especially at Leyton Stadium. Of the next ten home games we won eight and drew two. This run included an 8–0 thrashing of the hapless bottom club, Doncaster Rovers. At the end of the game I really should have been elated, which to a certain extent I was, but there was still a little disappointment on two counts. Firstly Taylor appeared to declare when it was 8–e0 with still twenty-five minutes to play. He substituted our two main strikers, the Welsh Wizard Carl, and two goal Tony Richards and as a result we did not add to our tally that afternoon. Eight – nil was our record victory and we could have gone past it, but he appeared to pass over the opportunity. The son of Peter Kitchen, Griffiths, had been taken off with a hat-trick under his belt, but he could well have gone on to notch four or five.

The second disappointment of the day I felt as I travelled home. Chingford Junior High School where I had been in the early seventies had sadly been shut down and was now a housing estate. Had it been open I would have stopped off at my old place of learning and gone into Mr Clegg's old classroom. I would have plastered 'Leyton Orient 8 Doncaster Rovers 0' over the left hand side of all the desks. It might have meant at least a month's detention to scrub them all clean, but boy, it would have been worth it to hammer home the result into the Doncaster supporting teacher.

Thanks almost entirely to the home form we climbed steadily up the table, so that as Easter approached we were actually on the fringes of the play-offs. On Easter Saturday we were away to fourth placed Barnet. I ventured over to Underhill for the game and a good 'un it turned out to be. We actually did a most un-Orient like thing and scored twice in the last ten minutes, coming from behind to win 2–1. Griffiths got the winner in the closing moments. How I loved the man.

Things really were looking up. But we were Leyton Orient. It was all too good to be true, something surely had to go wrong. And go wrong, of course it did, in spectacular fashion. Easter Monday saw Shrewsbury Town at home, a mid-table team with nothing to play for. After fifty-five minutes we were 2–0 up, with goals by Craig Maskell and Super Carl and cruising to a win, with the Shrews also down to ten men. So what happened next? In the next half-hour we committed three shocking defensive mistakes and ended up losing 3–2. A short chap called Lee Steele contrived to score a hat-trick for them. God how I hated him.

But if the Shrewsbury game was a setback, then even more catastrophic news was to follow. We had been getting lots of bookings throughout the season – at one point we were top of the table for yellow cards – yet strangely few of our players appeared to be getting suspended. Eventually though, some spoilsport at the FA appeared to notice this and investigated it. Yes, we had indeed been fielding players in matches when they should not have been playing. We got fined £20,000 for it, with £12,000 of it suspended for a year. The real hammer blow though came a few days after the Shrewsbury defeat when we were deducted three points for the offence. Leyton Orient secretary David Burton was duly sacked, but the damage had already been done. It was for sure the Leyton Orient cock-up to end all Leyton Orient cock-ups.

To cap, what was not the greatest week in the clubs history we lost 3–2 at Hull on the following Saturday. So after the elation of the victory at Barnet, in the seven days that followed we had had a record of: played 2, won 0, drawn 0, lost 2. Total points: minus 3. Just when a small push was needed to reach the play-offs, we got totally knocked down and condemned ourselves to yet another season in the bottom division. We ended the season tenth. Once again, it was a case of only at the Orient.

As I've said before, over the years you are spoilt for choice when it comes to picking frustrating seasons at Brisbane Road. This 1997–98 one though, is right up there with the best of them. With Griff scoring twenty-two in all competitions, though he still couldn't make it to twenty in the league, the defence being generally sound and Martin Ling outstanding in midfield, we really should have at least made it to the play-offs come May, but we did not. Mind you some of us had feared the worst from the start of the campaign when our Barry had pronounced 97–98 as; 'the season of no excuses.' If ever there was a kiss of death for the O's then that was going to be it. And so it proved.

Whilst we had the Shilton Saga to give us national coverage in 96–97, the main publicity that the club got in 97–98 came about through the food served at Brisbane Road. In February it was announced that we had come 93rd out of 93 in the *Coleman's Good Food Guide to Football Grounds*. The way that things had gone during the whole decade at the club, when the news broke that we had the worst food in the country, it came as no great surprise to anyone.

CHAPTER 34

1998–99 – THE VENUE OF LEGENDS (AND LEYTON ORIENT)

There had been a few signs in 97–98 that things were picking up a touch playing wise at Brizzy, but going into the new campaign most felt that it would probably be a typical Leyton Orient season in the nineties. ie bright in patches, with the threat of a play-off place, but with poor away form and a post Christmas collapse at some point putting us out of contention for a chance of promotion.

The only hint that the season might give us something out of the ordinary was the fact that Bazza was strangely silent at the start of it. Having of course famously pronounced 1997–98 as 'the season of no excuses', a statement which came back to haunt him in May, he was uncharacteristically muted in August. One wondered if this change of tactics from the great man would possibly lead to a change in fortune for the team on the pitch.

Well to begin with it certainly did not. Defeat at Cambridge on 12 September left us fifth from bottom. We had already been beaten 3–0 at home by Scarborough, a result which looked extraordinary come May the following year when they finished bottom and went out of the league. There was much abuse for the players emulating from the terraces, which moved Hearn to call some of the fans, 'mindless morons'.

We got drawn against Premier League side Nottingham Forest in the Second Round of the Worthington or League Cup, and I remember there was much optimism at the time that maybe we would see one of those Oriental Cup Classics. Forest were bottom of the top division, unable to score for toffees, and their centre-forward Pierre Van Hooijdonk was on strike. Yet after a quarter of an hour of the first-leg at our still three-sided ground, we were 3–0 down, and we subsequently went on to lose 5–1.

As Tommy Taylor celebrated two years in charge at the club in the autumn, the *Ilford Recorder* noted that in his time as manager an extraordinary forty-eight different players had been signed by him either full-time, or on loan. It would not have come as any great surprise at the time if we had turned up at Brisbane Road for a game, and found that Sid James, Kenneth Williams and Hattie Jacques had been signed up, and were in the starting eleven. Marking the tenth anniversary of Michael Marks playing for the O's, the club decided to celebrate by signing a forward who was just as bad. Steve McCormick came down on loan from Dundee reserves, and was truly awful. At 6ft 4in tall he naturally won the odd ball in the air, but unfortunately he had no idea where exactly to direct it. Like Marks he made his most telling contribution in an Orient shirt at Rochdale. In Mark's case it was his one and only shot for us, while with McCormick it was an attempted back-pass, which almost hit the corner flag. Marks-mark-two was initially due to be down from Scotland for a few months, but was sent back early, having been a complete failure. Indeed it was strongly rumoured at the time, that he took his Leyton Orient training kit with him when he went back up north, which the club subsequently had trouble trying to retrieve. 'Carry On Leyton Orient' in the nineties, continued.

The best thing about the start to the season in my eyes was the new kit. We had started playing in red and white checked shirts which were totally different to anything that we had ever worn before, and jolly classy they were too, in my opinion. It was not as good as the all-white with red braces shirt from the late seventies – our Cup run kit – but it was still very nice.

It actually prompted Sonia to start taking more of an interest in the O's. She is half-Croatian and the new kit was the same as the Croatian national side wore at the time, and she thus loved it too. Although she had come with me to games in the eighties she had not been for years, too busy she said looking after the kids. Barbara, despite Barry's ten-pound season ticket had no interest in joining me on a Saturday afternoon, and I had decided that I was not going to take our youngest Becky, who regrettably had shown no interest in football, either. Somewhere in their genes they had obviously inherited a dislike in footy from my Uncle Sir Roy. At least though, I did not have to worry about them being kept in detention after school to free the desks of any Leyton Orient graffiti, which they might have caused.

We all hoped that maybe despite all of the early season wows on the pitch, we might have a repeat of ten years before when the arrival of Kevin Campbell had been the catalyst for promotion. In fact rumours started to circle that we were indeed to sign a forward and one with international experience. The player was an ex-France international, Amara Simba. When his name was announced in the side for a Friday night game at home to Exeter City, many around the place were sceptical. The memory of Steve McCormick was still fresh in the mind. Amara was thirty-six so how motivated would he be playing for a crap bottom division English team? The last match he had played in England was for France at Wembley, when he was alongside Eric Cantona and Jean-Pierre Papin. Now he would be partnering Alex Inglethorpe and Tony Richards up front at Leyton Stadium.

Yet from the off he actually did look interested. The fans took to him straight away from the moment a header hit the bar in the first half of the Exeter match. Inglethorpe gave us a 1–0 half-time lead in the game, but the moment of the match came just after the restart as a Matt Lockwood cross was met by a bullet header from the Frenchman to double our lead. 2–0 was the final score and we had found a new hero.

Under Taylor, new players continued to come to the club on a regular basis. Steve Watts a forward from Fisher Athletic was an interesting one. He had beaten over eight hundred other entrants to win a 'search for a striker' competition run jointly by *The Sun* and the 'Bravo' satellite television channel. We had signed some rubbish from non-league teams over the years, but Watts actually looked quite useful. He scored a wonderful headed winner against Brentford, when we came from behind to win and quite remarkably we started to rapidly climb the table. In late autumn we went on a run of ten matches where we won seven and drew three. To add to the general fun in the league we had a memorable 4–2 victory in the FA Cup against Brighton with Tony Richards bagging a hat-trick.

As we entered December, Leyton Orient quite unbelievably were second. Would we have to wait long for the traditional Leyton Orient collapse? Of course not, we failed to win any of our next six and went down to eleventh at the end of January. And we had more bad news in that our new application for a lottery grant for the new South Stand was turned down. Our disciplinary record was bad, but at least players appeared to be missing games through suspensions, so that there would be no worries about having points deducted this time round, which was one piece of good news.

So going into February I think we all thought that the season was going to fizzle out into a mid-table one. We badly needed another good run, yet being Leyton Orient having already had one good run in 98–99, we all knew that the chances of a second in the same season were remote. Yet incredibly another fine run we did indeed have. We got knocked out of the FA Cup by Bristol Rovers, but following that we won six and drew one of our next seven to lift us back into a play-off place.

This included a magnificent win at home to top of the table Cambridge United, which was the first time we had beaten them since Tommy T. came down from the Abbey Stadium to manage us. Remarkably we actually started winning a few games away, a totally un-Orient like phenomenon in the nineties, of course.

At home there was an important addition to the Strong household in January 1999. We acquired teletext. For years after the days had ceased when I used to go to every game with the O's, when I was not present at the away games I used to follow our progress through local radio stations. I did not possess Sky at the time. Alas though as the decade neared its conclusion no one at the local stations bothered to send reporters to Orient games anymore. Thus getting to know how the boys were doing became very difficult if I was not present. All that changed with teletext however.

Many an afternoon was spent between three and a quarter to five staring at the television screen with the four pages of scores from the fourth division being updated continuously. I always found it very tense, indeed more so than if I had actually been at the game watching live. Your teams score came up on the screen for about fifteen seconds then you had an agonizing forty-five second wait while the other three pages in turn came up, before they returned to your team's page. The rest of the family found my antics on a Saturday afternoon a bit strange – staring at the television screen with the sound turned down and not watching any particular channel. However with the new tactics heralding an upturn in our away form I felt fully justified in my actions.

In March and April we continued to be in the top seven, and whilst automatic promotion appeared beyond us, there really did seem a chance of a play-off place, and that of course now brought the prize of a trip to Wembley if the Final was reached. Yes Wembley. That oh so elusive venue of legends where I had dreamed of watching my beloved club for over thirty years. I was though, not getting too worked up. We were after all Leyton Orient so we feared the worst. There had to be some kind of dip in form before May, surely. The club indeed did their best to initiate a collapse by selling 'Super' Carl Griffiths to Port Vale on transfer deadline day in March for £100,000. It was bad news indeed, though not entirely unexpected. I loved the bloke, viewing him as a Welsh-Kitch, especially in the 97–98 season, when he had scored twenty-two in all competitions. He had been troubled with injury in 98–99 however, and there were strong rumours that his relationship with Tommy Taylor was not good. Our boss had fined Carl when he got booked in a cup game at Southport, having jumped over a wall to celebrate with Orient fans after scoring. He sent him out on loan to Wrexham and eventually sold him to Port Vale.

Although we had lost one hero however, we had certainly found a new one in Amara Simba. The Frenchman scored two goals in each game in 3–1 and

6–1 victories against Scarborough and Shrewsbury respectively in May. There was incredibly no big end of season wobble this time round. I travelled up to Peterborough on 1 May for the last away game. We lost 3–0 yet despite the result our place in the play-offs was confirmed at the end of the afternoon. The final league game of the season saw a 2–2 home draw with Barnet, with Simba – the Lion King – again scoring twice, and we finished the regular season in sixth place.

Our new Frenchman ended the campaign as our leading scorer with eleven, though he admitted in an interview that he had never even heard of Leyton Orient until he played for us. As he was by now partnering Steve Watts up front, our strike partnership going into the play-offs consisted of a player who did not even know we existed eight months earlier, together with a forward whom we had acquired because he had won a competition in *The Sun*. It could surely only have happened at Leyton Orient.

We were paired to play Rotherham in the two-legged play-off semi-final. I must admit I was not overly confident at the time, as we had lost to them 3–1 and 4–1 in our two games against them in the proper season. They also had what was perceived to be the advantage of the second leg being at home for them. We were though, for just the third time in my Leyton Orient supporting career just one tie away from going to the twin towers to watch us play. We had failed against Arsenal in 1978 and Birmingham in 1995, but maybe that elusive road to Wembley was at long last nearing its end.

The first leg was played on a Sunday afternoon at Brisbane Road, and ended goalless. It shows what a really dull match it must have been in that although it was one of our most important games for years, to this day I can't remember anything about the match at all.

Before the first leg I had booked my place on one of the six coaches that were heading up to Millmoor for Rotherham part two the following Wednesday. After all that had gone on at the club in the previous few years we were all so desperate to see some kind of success for our beloved team. Standing behind the goal that night in Yorkshire, prior to kick-off there were just a few signs that we might just end up the evening with something to celebrate. The Rotherham programme had devoted half a page to Play-off Final souvenirs that they were going to sell after they had defeated us. They were even advertising the official Rotherham Wembley video that would be on sale there from early June. Talk about tempting fate. If Tommy Taylor had wanted to gee our boys up before the big match, he only had to pin those pages up in our changing room prior to kick-off.

Also, as I stood on the terrace that night, I thought to myself how similar it all was to that wonderful night up at Scarborough some ten years earlier, when we had also secured a Play-off Final place in 1989. Now, as was the case then, there was the prospect of a backs-to-the-wall resistance on a Yorkshire ground, and indeed at Scarborough, as was the case now at Rotherham, kick-off had to be delayed due to the size of the crowd.

The match was always going to be tight with so much at stake. Amara had an early chance, firing over the bar, but shots from both sides were few and far between. As the game entered its final phase it remained goalless, with extra-time looking more than likely. Then, with the game entering its fourth minute of injury time Rotherham were awarded a free-kick on the edge of our area. Everyone knew that it would be the last kick of the game, one we just had to keep out. Lee Glover stepped up and curled the ball over the wall towards the top left hand corner. Our 'keeper, Scott Barrett flew through the air however to magnificently tip the ball wide of the post. As saves go, to this day I still consider that save to be the best I've ever witnessed by an O's custodian, due in part to the circumstances that it was made under. He certainly kept us in the tie as the referee blew for time straight after.

Predictably the thirty minutes of extra-time did not produce a goal, so it all came down to penalties. The referee – apparently on the instructions of the police – ordered the kicks to be taken in front of the goal where the home fans were congregated, up the other end to where we all were. Rotherham then won the toss to take the first penalty, so the omens did not look promising for us. Though our record in penalty shootouts had improved over the years, we had still lost more than we had won.

The Yorkshiremen scored with their opening kick, but our Dean Smith retaliated to make it 1–1. Lee Glover stepped up for Rotherham's second attempt, but Barrett anticipated brilliantly, diving to his right to parry away. Martin Ling then scored our second to put us in charge. Paul Hirst stepped up to take the all-important third for the opposition. His penalty was not at all bad, but once more Scotty read it magnificently, diving to his left this time to brilliantly palm the ball away. The rest of the O's followers around me I remember celebrated wildly. We were in the ascendancy but we had not yet won it. I just stood there passively. I had supported us for thirty years and knew our club too well for any premature ecstasy. The next two kicks were successfully converted, meaning that Matt Lockwood just had to score our fourth to take us to Wembley.

The Locky pen.

As he left the centre-circle and approached the penalty area I looked out over the Yorkshire countryside. There in the distance I'm sure I could see those twin towers in north London, with flags flying around them. My mind was cast back some thirty-three years. I could see Bobby Charlton entering the Mexico half and letting fly from thirty yards out, the ball screaming into the top corner. He had scored the first goal that I had ever seen, and it had been enough to make me instantly fall in love with Wembley. Almost a year later, I had seen a goalless draw with Swindon Town at Brisbane Road, and on that afternoon I had fallen in love with Leyton Orient. Now some thirty-two years later those two loves of my life were finally just one penalty kick away from finally colliding.

Matt placed the ball down. He stepped up, calmly stroked the ball to the right of the 'keeper and duly scored. The Orient contingent, myself now included went totally delirious. We had done it. A Play-off Final and a trip to Wembley to see it. My lifelong dream had finally come true after over three decades. It was just amazing. The atmosphere on the away terrace after the victory was I have to say, the best I have ever known at any away game. It beat even that encountered after the Northampton triumph in 1995. Whilst this time there was no pitch invasion, we all hugged and kissed one another, shook each others hands and generally just shared the ecstasy with those fellow O's around us.

Despite the fact that it was already very late, we all remained in the stand for some ten minutes, everyone just trying to take it all in, before we headed back to our coaches and cars to take us back to London. It was such a wonderful feeling for us all. Folk like George and Lotte who had been following us since the forties were at last going to see us play at the venue of legends. Folk like Charlie Hasler, our magnificent groundsman, who had stayed loyal to the O's despite receiving offers to work at bigger clubs and was now getting his just reward, and of course there was the great man Barry Hearn. He had come to Leyton Orient some four years earlier when we could not pay the milkman and now he was going to be able to sit in the Royal Box at Wembley. I even imagined that somewhere that evening even Herb Alpert was celebrating somewhere. Magnificent stuff.

I finally got home at 2.45am and I was up again at 5.30am to go into work in the city. I was still on a high, of course. I was tired but did not care. A thirty-two year journey was finally over. Our opponents in the Final were to be Scunthorpe United, who had beaten Swansea 3–2 on aggregate in the other semi. Tickets for the game went on sale two days after the Rotherham game. Who would ever have believed it? I was going to Brisbane Road to get tickets to see us play at Wembley. I rang the club on Saturday to find out the prices and when the tickets would go on sale. The lady on the other end was very helpful. She explained that we had plenty of tickets, that Scunthorpe had only requested twelve and a half thousand so that there would be no problem at all getting any number that we wanted. The match in the 80,000 capacity stadium was hardly going to sell out. Though they would be on sale at Brisbane Road on Sunday, she told me to leave it till later in the week to go and buy them, when I would be able to get them straight away. From the phone calls she had received, she knew that people would panic and that there would be long queues the following day. She advised me to wait. What? I was not having that. This was Wembley we were talking about. I had waited over thirty years to queue for Wembley tickets to watch my boys play there. I wanted to make the most of every moment leading up to the big day. I wanted to spend at least a few hours outside Leyton Stadium, waiting to purchase one of those magical pieces of paper, our passport to heaven the following Saturday.

I could easily have left it and gone a few days later to get one, but early on Sunday morning I filled my thermos flask with coffee, and set off for the ground. It was, for sure, a relief when I reached my destination to see so many people lined up and waiting, even at ten o'clock in the morning. I was clearly going to be there a few hours, which was good news. I felt such a proud man. Here I was actually queuing up for Leyton Orient Wembley tickets. It was all just so wonderful. There were plenty of people in front of me who you could tell

were not proper O's fans but followers
of other London clubs. Folk who just
fancied a day out at the twin towers.
I saw nothing wrong with that. Come
the big day they would all be decked in
red and white cheering on our lads. My
ticket finally entered my hand at about
midday and I arrived home an hour
later a more than happy man.

The big question in the six days leading up to the big day was what was I to
wear for the historic occasion? It was tempting a buy a replica top, but I figured
that the kit would more than likely be changed at the start of the new season. I
opted instead for a 'Leyton Orient Wembley 1999' T-shirt. Next question: should
I wear my red and white scarf? It was an extra thick garment, and as such would
be far too hot for late May, yet as it had accompanied me to hundreds of games
over the years, I decided that it had to be there, and it would thus be worn. Then
there was the headgear. I had a wonderful old red and white cap, a real Orient
antique, yet was I to buy one of those 'Wembley 1999' caps that were available
in the club shop? Once more I became sentimental and took the former option.

I anticipated that the few days before the game would be great news for my
cuttings collection with the O's getting plenty of publicity in all the nationals as
well as the local papers. Our game was surely the biggest that English football

Play-off uniform.

had seen for years. For some strange reason however, the media seemed more preoccupied with Manchester United's dramatic late win over Bayern Munich in the Champion's League Final on the Wednesday that preceded our match. There were eight page United supplements in many of the nationals on Thursday and Friday, which meant that there was little room for any coverage of Leyton Orient versus Scunthorpe United. I had, of course hated Man. U. since 17 August 1974 but now I hated them even more.

The big day finally arrived. Saturday 29 May 1999. Third Division Play-off Final. Venue : Wembley Stadium, London. The anticipation as I got up that morning was huge. Probably the nearest comparison to any other match I had gone to was for the infamous Villa game in 1974. Ok so we had had the cup games in 1978 and the Play-off Final in 1989, but we were talking Wembley here. Just as with the Aston Villa match some quarter of a century earlier, I felt I just had to get to the ground early. I wanted to be there at Wembley as soon as possible to take it all in just in case, heaven forbid, I had to wait another thirty-two years to see us play there again. The last time that I had walked along Wembley Way was back in 1982, when O's manager Ken Knighton had presented all the Orient player's FA Cup Final tickets to the fans after such a wretched season. Back then the place was awash with blue and white for the big game, with the teams being Spurs and QPR. As I now walked towards those twin towers in 1999 however, among the claret and blue of Scunthorpe, there was a mass of red and white. In 1982 there were just forty-five Orient supporters present who had been given tickets for the game. Now though, there were over twenty thousand O's fans there. And this time we were all there to actually see our own team play. How proud I felt.

I arrived at the top of Wembley Way at around eleven o'clock, a mere four hours before kick-off time. It was early for sure, yet a lot of other folk had followed my lead and had also turned up at a ridiculous hour. I spent the next wonderful two and a half hours milling around outside the ground. Indeed I reckon that of the twenty thousand or so Leyton Orient fans present, I must have shaken hands with around eighteen and a half thousand of them before the game. We all congratulated each other on finally having made it there with our beloved team. The long road had at long last come to an end.

I bought the official souvenir brochure for the game. It was the one hundred and sixth different ground on which I had acquired a programme for a Leyton Orient match. My dad had parted with a sixpence for the first one some thirty-two years previously, though now I was paying £3.50 for a glossy magazine. And the newer, more expensive edition still managed to contain some mistakes. Among the pen-pictures of the Orient team was one of Mark Warren, who had left us eight months before. I decided however, that I was not going to let this little detail spoil my day.

Outside the stadium there was a fine selection of Leyton Orient drummers, along with a wide range of horns and a bugler who had obviously spent most of the time since the Rotherham victory practicing *Tijuana Taxi* on his instrument. The whole occasion was just magnificent. I can remember commentating at the time however, that it was maybe just a pity that the game had to start. Although I was half-joking, I was a Leyton Orient supporter and I had been in similar situations before. There was the Villa game some twenty-five years earlier, as well as the cup Semi-Final in 1978. I knew that there was a very good chance that the day could end in disappointment.

I eventually passed through the turnstile and took my seat at 1.45pm. Over the next hour it was shear bliss to see almost half of Wembley fill up with the colours of Leyton Orient. A lump came to my throat at around 2.10pm when *Tijuana Taxi* came blasting over the PA. My mind went back to that 3–3 draw with Rotherham back in 1968 when *Taxi* had made its Brisbane Road debut, with my dad sitting next to me, roaring with laughter. There had been eight thousand present at Leyton Stadium that day, now though there were eventually to be 36,985 inside Wembley. What a proud day for sure this was for the great man, Herb. We cheered each player as they came out to warm up and eventually gave an almighty roar as the two teams were led out at ten to three. Yes, I remember there was a tear running down the old cheek.

In hindsight it would have been nice to have stopped the clock at three o'clock on 29 May 1999. What a shame that the referee had to blow the whistle for the start of the game. By six minutes past the hour we were one down. For the whole of the first half indeed we were poor. Very poor, in fact. Whether it was the early goal that knocked us for six, or whether the players were just nervous we shall never know. We were not helped though, in my opinion, by the strange tactics employed by Tommy Taylor. Our top scorer Tony Richards was playing on the right wing, whilst a thirty-six-year-old Amara Simba was all alone up front in the middle. He appeared to be struggling with the vast spaces of the Wembley pitch. It was actually a relief when the half-time whistle was blown and we were only one down.

Taylor unsurprisingly made two changes at the break with Craig Maskell and Alex Inglethorpe replacing Richards and Hicks, though he could actually have taken off any of the outfield ten players, they had been so bad. Things improved slightly but we still had to wait until five minutes before the end of the game before our first really good move of the afternoon, with an Inglethorpe shot resulting in a fine save from the Scunny 'keeper. It was not to be our day however, the early goal proved crucial and we ended up losing 1–0. Sadly, as a result we were to spend at least one more season in the basement division.

After such a magnificent build-up, at the end of the match I felt gutted. It was a feeling once more comparable to that following the Villa game in 1974. Both times we had been so close to achieving something special, yet on both occasions we had blown it. As was the case some twenty-five years earlier I just wanted to be left alone, though this time around it seemed impractical to walk all the way home, as I had done after the Villa match two decades earlier. I declined a few offers of a lift home though and travelled alone on the tube. The only consolation now was that my dear mum could not turn round and say to me, 'at least they did not lose' as she had done after the Villa draw back in 1974, because this time round we did lose.

Looking back now in 2016, some seventeen years later I really don't know why I took the defeat so badly that day back in 1999. That monkey on my back that I had not seen the O's play at Wembley had been taken away after three decades of waiting. One of my Oriental dreams had been realized. Back in 1974 when it had all gone wrong it was different. I think then that I knew deep down that there was a very good chance that there would not be another opportunity as good as that one for the O's to make it to the top division. It was different in 1999, however. Though we had missed out on going up to the third tier, there would surely be another opportunity to get it right in the seasons that followed.

I suppose the thing was that it had all gone so badly so quickly. There had been the monumental build up in 1999, yet it really all went wrong within six minutes of the game starting, when we had conceded the goal. I got home around seven and the champagne remained in the fridge unopened. Sonia, Barbara and Becky wisely decided to leave me alone for the evening.

Interestingly though, comparisons with the Villa debacle ceased somewhat the next day. Back in 1974 of course I had sulked during the whole of Cup Final day, which was the day after the match. In 1999 however my mood picked up quite dramatically the morning after the afternoon before. It picked up at precisely nine minutes past nine. It was then that I heard an interview that Barry Hearn had done with Capital Radio just after the Scunny game had finished the day before. He said that he was not down at all that we had lost, and that he had had a great day out with the O's at the venue of legends. He said that he was going to have a party that evening to celebrate what the club had achieved to get there.

Stopping to thinking about it all philosophically, I came to the conclusion that the great man was indeed one hundred per cent correct. Only four years previously when Barry Hearn had taken over at our club, Leyton Orient could not afford to pay the milkman. We were, to put it mildly in a bit of a mess. Despite Phil Wallace (and Rod Stewart) we were close to going out of business. In Hearn's first year at the club we had lost £650,000. We then proceeded to come fourth from bottom of the entire league. It was no fun at all supporting Leyton Orient Football Club. Yet here we were now in 1999 and we had just taken over twenty thousand to our first visit to Wembley - apart that is from a couple of league games that we had played there in 1930. There were articles a plenty in the papers at the time about certain clubs that were in crisis, yet just for a change Orient were not one of them. Unbelievably for the O's we actually appeared financially secure as the decade drew to a close. The money that we had made from the play-offs would further boost our coffers, and work had finally begun on building a new stand at the south side of the ground in Leyton. We were once more to have a four-sided stadium.

On the park we had been just one agonizing match away from gaining our first promotion for ten years and we had an ex-French international playing for us up front for us who had just signed another one year contract. Yes, Barry was quite right. This was not a time for any of us to be despondent. And now that we had graced Wembley once, further trips there would doubtless quickly follow and these would be winning ones. It would not be long, surely, before I would be able to write my next book, 'Leyton Orient – the winning road to Wembley'. Yes, I just could not wait for the 1999–2000 season to start, when we would surely get it right.

CHAPTER 35

2016 – WHERE ARE THEY NOW?

Seventeen years have now passed since that first Wembley day back in 1999 and a lot has happened in that time to myself and the O's. My job at the ANZ was moved to Bangalore in 2009 and as I was unable to make it back to Brisbane Road from India every other Saturday, I took early retirement and a nice little pension from the bank. It was temping to stay at home for the rest of my life and spend every day reading through my old Orient programmes and newspaper cuttings, but I elected instead to get a part-time job. To pass away thirteen hours a week, I got work as a sales assistant in our local WH Smith store in Loughton, selling Panini stickers to kids wearing Barcelona shirts, and I am still there today, working hard to earn every penny of my £7.20 minimum living wage.

Some things in my life have still remained the same, however. My mum and dad still live in Chingford, having just celebrated their sixty-second wedding anniversary and their garden still gets tended to every Saturday. Neither of them have ventured to Brisbane Road in the last seventeen years, the same of which can be said of Sonia, Barbara and Becky, who still all reside with me in Roundmead Close, Loughton.

Uncle Sir Roy was honoured again recently when he was made a 'Member of the Order of the Companions of Honour' by the Queen (whatever that is) in the 2016 honours list, for services to culture. This apparently is the equivalent of winning the 'Ballon d'Or' in the arts world. And he still hates football.

My Leyton Orient programme collection is now approaching three thousand, though with the advent of DVD's and YouTube, alas my video cassette collection has somewhat stagnated. It goes without saying of course that I still see the O's play at all of their home games, and indeed I go to a good many of the aways now. (Though I have not yet challenged my personal record of 244 consecutive matches.) I still write all of the games that I go to in my little black book and I still hate Newport County, Manchester United and Peru, and love Peter Kitchen.

After half a century, it has to be said that I still get a buzz when I wake up knowing that I'm going to Leyton Stadium to watch my lovely little team play. I'm always one of the first in the magnificent supporter's club at around 12ish on a Saturday if we are playing at home, longing to hear *Tijuana Taxi* some three hours later. We may still be in the bottom division, we may still be rubbish on the pitch, but we are still a wonderful little club watched by wonderful people at a wonderful piece of east end heaven that is Brisbane Road.

Here's to the next fifty years of supporting them, with maybe a Leyton Orient Wembley win thrown in there for good measure, sometime. (Or at the very least another Anglo-Scottish Cup Final appearance.)

Up the O's!

Martin.

ND - #0196 - 270225 - C0 - 229/152/12 - PB - 9781780915388 - Gloss Lamination